this CHANGES everything

This Changes Everything fearlessly tackles theologically profound and extremely important biblical subjects in a clear, lucid and practical way. C. Peter Wagner brilliantly distills the paradigm shifts that have transformed his life and a theology that has been the foundation for more than 50 years of fruitful ministry around the world. This is a must-read for those who want to hear what the Holy Spirit is saying to His church today!

Dr. Ché Ahn
President and Founder, Harvest International Ministry
Senior Pastor, HRock Church, Pasadena, California

My approach to my personal relationship with God and to ministry is that of simple, childlike faith. However, Dr. Wagner's scholarly and strategically written book *This Changes Everything* has both provoked and invited me to deeply examine mindsets that might have restricted my experience in God. When I started reading it, I could not put it down. I am convinced you won't either . . . and don't be surprised if you encounter some profound paradigm shifts.

Patricia King
Founder of XPministries and XPmedia

Peter Wagner has done it again—but this time bigger, better and deeper! In this book, he provides us with a detailed yet intimate roadmap that reveals how he expanded from one theological paradigm to the next. He shows how he bridged what to many would be irreconcilable positions, and in so doing provided a way for the Church to get closer to displaying the fullness of Christ in the heavenly places without being tossed by every wind of doctrine. A true apostolic work!

Ed Silvoso
Author and Founder of International Transformation Network

This Changes Everything will cause you to take a step back and really think about what you believe. At times challenging to classic doctrinal thinking, it will cause you to dive into the Scriptures, wrestle with deep truths, and empower you to know why you believe what you believe. Whether you agree with everything written in these pages or not, it will compel you forward in your pursuit of truth, revelation and understanding into some of the most crucial paradigms of thought facing the church today. C. Peter Wagner magnificently communicates these paradigms in a down to earth and understandable way.

Matt Sorger
Prophetic and Practical-life Minister
Head of Matt Sorger Ministries
Author and TV host of *Power for Life*

C. Peter Wagner has been my friend for more than 30 years. Since I meet him during the 1980s, I have seen him change the emphasis of his ministry on occasion—changes he described as "God giving him a new assignment." Those who want to follow his growth in ministry over the years will understand these changes by the "new paradigms" he explains in this book. Here you will find insight into Dr. Wagner's heart.

Elmer L. Towns
Co-founder, Liberty University, Lynchburg, Virginia

this
CHANGES
everything

HOW GOD CAN TRANSFORM
YOUR MIND AND CHANGE YOUR LIFE

"Be transformed by the renewing of your mind."
ROMANS 12:2

C. PETER WAGNER

Regal

For more information and
special offers from Regal Books, email us at
subscribe@regalbooks.com

Published by Regal
From Gospel Light
Ventura, California, U.S.A.
www.regalbooks.com
Printed in the U.S.A.

Library of Congress Cataloging-in-Publication Data
Wagner, C. Peter.
This changes everything : how God can transform your mind and change your life / C. Peter Wagner.
pages cm
Includes bibliographical references and index.
ISBN 978-0-8307-6627-7 (trade paper : alk. paper)
1. Thought and thinking—Religious aspects—Christianity. 2. Theology. I. Title.
BV4598.4.W34 2013
248.4—dc23
2013003205

Rights for publishing this book outside the U.S.A. or in non-English languages are administered by Gospel Light Worldwide, an international not-for-profit ministry. For additional information, please visit www.glww.org, email info@glww.org, or write to Gospel Light Worldwide, 1957 Eastman Avenue, Ventura, CA 93003, U.S.A.

To order copies of this book and other Regal products in bulk quantities, please contact us at 1-800-446-7735.

Contents

Introduction: Paradigms and Paradigm Shifts 7

1. From Two Channels to Jesus as a Real Man 19
2. From Human Abilities to Spiritual Gifts 29
3. From Theological Education to Equipping the Saints 41
4. From Passive Evangelism to Pragmatic Evangelism 53
5. From Mono-cultural Theology to
   Cross-cultural Theology 65
6 From Programmed Evangelism to Power Evangelism 77
7. From Tolerating Satan to a Declaration of War 89
8. From Reformed Sanctification to Wesleyan Holiness 101
9. From Denominational Government to
   Apostolic Government 113
10. From a Greek Mindset to a Hebrew Mindset 127
11. From Classical Theism to Open Theism 137
12. From a Church Vision to a Kingdom Vision 149
13. From Ministry in the Church to
    Ministry in the Workplace 161
14. From Extending the Church to Reforming Society 173
15. From Society as One Mass to the Seven Mountains 183
16. From Escapist Eschatology to Victorious Eschatology 195
17. From a Spirit of Poverty to a Spirit of Prosperity 207

Scripture Index 219
Subject Index 223

Paradigms and Paradigm Shifts

Let's talk about paradigms.

A paradigm, in the way I am going to use the word in this book, is a mental grid through which certain information is processed while it is being absorbed. Did you ever notice that two people can receive the same information but interpret and use it in different ways? It happens all the time, and it is because they have different paradigms.

Don't think that certain people have paradigms while others do not. Everyone lives under the influence of not one, but many, paradigms. Most of us are aware of how this works in politics, just to take a common example. In a democratic, free-speech society such as ours, it is often perplexing to observe Democrats interpreting certain facts in one way and Republicans interpreting the exact same facts in another. Our tendency is to think that certain politicians are right and the others are wrong, but, as a matter of fact, they may both be right according to the paradigm that each one has previously adopted. Those whom we believe are right and for whom we vote, of course, would be those whose paradigm is most similar to our own.

Paradigms Relating to Abortion

Let me be specific, just so we are all on the same page. Let's take abortion as an example. I don't know about you, but I personally interpret whatever is being discussed about abortion through my paradigm that human life begins at conception. Those who disagree with me would have adopted a different paradigm that assumes that whatever is in the womb before birth is a zygote or a fetus or some accumulation of tissue that has no independent life or personhood and may be removed much like an unwanted appendix.

One of the reasons I chose abortion as an example is that any-one can easily see what a huge difference one's paradigm can make. I consider abortion to be murdering a human being. My opponents see it as a woman's exercising her rights of disposing some bothersome tissue. Yes, we have different paradigms, but I bring this one up because I am convinced that my paradigm, in this case, is *morally* right and that society should make laws that protect the life of the unborn baby just like it protects the life of all other human beings.

I derive this from a previous and overriding paradigm that there is a God who created the universe, including the human race, and who revealed the basic principles guiding human society in the Holy Scriptures. One of the things I read in Scripture, for exam-ple, is the occasion in which Mary, recently impregnated with Jesus by the Holy Spirit, visited her relative Elizabeth, who was then preg-nant with John the Baptist. The moment they greeted each other, John physically jumped up in Elizabeth's womb. She felt it and said, "As soon as the voice of your greeting sounded in my ears, the babe leaped in my womb for joy" (Luke 1:44). Obviously, Elizabeth was carrying a human being, not some blob of tissue.

More could be said about abortion, but that is not my theme. I am attempting to explain the nature of paradigms and paradigm shifts. Abortion paradigms are obviously an extreme, because if abortion is murder, then it is clearly a criminal offense. As an or-dained minister, I must hasten to add that it is not an unforgiv-able sin and that with repentance and confession from a contrite heart, God can and will forgive a woman who has an abortion.

Why do I bring this up? I bring this up in order to deal with a further principle. Not all paradigms involve choices between moral absolutes as does abortion. Go back to politics, for example. This is somewhat oversimplified, but let's say that the Democratic par-adigm leads its adherents to believe that government has the re-sponsibility of regulating the lives of citizens to a higher degree than the Republican paradigm, which values freedom of the indi-vidual and free enterprise economics. Following their paradigm, Democrats typically lean toward higher taxes than do Republicans. Here we have an important political difference, but I hope that most would agree that neither position is *morally* right or wrong.

The Paradigm Spectrum

This leads us to recognize the fact that paradigms can be placed on a spectrum that would run from what we could call moral imperatives on the left end to personal preferences on the right. When you think about it, you would probably agree that your own personal paradigms could be placed on many points across that spectrum. The farther you go toward the right end of the spectrum, the more tolerance you would have for those who entertain paradigms that are different from yours.

This is important to me, as you could see from the subtitle of this book: "How God Can Transform Your Mind and Change Your Life." My life pathway has been quite long since I have passed the biblical "threescore years and ten" (Ps. 90:10, *KJV*) and reached "fourscore," which in modern language is 80 years. As I look over the list of my paradigm shifts in the rest of the book, I recognize that none of them would be located clear over on the left hand side of the paradigm spectrum. What does this mean? It means that I would not regard those who disagree with me on any of these issues as morally deficient. Our issues, rather, would be things upon which we could agree to disagree and still be friends.

Cultural Paradigms

One of the personal advantages I have in understanding the paradigm spectrum comes from my 16-year missionary experience in Bolivia. After my wife, Doris, and I arrived in the Bolivian jungles in 1956, we endured a stressful period of culture shock. That means that we found ourselves in a society in which individuals were operating through paradigms radically different from ours.

One of the constant challenges of cross-cultural ministry is to adapt to the paradigms of the second culture as rapidly and as thoroughly as possible. However, it also involves the sometimes agonizing decision of whether or not to locate some of the paradigms of the second culture on the left end, the moral imperative end, of the spectrum. The tendency, particularly of missionaries not versed in cultural anthropology, has been to locate too many of the native paradigms toward the left.

Let's choose an example that, intentionally, may turn out to be controversial and not politically correct for most Americans, including me. I have always been a champion for women's rights and women in Christian leadership at any level. In fact, when one woman apostle who is aligned with me first saw the outline of this book, she said, "Peter, why don't you have a chapter on women in leadership?" I simply smiled and responded, "This is a book on paradigm shifts. I never needed a paradigm shift on the issue of the ministry of women!" She understood what I meant.

I want to go to my friend Charles H. "Chuck" Kraft's book *Christianity in Culture,* which I consider the best book on cultural paradigms that we have. At one point, Kraft discusses the role of women in culture. He begins by accurately describing our American paradigm, namely, that women should have equality to men by being free to do anything that men are free to do. He writes, "*We link equality with freedom.*"[1] He goes on to explain, "We judge that men have heretofore been allowed greater freedom than women, and we conclude, therefore, that the position of women is unequal to that of men, since it is not the same with respect to the possession of individual freedom."[2] He concedes that, because this is our American paradigm, we Americans feel we must take whatever action is necessary to secure more freedom for women. No problem.

Kraft then asks us to imagine a different paradigm that actually is characteristic of a large number of other cultures in the world today—namely, that the most valuable thing for a woman is *security,* not *equality.* "Whereas we might say, 'A woman is so valuable as an individual that she should be as free as possible,' such a society, on the other hand, might reason: 'A woman is such a valuable member of society that she should be made just as secure as possible.'"[3]

In that case, the main things to provide for women would be a secure marriage and home, a routine set of behavior expectations, and the responsibility to provide security for children. In these societies, men have maximum freedom (in some, for example, men can go with bare heads, while women must wear scarves) and women end up with maximum security. Kraft concludes, "There seems to be no feeling of compulsion on the part of these societies to give both men and women the same kind of thing, since they regard male and female roles as complementary (i.e., non-overlapping)."[4]

Of course, this raises the question as to whether one of these paradigms might be morally *right* and the other morally *reprehensi-*

ble. My purpose here is not to argue the point one way or another but simply to illustrate how profound certain paradigms can be.

"We Work to Live"

Getting back to the jungles of Bolivia, one of my most interesting introductions to a different paradigm had to do with a chain saw. We lived in a small town on the railroad line between Corumbá, Brazil, and Santa Cruz, Bolivia. The trains were driven by wood-burning steam engines. (By the way, we had to have a special set of clothes specifically for traveling because the sparks from the engine continually fell on us and burned multiple holes in our clothing . . . but I digress.)

A friend of ours named Bernardo made his living by cutting firewood in the jungle and selling it to the railroad. His tools were axes and handsaws. It happened that a friend of ours in the United States, who knew that I had to see that Doris had enough firewood for cooking and baking, decided to ship us a chain saw, the first one ever to be seen in that region. I couldn't wait to show it to Bernardo. I felled and trimmed a couple of small trees, and then I let him try it. He was thoroughly amazed. I'll never forget his comment. He said, "With this saw I could get a whole week's work done in less than one day!"

I could hardly believe it. With my paradigm I would have expected him to say, "With this saw I could produce and sell six times the amount of firewood I can cut with my axe and handsaws!" But, no! He was more interested in six times the amount of leisure on his calendar than increasing his firewood production. He was happy with his lifestyle as it was. After a while, with some cultural probing, I learned how this difference in paradigms was being verbalized among themselves in that part of Bolivia: "Americans live to work, but we work to live!" It was a profound lesson, but I must admit that I still live to work! Even though part of me envies Bernardo, I still have not made a paradigm shift in his direction!

Paradigms Can Quench the Spirit

When it comes right down to it, the differences between paradigms of working to live or living to work are rather benign. However, let's take a look at a more serious difference, this time one that actually prevented the communication of the gospel of salvation. For this interesting case study, which I will paraphrase, let's go back to Chuck Kraft, who was for a time a missionary to Nigeria.

It turns out that some missionaries had been assigned by God to evangelize a certain tribe in northeastern Nigeria. They were good missionaries, faithful to God, up to date on their prayer lives, and passionate for souls. However, something was wrong. While missionaries in many other tribes were planting churches and seeing people saved, relatively little was happening in this tribe. The people were friendly enough, but they didn't want anything to do with the Jesus that the missionaries preached.

Much later, the missionaries discovered the problem, and it had to do with paradigms. The missionaries had made the mistake of telling the people that Jesus was the Good Shepherd. What the missionaries didn't know was that most people in that tribe would not be inclined to commit themselves to a shepherd. Why not? It was because in their culture, the only ones who were shepherds were either young boys or mentally deficient adult men! They knew Jesus wasn't a young boy, so they concluded He must have been a mentally deficient man. Who would want to follow such a person?

In the Hebrew culture of the Bible, the Good Shepherd would have been admired, but in this African tribe, He would be scorned. Different paradigms! Until the problem was corrected, which it eventually was, the African paradigm had effectively quenched the Spirit and inhibited evangelism![5]

Once the people in Africa began to realize that the Jesus the missionaries were preaching could be a Good Shepherd without being mentally deficient, they had to revise their view of a typical shepherd. In other words, at least those who became Christians had to make a paradigm shift.

Shifting Paradigms

Now that we have been thinking about paradigms themselves quite a bit, let's begin to imagine what is involved in changing a paradigm. This process may not be as simple as it seems. Let's take, for example, an uncomplicated, non-moral paradigm concerning the process of getting food from your plate to your mouth. My paradigm, instilled from childhood, was that you use a fork to eat your food. I always knew that some people's paradigm was to use chopsticks. I even experimented once or twice with chopsticks, but with no success. Consequently, whenever I ate in a Chinese restaurant I asked for a fork, and I enjoyed my food.

Life in this respect was comfortable until one day in the 1960s when I was invited to minister in Taiwan for the first time. The venue for the meeting was not in a city like Taipei or Taichung, but in a hotel retreat high in the mountains. When I sat down at a large, round table with my Taiwanese hosts for my first meal, I asked for a fork. To my dismay, there was not a fork within miles! I was forced into, what I considered at the moment, a radical paradigm shift. Chopsticks were my only choice of an eating tool. My friends saw what a mess I began making of things, and they instructed me, the best they could, on the basics of chopsticks management. I bumbled my way through, but, at least by the end of my four days there, I was able to eat my fill most of the time. However, the experience was so painful and embarrassing that I remember it clearly 40 years later. For the record, I have since made a paradigm shift to the extent that now if I am given a fork in a Chinese restaurant, I ask for chopsticks!

As you read this story, I'm sure that you will recall experiences in your own life when similar things have happened. You, undoubtedly, have shifted more than one paradigm over the years. So let's analyze a bit what happens in a paradigm shift.

Where Does the Shift Begin?

A good starting point is to ask the question, "Where does a paradigm shift begin?" The answer is that it begins in the mind. At the outset of this chapter I said that a paradigm is a *mental* grid through which certain information is processed while it is being absorbed. This is so basic that we could say that without changing your mind, there cannot be a paradigm shift. A paradigm shift is not so much an issue of the emotions, the will or the heart as it is of the mind. Granted, all those other things might be involved, but they are secondary.

What does the Bible say about this? Most of us know this verse: "Do not be conformed to this world, but be transformed by the renewing of your mind" (Rom. 12:2). "Renewing your mind" is another way of describing what happens in a paradigm shift. In this case, it is not referring to a trivial thing like eating with chopsticks, but to something important enough to "prove what is that good and acceptable and perfect will of God." Some of the most important steps forward in our Christian service may well involve a willingness to undergo paradigm shifts.

But this isn't always easy. In fact, most of the time it is quite difficult. Why? Because a paradigm shift inevitably pulls us out of our comfort zones. Just about everybody prefers comfort to discomfort. Most people resist paradigm shifts because they know ahead of time that renewing their mind will be uncomfortable for them. Maintaining the status quo seems like the best choice.

I know this by experience. I happen to be one of those people who harbor a favorable view of change. I do realize that I may not be typical in this respect because many people whom I considered to be friends have actually turned against me after I made certain paradigm shifts. Obviously, they did not like the prospect of change, and seemingly, they were upset because I shifted paradigms without obtaining their consent. One way to express their discontent was to criticize me and become my opponents. Those who did this, of course, relieved themselves of any compulsion to make a similar change.

Somehow, even though I have known that at times it might be painful, I have always tended to be receptive to renewing my mind, as I believe the Bible says we should be. In fact, if you look at the table of contents you will see quite an extensive list of paradigm shifts drawn from my personal life and ministry. As you read about each one, you will see how my change tended to pull others out of their comfort zones. Consequently, I entered into debate, dialogue, arguments and even conflict over my new views. I will detail some of them as we go along.

A Biblical Example

Do we have any biblical examples of paradigm shifts? Of course we do. There are many of them. One of the most dramatic would be

Jonah after the whale coughed him back up. Another would be Saul on the Damascus Road. I don't want to extend this list because I want to bring up, as my example, what I consider one of the most significant biblical paradigm shifts on record and one that actually few Christian leaders have paid much attention to.

I'm referring to James of Jerusalem and the famous Jerusalem Council that we read about in Acts 15. Please permit me to spend a bit of time telling this fascinating Bible story as a way of concluding my opening chapter on paradigms and paradigm shifts.

The story begins in Antioch when Barnabas and Paul (Saul) were sent out on their first missionary assignment to the Gentiles.[6] It is important to keep in mind that up to this point virtually all believers in Jesus had been Jews, what today we might call Messianic Jews. It was taken for granted that since Jesus was circumcised, His followers likewise would be circumcised. I am taking the liberty of using circumcision as a specific symbol of the much broader and deeply penetrating concept of Jewish ethnicity. The cultural gap between Jews and Gentiles in those days was enormous, rivaling what we have known as apartheid in our day. I will spare details except to note that Jews were not allowed to enter Gentile homes or vice-versa; they could never eat together; and Jews were not even permitted to drink milk if a Gentile had milked the cow! Enough said.

This is why Barnabas and Paul's mission to the Gentiles was so historic. How would they handle this? If a Gentile heard the gospel and wanted to be born again and enter the family of God, would he or she first have to become a Jew? If it was a man, would he need to be circumcised in order to be baptized? Following the leading of the Holy Spirit, Paul and Barnabas, both circumcised Jews, decided that they would respect the Gentile culture and baptize Gentiles on their own terms without circumcision, which they did with amazing results. The gospel spread and churches were multiplied in many areas, one of which was the region of Galatia.

I mention Galatia because that was the place where things blew up, at least according to the information we have in the Bible. Paul and Barnabas finished their first missionary assignment and returned for a time to Antioch, where some Gentile house churches had also been started. That was when Paul's terrible nightmare occurred, and the main instigator of this worst-case scenario was none other than the apostle James of Jerusalem. Let me remind you that I am bringing this up in order to describe James's subsequent paradigm shift.

Who Was James?

James was not one of the original 12 apostles. He was a son of Mary and Joseph, namely, the brother of Jesus. He had risen to a position of apostolic leadership in the church of Jerusalem. He was the author of our New Testament Epistle of James. The church of Jerusalem, as would be expected, was thoroughly Jewish and quite ethnocentric. In their opinion, every true follower of Jesus should convert to Judaism and, if a man, should prove it by being circumcised before baptism.

As you would expect, James did not like the news that Gentiles in Galatia were being baptized without circumcision, so he took the radical step of sending a company of Judaizers to Galatia, behind Paul's back, to tell them that Paul was wrong and that they should be circumcised as soon as possible if they really wanted to be saved. Guess what? When this news got to Paul in Antioch, he was infuriated! He responded by writing the epistle of Galatians and saying, among other things, "Who has bewitched you . . . ?" (Gal. 3:1). Strong language!

If any might doubt that James was the instigator of this blowup, allow me to quote Paul. First, let me mention that this also precipitated a serious rift between Paul and Peter and even between Paul and Barnabas, as you will see from this quote: "Now when Peter had come to Antioch, I withstood him to his face, because he was to be blamed; for before certain men came from James [note that James was the instigator], he would eat with the Gentiles; but when they came, he withdrew and separated himself, fearing those who were of the circumcision [i.e., the Judaizers]. And the rest of the Jews also played the hypocrite with him, so that even Barnabas was carried away with their hypocrisy" (Gal. 2:11-13). Things must be pretty tense if Paul blatantly called Peter and Barnabas hypocrites!

All this led to the Council of Jerusalem, convened by none other than our friend James. Would the fact that he even called a council to discuss the matter indicate that his paradigm might have been shifting? Who knows, but look what happened. A Who's Who of apostles showed up, including Paul, Barnabas and Peter, the only three whom Luke quotes in Acts 15, except James. No one knows how long the council lasted, but it must have been a long time because James let all of the apostles say all they wanted to say about the matter. Then, "after they had become silent," James took the floor. He said, "Men and brethren, listen to me" (Acts 15:13).

The Paradigm Shift

Here is the paradigm shift. James was one of those not afraid to renew his mind. He listened thoroughly to his peer-level apostles, and he obviously was submitted to the revelation of the Holy Spirit through them. I wrote earlier that this was a significant paradigm shift. Let me go a bit further and say that, in my opinion, this resulted in the most important missiological decree this side of the cross. In fact, when you think of it, it could be argued that all of us who are not Messianic Jews today owe our salvation to James's decision.

Here it is: "Therefore I judge that we should not trouble those from among the Gentiles who are turning to God" (Acts 15:19). This means, as you would guess, that Gentiles did not have to convert to Judaism and be circumcised in order to be fully accepted into the family of God! For James it was a 180-degree shift!

As you would anticipate, James of Jerusalem is one of my biblical heroes and role models. You will see in the following chapters that from time to time I also went so far as to send the equivalent of Judaizers to disrupt the camp of my opponents before I underwent certain paradigm shifts. I think I understand James. Whenever it is necessary, I want to continue to be transformed, and I am sure that you do as well. How? As the Bible says, it will be by the "renewing of your mind" (Rom. 12:2).

Notes

1. Charles H. Kraft, *Christianity in Culture: a Study in Dynamic Biblical Theologizing in Cross-Cultural Perspective* (Maryknoll, NY: Orbis Books, 1979), p. 59. Emphasis in the original.
2. Ibid.
3. Ibid.
4. Ibid.
5. Charles H. Kraft, *Anthropology for Christian Witness* (Maryknoll, NY: Orbis Books, 1996), p. 25.
6. I am abbreviating this story considerably here. I suggest that anyone who wants to study it in detail see chapters 15 and 16 of my book *The Book of Acts: A Commentary* (Ventura, CA: Regal Books, 2008)

1

From **Two Channels** to **Jesus** as a **Real Man**

We all know that Jesus was both God and a human being. The Bible teaches this very clearly, and consequently it has become a part of classic Christian theology. However, it is one thing to assert that we believe it, but it is another thing to begin thinking through the implications of that statement and then try to answer some of the interesting questions that it raises.

This is taught in theology classes as the doctrine of the two natures of Christ. Jesus had a divine nature and a human nature. Please don't confuse the word "nature" with the word "person." Jesus was never two persons; He was always one person, known as the second Person of the Trinity. The first Person is God the Father, and the third Person is God the Holy Spirit. Jesus is God the Son. However, beginning with the incarnation, when Jesus was born of Mary, the Son acquired what neither the Father nor the Holy Spirit had, namely, a human nature to go along with His divine nature.

We may agree with Jesus' having two natures, but we mustn't fall into the supposition that He was half-God and half-human, like certain creatures we read about in Greek mythology. No. Jesus was 100 percent God and 100 percent human. I know that this does not compute mathematically; nevertheless, it is what both the Bible and orthodox Christian theologians teach. To underscore the long history of this doctrinal conclusion, many theologians like to use the ancient Latin phrase *vere deus et vere homo,* meaning totally God and totally human.

The reason I have gone into that much theological detail in the beginning of this chapter is that I do not want my paradigm shift to be misunderstood. I have no intention of questioning the fact that Jesus has (notice the present tense) two natures: a divine nature and a human nature. For me that is a theological non-negotiable. I am going to stress the human nature a great deal, but that does not nullify the divine nature. Watch and see what I mean.

The Relationship of the Two Natures

Undoubtedly, the most interesting question that arises when we consider Christ's two natures is how they relate to each other. When we think about His time here on earth, was Jesus using mostly His divine nature, His human nature or both?

Before I answer this question, let me paint a picture very clearly by referring to Mark 13. There we have Jesus up on the Mount of Olives talking privately to Peter, James, John and Andrew. They ask Him when the end will come. Jesus begins by listing some of the signs that will show when the end times are approaching, such as wars and rumors of wars, earthquakes, persecutions, false prophets, and the like. But the disciples' question had to do with the time. *When* would all this happen? Look at Jesus' rather surprising answer: "But of that day and hour no one knows, not even the angels in heaven, *nor the Son*, but only the Father" (v. 32, emphasis added).

Why is this so surprising? Jesus actually said that there was something that He, the Son, the second Person of the Trinity, didn't know! Wasn't He God? Isn't God omniscient, knowing everything? If so, how could there be anything at all that Jesus didn't know? These questions have perplexed theologians for a long time. Generally speaking, they have proposed four different answers. Let's look at them one at a time.

The Total Mystery Theory

> *For some theologians the way that the two natures of Jesus related to each other while He was on earth is beyond the pale of human understanding. We must reconcile ourselves to the fact that we will never be able to explain it.*

In response, I would first admit that some areas of theology are indeed a mystery. An example would be how the Trinity could be three persons in one essence, just to mention something that no theologian has ever been able to explain completely. However, I do not agree that the relationship of Christ's two natures should be placed in the mystery category. To the contrary, the purpose of this chapter is to make the issue very understandable.

The Human Jesus Theory

There are some liberal-leaning theologians who actually doubt that Jesus was ever God in the first place. They consider Him a wonderful person, a brilliant teacher, a prophet of God, perhaps the greatest man who ever lived, but something less than God. Mormons and Jehovah's Witnesses would join some Christian theologians in denying the divinity of Christ. To them, Jesus had only a human nature, and the fact that He didn't know the date of His own return was something that they would cite to help prove their point.

I cannot relate to that position because of my faith in the authority of Scripture. The Bible addresses Jesus' deity directly when it says, "In the beginning was the Word, and the Word was with God, and the Word was God. And the Word became flesh and dwelt among us" (John 1:1,14). Jesus was really God as well as a real human being.

The Two-Channel Theory

I will spend a bit of time on the two-channel theory because it is the one that most evangelical leaders currently espouse. If you have heard a sermon on the subject or even a reference to Jesus' two natures, you probably heard this view. When I was a new Christian, this is what I was taught, and naturally, it is what I believed. On the surface, it seems to explain all that we read in the Bible.

The basic idea is that sometimes Jesus spoke or acted from His divine nature, but other times He spoke or acted from His human nature. It is as though Jesus constantly switched from one channel to another and then back again. You never knew ahead of time which channel He might use next. In other words, when He changed water into wine or when He raised Lazarus from the dead, He was using His divine nature with its accompanying supernatural power. When Jesus got hungry or when He wept, His human nature had taken over.

This is a very popular theory because, if it were true, it would help us understand all the areas of Jesus' behavior. However, even though I was comfortable with this explanation for several years after I had become a believer, I no longer am. I went through a paradigm shift that, to my recollection, was the first one of my career. I was beginning to learn how to renew my mind!

For one thing, just by way of explanation, look again at what Jesus said in Mark 13:32: "But of that day and hour [of My second coming] no one knows, not even the angels in heaven, nor the Son, but only the Father." Those who hold the two-channel theory would argue that Jesus really meant that, *humanly speaking*, He, the Son, did not know when He was returning, although as God in His divine nature, He really would have known it because God is omniscient. Notice one thing though: If Jesus were speaking here from His human nature channel, how did He know that the angels also were ignorant of the date? There is no human way to know what angels think! The only way to explain this would be to suppose that Jesus switched channels in the middle of one sentence. I would not be happy with this rather devious explanation, and consequently, I think there must be a better way to understand the relationship of Jesus' two natures.

The Incarnation-Theology Theory

The incarnation-theology theory is the view of the relationship between Christ's two natures that I now hold, even though it may not yet be the majority view. When I say "not yet," I am implying that I hope someday to be able to convince all of my friends and readers that this is the most biblical position. I say this, of course, with my tongue in my cheek because I am realistic enough to know that I won't live long enough to accomplish such a feat, but I can still try! This chapter might help some, and what I especially want to point out is why I think that incarnation theology is not only right but also very important for each one of us who wants to end up serving God in the most productive and fulfilling way possible.

How did I make this very significant paradigm shift? Back in the 1950s I received my training for missionary service at Fuller Theological Seminary, when it was still a relatively new school. For almost all of us who were students at that time, our favorite professor was Edward John Carnell, who taught systematic theology. It was in one of Carnell's classes that I first heard incarnation theology, although I do not recall that he used the exact term. I use it now because he based his teaching on Philippians 2, which is a major passage on Jesus' incarnation. By the end of Carnell's one-hour lecture, I had shifted my paradigm from the two-channel theory to the incarnation-theology theory. It was as simple as that!

Let's consider Philippians 2:

> Let this mind be in you which was also in Christ Jesus, who, being in the form of God, did not consider it robbery to be equal with God, but made Himself of no reputation, taking the form of a bondservant, and coming in the likeness of men. And being found in appearance as a man, He humbled Himself and became obedient to the point of death, even the death of the cross (vv. 5-8).

By stating that Jesus was "equal with God," this passage clearly affirms His divine nature. As God, Jesus would have all the divine attributes, including omniscience, or knowing everything there is to know.

However, after Jesus became a human being (the incarnation), He was then different from the Father because He took on a human nature, something that the Father never had. Jesus took the form of a servant, and came in the likeness of man. It is important to remember that, through all of this, Jesus still possessed His full divine nature.

Part and parcel of Jesus' accepting His incarnation and taking on a human nature was that He agreed to become obedient throughout His life on earth. He "became obedient to the point of death, even the death of the cross." Let's take a closer look at this obedience. First, it was voluntary. It had to be. Nothing forced Jesus to do this against His will. Second, it was temporary. It would end at His death, namely, "the death of the cross." What did the obedience consist of? Jesus entered into an agreement with the Father that He would suspend the use of His divine attributes for the duration of His earthly ministry. He came in "the likeness of men." I use the word "suspend" because Jesus never gave up His divine attributes.

However, although He always had them, He voluntarily agreed not to use them.

By the end of Carnell's lecture I had adopted this theological conclusion: *The only nature that Jesus used between His birth and His death here on earth was His human nature.*

Back in those days, I was naive enough to suppose that anyone else who heard this would quickly agree. I soon discovered how wrong I was. In fact, I almost failed my ordination examination because of my paradigm shift. It turned out that all of the six pastors on my ordination committee held to the two-channel theory of the relationship of Jesus' two natures. They were quite shocked when I expressed my opposing point of view. After an ominous amount of deliberation, they finally agreed to ordain me, but they gave me the stipulation that I agree to visit a seminary library and read theological works on Christology for six hours. I kept my promise, but after the six hours, I was more convinced than ever that my incarnation Christology was the correct interpretation of biblical data.

Years later when I joined the faculty of Fuller Seminary, I was elated to find that Colin Brown, a highly respected theologian, agreed with me. In his book *That You May Believe,* he calls it Spirit Christology. With skillful detail he rejects the two-channel theory "put together by traditional apologetics of Jesus the divine Son of God, doing miracles in his own right."[1] Brown continues, "Jesus miracles are given a prominent place, but they are not attributed to Jesus as the Second Person of the Trinity. They are not presented as manifestations of his personal divinity."[2]

Jesus as the Last Adam

Jesus is referred to as the "last Adam" and the "Second Man" (1 Cor. 15:45,47). Both the first Adam and the last Adam were created beings. Adam was created from dust, and Jesus was created as an embryo and implanted in Mary's womb to begin a normal gestation process. Since we know for sure that Jesus wasn't genetically related to Joseph, there is no compelling reason to believe that He was genetically related to Mary either. Neither Adam nor Jesus was contaminated with original sin, unlike the rest of us who all have inherited a sinful nature as a result of Adam's fall. Any sin from either Adam or Jesus would not have come from a sinful nature; rather, it would have to have been their personal choice.

This brings up their temptations. Both Adam and Jesus were tempted to disobey God. They each had a covenant of obedience with the Father. Adam had agreed not to eat the forbidden fruit, and Jesus had agreed not to use His divine attributes. Satan tempted Adam to disobey God and eat the fruit, which he did. Satan also tempted Jesus to disobey God and use His divine attributes. This will be a new thought to some, so let's take a closer look.

If we believe that Jesus' temptations were real, we have to believe that He could have sinned. Otherwise, the temptations would have been mere charades. Since God, by definition, cannot sin, we know that Satan's temptations had to be directed at Jesus' *human* nature, not His *divine* nature. In all three temptations, Jesus was tempted to break His covenant of obedience with the Father and use His divine attributes. He could have turned the stones into bread, but only through His divine attributes. He could have jumped off the temple and called angels to rescue Him, but only through His divine nature. Since Jesus was God, He could have taken all the kingdoms of this world back from Satan without worshiping him. Unlike the last Adam, however, the second Adam resisted the temptations, and His obedience to the Father remained intact.

Power from the Holy Spirit

Jesus did extraordinary miracles: He healed the sick; He raised the dead; He cast out demons. Where did He get the power to do this? Humanly speaking, He couldn't do it. He had agreed not to use His divine attributes, so they were not the source of His power. All of Jesus' supernatural ministry was done by the power of the Holy Spirit working through Him.

The apostle Peter understood this well, and he explained it when he preached in the house of Cornelius. He told how Jesus "went about doing good and healing all who were oppressed of the devil" (Acts 10:38). But did Jesus do it on His own? No. He did it only because "God anointed [Him] with the Holy Spirit and with power" (v. 38). That's why Colin Brown calls it Spirit Christology.

Jesus Himself made it clear that He needed outside power to do what He did. He said, "The Son can do nothing of Himself, but what He sees the Father do" (John 5:19).

Did you ever think what Jesus was like when He was growing up? He probably cried when He was hungry just like all the babies we know. He needed potty training. He had to learn to talk Aramaic by trial and error. He couldn't understand a word of Chinese or Aztec or Hindi, simply because He had never learned those languages. I imagine that His parents scolded Him from time to time. He probably made His share of apprentice mistakes in His father's carpenter shop. He got indigestion when He ate bad food. In fact, the people of His hometown of Nazareth thought He was such a normal Jewish boy that, later on, they had little or no faith that the Jesus they knew could actually be the Messiah (see Matt. 13:54-58).

Jesus Was Different

While Jesus may have been a lot like the other boys His age, He was also different from them in that He was totally obedient to the Father. The first out-of-the-ordinary incident that we know about was when He once stayed behind in Jerusalem to dialogue with the Jewish teachers. Remember what He said to His parents by way of explanation? "Did you not know that I must be about My Father's business?" (Luke 2:49). Mary and Joseph didn't seem to understand at the time, but we do because we remember John 5:19, where Jesus said that He only did what He saw the Father doing.

We might think that Jesus' obedience was automatic, but that could not be the case. He was human, and He had to make His own choices. He had to *learn* obedience just like we do! Look at Hebrews 5:8: "Though He was a Son, yet He learned obedience by the things which He suffered."

Now let's focus on Jesus' power. When He cast out demons, it was not with His own power. He said, "I cast out demons with the finger of God" (Luke 11:20). When He passed judgment, it was with the authority delegated to Him by the Father. He said, "For the Father judges no one, but has committed all judgment to the Son" (John 5:22). And then, "I can of Myself do nothing. As I hear, I judge" (v. 30). Where did Jesus' wonderful teaching come from? "Whatever

I speak, just as the Father has told Me, so I speak" (John 12:50). No one had power to take Jesus' life without His personal agreement. He said, "I have power to lay it down, and I have power to take it again" (John 10:18). Where did He get this power? He went on to say, "This command I have received from My Father" (v. 18).

However, let's keep in mind that Jesus did something that no other human being or angel is allowed to do, namely, He accepted the worship of others. Jesus was always 100-percent God, even though He was not using His divine attributes. The wise men came to worship Him (see Matt. 2:2). A blind man whom Jesus healed worshiped Him (see John 9:38). A demonized man worshiped Him even before the demons were cast out (see Mark 5:6). Jesus never refused the worship of others.

The End of the Obedience

As I have written, Jesus' pact of obedience to the Father was not supposed to be forever. We read in Philippians 2:8 that He "became obedient to the point of death, even the death of the cross." Many who do not understand that Jesus was operating solely from His human nature have a hard time with His agonizing statement from the cross: "My God, My God, why have You forsaken Me?" (Matt. 27:46). However, it makes good sense if we suppose that, at this particular point, the Father chose not to reveal to Jesus what was actually happening and that Jesus' question was a normal human reaction.

When Jesus said, "Into Your hands I commit My spirit" (Luke 23:46), the covenant of obedience was all over. Jesus once again began using His divine attributes.

One clue that we find for understanding that a change took place at that time came after Jesus' resurrection when He was giving a final teaching to His disciples. Once again they asked Him, "Lord, will You at this time restore the kingdom to Israel?" (Acts 1:6). Notice that this question was almost identical to the one that earlier precipitated the questions surrounding Mark 13:32. At that time, before His death, Jesus did not know the answer as to when He was coming again, and He said so. This time, however, after His death, He did actually know, because, once again, He was using His divine attributes. Therefore, He simply said, "It is not for you to know

times or seasons which the Father has put in His own authority"
(Acts 1:7).

What Does This Mean for Us?

If Jesus used only His human nature while on earth and if His supernatural ministry was done by the power of the Holy Spirit working
through Him, the good news is that you and I today have access to
the same Holy Spirit and the same power. Knowing this helps us
greatly in understanding how Jesus could make the remarkable
statement, "He who believes in Me, the works that I do he will do
also; and greater works than these he will do, because I go to My Father" (John 14:12).

As I mentioned earlier, I went through the paradigm shift from
the two-channel theory to the incarnation-theology theory when I
was a young seminary student. However, I did not apply the implications of this to myself or accept the supernatural ministry of the
Holy Spirit until much later. I will explain that in chapter 6, "From
Programmed Evangelism to Power Evangelism."

Meanwhile, do not forget that Jesus ministered as a real man.

Notes

1. Colin Brown, *That You May Believe: Miracles and Faith Then and Now* (Grand Rapids, MI:
   Wm. B. Eerdmans Pub. Co., 1985), p. 97.
2. Ibid.

From **Human Abilities** to **Spiritual Gifts**

I'm sure that this will turn out to be the most basic chapter in this book. At least such would be true for me personally. I can safely say that, since being born again, no other biblical teaching has helped me live the Christian life and engage in productive ministry more than understanding spiritual gifts. Not only has it helped me know myself much better than I could have otherwise, but also it has enabled me to affirm and encourage a notable variety of brothers and sisters across a broad spectrum. Working with a biblical mindset for spiritual gifts makes life considerably more enjoyable.

When someone asks me which is the most helpful book for the body of Christ that I have written, I immediately respond with *Your Spiritual Gifts Can Help Your Church Grow*. It was first published in 1979 and is still in print; it has sold more copies than any other book I have written; it has been translated into many, many languages; and it is used across denominational lines from Episcopalians to Pentecostals. Part of the book's attraction is that it contains dictionary-type definitions of 28 spiritual gifts plus a 135-question, self-graded inventory that helps people take concrete steps toward discovering what gifts they might have.

Ignorance of Spiritual Gifts

But I'm getting ahead of my story. When my wife, Doris, and I were saved in the late 1940s, we found ourselves in the traditional evangelical stream of Protestantism. At that time, few, if any, of the leaders with whom we came into contact were teaching about spiritual gifts. Spiritual gifts were not discussed in my Inter-Varsity Christian Fellowship group in college. Pastors of the churches we attended did not sermonize on spiritual gifts. In order to train for the mission field, Doris enrolled in the Bible Institute of Los Angeles (Biola), and I enrolled in Fuller Theological Seminary. None of the professors under whom we sat instructed their students on the need to discover, develop and use their spiritual gifts. The committee of pastors who ordained me did not ask me what spiritual gifts I might have had. Even though Paul said, "Now concerning spiritual gifts, brethren, I do not want you to be ignorant" (1 Cor. 12:1), when we left the United States for missionary service in Bolivia in 1956, we were clearly ignorant of our spiritual gifts.

How did we know we were supposed to be foreign missionaries? Why did we choose Bolivia? Yes, we prayed and asked God to guide us. Back then we were taught that the truest display of consecration to God for any believer was to offer your life for foreign missionary service. Preachers would say, "Don't trade missionary service for an offer to be a king!" We were both young and consecrated, so we chose that route. We took out three years for training. We attended the Urbana Missionary Conference to become informed as to the mission boards and the mission fields. Since we both had a farming background, it was reasonable to conclude that we should be agricultural missionaries. We really didn't care what part of the world we went to, so when we read the literature of the South America Indian Mission (SAIM) and discovered that they advertised for agricultural missionaries, we applied and were accepted. They assigned us to a mission station in eastern Bolivia, and off we went.

Now, I'm sure you would have noticed that in that brief description of how we received the leading of the Lord to be career missionaries to Bolivia, not a mention was made of spiritual gifts. Prayer, consecration, sacrifice and obedience were the qualities stressed by our mentors. We believed that these virtues, combined with our consecrated human abilities, would keep us in the will of the Lord. We set forth to serve God, not because of certain spiritual gifts that He had given us, but because we loved Him and were willing to pay whatever price to serve Him. Permit me to pause and point out that I am not just describing ourselves here; I am accurately reflecting the environment of evangelical Christianity at that time—in a word, ignorance of spiritual gifts!

I must say that I was quite satisfied with the way things were going around our first mission station, Santiago de Chiquitos. We learned Spanish, and I did a bit of agricultural work; but my senior missionary felt that a greater need was for me to run a Bible Institute, since I was the first seminary-trained missionary to arrive in that part of the world. I assured him that I was ready to go wherever and do whatever the Lord directed, so from then on, that became my primary assignment. No longer was I an agricultural missionary!

Beginning the Shift

Soon after that, the paradigm shift began. In the providence of God, Doris and I became friends with another nearby missionary couple our age, Ken and Ruth Decker of the New Testament Missionary Union (NTMU). A British missiologist named Alexander Rattray Hay, who lived in Buenos Aires and was considered somewhat of a maverick by traditional evangelicals, founded the NTMU.

One of Hay's suspicious characteristics was that he based much of his mission strategy on spiritual gifts. Hay was by no means a Pentecostal; in fact, he was as anti-Pentecostal as we were at the time. However, he aggressively stressed employing most of the biblical spiritual gifts. I highly respected Ken Decker, so I followed his advice and read Hay's textbook, *The New Testament Order for Church and Missionary*. I was fascinated by what, for me, was brand-new teaching!

Back in 1947, when he wrote his book, Hay had noticed the same thing I have been describing. He writes, "[Spiritual gifts] is one of the subjects least understood by Christian people today. It is seldom adequately taught."[1] This caught my attention, and the pages that followed gave me a solid biblical framework on which to build my own teaching on spiritual gifts, a framework that I have used ever since.

As I began to absorb these new ideas, I gravitated toward specializing in 1 Corinthians in my Bible school teaching because 1 Corinthians has more detail on spiritual gifts than any other book in the Bible. Studying and developing teaching notes on a given subject is one of my preferred ways of deepening my understanding of whatever issues God is bringing to my attention at the moment. This, characteristically, would lead me to putting my thoughts in writing, which I did in a series of articles for *Eternity* magazine. Just as an aside, this became my first significant experience in publishing my material.

Stedman Legitimizes Spiritual Gifts

Spiritual gifts remained one of my major areas of concentration as I returned from Bolivia to begin teaching at Fuller Seminary in 1971. In fact, that was also the year that I published my thoughts on 1 Corinthians in *A Turned-on Church in an Uptight World*. I was more convinced than ever that the idea that God would lead us in our ministry direction through consecrated and sacrificial use of our human abilities alone was a misguided thought. However, my spheres of influence were so limited that I felt I was making very little progress in helping others consider making the same paradigm shift I had experienced. It seemed like I was a small voice crying in the wilderness. With this, you can imagine my elation when Ray Stedman, a high-profile evangelical pastor in Palo Alto, California, published his book *Body Life* in 1972.

Body Life was an instant Christian bestseller. It became the talk of the evangelical world. The fact that Peninsula Bible Church was one of the most vigorously growing churches in the nation helped its visibility a great deal. Stedman unfolded a philosophy of ministry revolving around the biblical teaching of spiritual gifts. He writes, "The church is primarily and fundamentally a body designed to express through each individual member the life of an indwelling Lord and is equipped by the Holy Spirit with gifts designed to express that life."[2] It was not long before the paradigms of church leaders across the nation began shifting. Suddenly spiritual gifts were cool!

A Curious Silence Through History

With all this, one question that began bothering me was why Christian leaders up to that point had not unearthed and taught this obvious and clear biblical truth through the ages. The Roman Church did not see it; the Eastern Orthodox did not see it; Martin Luther did not see it; John Calvin did not see it; John Wesley did not see it; Jonathan Edwards did not see it; and on and on. Alexander Hay did see it, and he wrote about it, but he was marginalized by the evangelical establishment. Later on, I saw it, and undoubtedly some others did as well, but few were listening. This lasted until Ray Stedman single-handedly brought the teaching about spiritual gifts into the mainline.

The Pentecostal Movement

An obvious exception to what I am saying was the birth of the Pentecostal Movement right after the turn of the twentieth century. From the outset, Pentecostals began teaching and preaching on spiritual gifts and demonstrating their use in their churches and ministries. With the current explosion of worldwide Pentecostalism today, it is hard to believe, but the fact of the matter is that at least for the first half of the twentieth century, Pentecostalism grew very slowly and had virtually no influence outside of its own well-defined spheres. It was not uncommon for influential evangelical leaders to pronounce Pentecostalism a false cult. Many who didn't want to put it that strongly would relegate them to the lunatic fringe of Christianity. Pentecostalism was labeled Hillbilly Religion, and Pentecostals were called Holy Rollers.

After Alexander Hay lamented the paucity of teaching on spiritual gifts, he went on to write, "Unfortunately, the teaching of it is left to groups [undoubtedly referring to Pentecostals] whose presentation of it is extravagant and unsound."[3] Of course, the one spiritual gift that terrified traditional believers more than any of the others was speaking in tongues. The practice was frequently attributed to demonic activity by respected evangelical leaders. Such attitudes toward Pentecostals on the part of the body of Christ in general were enough to cause aversion to any teaching on spiritual gifts at all, at least until Ray Stedman came along.

The stories I have been telling go back a generation or two. Fortunately, our present generation of believers now accepts Pentecostalism as a legitimate, and frequently envied, form of biblical Christianity. I feel that I should say that I was honored to have had a small slice of the action when, in 1973, I published *Look Out! The Pentecostals Are Coming*. In it, I tried to help legitimize Pentecostalism among my traditional evangelical friends. Pentecostal leader Jack Hayford told me that, for him, it was the most influential book I have ever written.

Enough of history. Let's get to substance.

The Body of Christ

The three major passages on spiritual gifts in the New Testament are found in Romans 12, 1 Corinthians 12 and Ephesians 4. Each one of them highlights "the body of Christ" as a key metaphor for understanding how spiritual gifts function. This obviously means that if we are going to grasp this paradigm of spiritual gifts, we must be sure we know the meaning of "the body of Christ."

It's not a difficult assignment. Ephesians 1:22-23 reads, "He [God] put all things under His [Jesus'] feet, and gave Him to be head over all things to the church, which is His body." The church is Jesus' body, the body of Christ. If there is any doubt, Colossians 1:24 goes on to say, "I now rejoice in my sufferings for you, and fill up in my flesh what is lacking in the afflictions of Christ, for the sake of His body, which is the church." Enough said. Jesus' body is the church. Every major passage on spiritual gifts relates using them to the function of individual members of the church. And let me add what will come up in detail later in the book. The church, which I will refer to frequently, will always include not just the traditional local church as we know it but also the church in the workplace.

With this in mind, we have an important clue as to God's original design for the day-to-day operation of the church. He did not intend that it would be a dictatorship, with one person running the church and doing all the ministry. On the other hand, He did not foresee a democracy in which every member has a part in running the church or votes for those who do. Rather, God chose to make the church, the body of Christ, an organism with Jesus Christ as the head and every member functioning with one or more spiritual gifts. It is hard to believe, but, as I have pointed out, this simple, biblical concept of the basic dynamics of the church only began to be broadly highlighted with Ray Stedman's book published in 1972. It was definitely a new paradigm as far as the sweep of church history is concerned.

What Is a Spiritual Gift?

Precisely what is a spiritual gift? A spiritual gift is a special attribute given by the Holy Spirit to every member of the body of Christ, according to God's grace, for use within the context of the body.

Let me explain a couple of things in that definition. First look at "the context of the body." This includes whatever the church is assigned by God to do, including outreach to the community, not just ministering to the faithful. It also encompasses God's assignments to the church in the workplace as well as to our traditional local churches.

Second, look at the phrase "according to God's grace." The biblical word for grace is *charis*. The word for spiritual gift is *charisma*. Do you see how grace is an integral part of any spiritual gift? The only way you ever get a spiritual gift is by the sovereign grace of God. You cannot generate it yourself. "But now God has set the members, each one of them, in the body just as He pleased" (1 Cor. 12:18). Spiritual gifts are *received*, not *achieved*!

I want to stress the fact that every single true believer has one or more spiritual gifts. Look at 1 Peter 4:10: "As each one has received a gift, minister it to one another, as good stewards of the manifold grace of God." Look also at 1 Corinthians 12:7. About spiritual gifts Paul writes, "But the manifestation of the Spirit [spiritual gifts] is given to each one for the profit of all."

Knowing Your Spiritual Gifts

There are many advantages for you to know about your spiritual gifts. They will benefit you in your personal life, and they will help you to be a better all-around person that you ever have been. If they benefit you and other believers as well, they will then benefit the whole church. Knowing your spiritual gifts is a key to helping you know God's will for your life.

For example, in Romans 12:2 Paul says that you're supposed to be transformed by the renewing of your mind to do God's perfect will. How do you do that? The next few verses tell us to think soberly of ourselves because we have "gifts differing according to the grace that is given to us" (Rom. 12:6), followed by one of the chief lists of spiritual gifts in the New Testament.

Speaking of God's will, I think that every believer should strive for what Fuller Seminary professor Bobby Clinton calls convergence. He stresses convergence for leaders, but there is also a sense in which we all would do well to set convergence as a life goal. If we do, "God moves the [believer] into a role that matches his or her gift-mix and experience so that ministry is maximized."[4]

This not only helps you know what you're supposed to be doing, but, just as important, it also helps you know what you should *not* be doing because God has not chosen to gift you for that ministry. I personally reached convergence around age 50; but, unfortunately, according to Clinton's research, a relatively small percentage of leaders, never mind believers in general, reach convergence at all. The major reason that I was able to do so was because I had gone through the paradigm shift that I am describing in this chapter.

If all this is correct, it becomes obvious that one of the most important spiritual exercises in your Christian life should be to discover, develop and use your spiritual gifts. Notice carefully that "discover" comes before "develop." You can't develop what you do not have.

Constitutionalists vs. Situationalists

When I just wrote that this is obvious, I meant that it is obvious to me. I have some friends who do not fully agree with me at this point. I think I should pause to address this issue because it is the most crucial point of disagreement among those of us who believe in and teach about spiritual gifts. To use theological terms, it is the difference between the *constitutional* view of spiritual gifts (which I hold) and the *situational* view of spiritual gifts.

The situational view, which is the position of most Pentecostals and charismatics, is that when a believer receives the indwelling of the Holy Spirit, the Holy Spirit brings all the gifts of the Spirit. Therefore, if you are filled with the Holy Spirit, you have all the spiritual gifts, not just some of them. This means that there is no need to discover which gifts you have and which you don't have, because you have them all. You just depend on the Holy Spirit to activate the particular gifts that you need for a given *situation*.

For example, if you are praying for a sick person, the Spirit will activate the gift of healing. If you are praying for someone who needs direction, the Spirit will activate the gift of prophecy. If you are witnessing to an unbeliever, the Spirit will activate the gift of evangelist. If you need to make a crucial decision, the Spirit will activate the gift of wisdom.

As I hinted previously, I cannot agree with this situational view. While I do not think it is a heresy, I do think that it is biblically misinformed. It does not hold up to the main biblical analogy for understanding spiritual gifts, namely, the way the human body is constituted. Our bodies have many different members, each of which has its own function and does not attempt to do what the other members are supposed to do. The ears hear, but they cannot chew; the teeth chew, but they cannot breathe; the lungs breathe, but they cannot digest food; and so on.

This is the way the body of Christ is supposed to operate. Take my own case as an example. My two main spiritual gifts are apostle and teacher. These gifts have become a part of my personal *constitution*. That's who I am because God has chosen to constitute me that way. No one has ever confused me, for example, with a prophet, an evangelist or a pastor. I actually hate the thought of trying to be any of those three because I know I have no supernatural gifts for doing those tasks. If I didn't understand that, I would never have reached convergence. I would still be trying to do everything and, in the process, attempting many things poorly with only human abilities.

I am currently known as a leader in the charismatic movement. I am ordained by Glory of Zion International, a charismatic apostolic network. However, I feel that I should go on record here by saying that one of my greatest disappointments since, years ago, I moved from the traditional evangelical stream to the charismatic stream has been discovering the anemic view of spiritual gifts among many, if not most, charismatics. Research in the sociology of religion has uncovered the ironic fact that evangelicals in general hold a stronger and more biblical view of spiritual gifts than typical charismatics, even though charismatics usually talk about them more. A part of the charismatic weakness comes from their tendency to limit the list of spiritual gifts to the 9 gifts found in the first part of 1 Corinthians 12. That is a short list. My list of gifts numbers no fewer than 28!

Let's see what they are.

A List of Spiritual Gifts

As I have said, the three major lists of spiritual gifts are found in Romans 12, 1 Corinthians 12, and Ephesians 4. If we collate the spiritual gifts mentioned in those passages, we come up with 20 of them: prophecy, ministry (or service), teaching, exhortation, giving, leadership, mercy, wisdom, knowledge, faith, healings, miracles, discernment of spirits, tongues, interpretation of tongues, apostle, helps, administration, evangelist and pastor. Five more gifts are mentioned in other Scriptures, including celibacy (see 1 Cor. 7:7), hospitality (1 Pet. 4:9), martyrdom (1 Cor. 13:3), voluntary poverty (1 Cor. 13:3), and missionary (Eph. 3:6-9). A total of 25 is all I have found in Scripture.

But are these all the spiritual gifts? Could there be some other gifts that God is actually giving to believers that might not be mentioned as such in Scripture? I don't see why not. In fact, there are three spiritual gifts that I have been observing through the years that are not mentioned specifically as gifts in the Bible, yet the ministries are clearly biblical ministries. Some may disagree, but the three that I have personally become convinced about are intercession, deliverance and leading worship, bringing us to a total of 28 spiritual gifts. Yes, there may be more or there may be fewer, but I think we have a fairly reasonable list here.

Five Steps Toward Discovering Your Spiritual Gifts

Since I first went through this paradigm shift in the 1950s, I have been teaching the subject regularly, and I have read dozens of books on gifts as well. My experience coincides with most other experts, and we agree that these are five essential steps toward discovering your spiritual gifts.

1. *Explore the possibilities.* You need to know what is the range of gifts and their definitions. I provide dictionary definitions of all 28 spiritual gifts in my books and my questionnaire.

2. *Experiment with as many as you can.* As you try the gifts out, ask yourself two questions: (1) Do I have the gift? (2) Do I not have the gift? In a way, they are equally important questions, and you are looking for the answers.

3. *Examine your feelings.* If you really have the gift, you will like using it. That's why the Bible says, "For it is God

who works in you both to *will* and to do for His good pleasure" (Phil. 2:13, emphasis added).

4. *Evaluate your effectiveness.* If you have a certain spiritual gift, it will accomplish its purpose because of the special, supernatural help that God gives you in using it.

5. *Expect confirmation from the body.* If you truly have a certain spiritual gift, others in your circle of friends will recognize it and encourage you to use it more.

If you know your spiritual gifts and have been using them, this chapter will be an encouragement to you. If you don't, I've given you some concrete action steps to begin to take now. Follow this basic advice, and I promise you that when you discover your gifts, it will turn out to be your most important spiritual advance since being born again and getting filled with the Holy Spirit.

Notes

1. Alexander Rattray Hay, *The New Testament Order for Church and Missionary* (Temperley, Argentina: New Testament Missionary Union, 1947), p. 175.
2. Ray C. Stedman, *Body Life* (Ventura, CA: Regal Books, 1972), p. 51.
3. Hay, *The New Testament Order of Church and Missionary*, p. 175.
4. J. Robert Clinton, *The Making of a Leader* (Colorado Springs, CO: Navpress, 1988), p. 46.

From **Theological Education** to **Equipping** the **Saints**

Picture the early 1950s. My wife, Doris, and I were new converts and were called to serve as foreign missionaries. We found ourselves in the traditional evangelical stream of Protestantism. Doris had a high school diploma, and I had just graduated from college. We had been informed that if we expected to be accepted by a recognized mission board, we would need the proper training. That was all right with us. We were ready to do whatever it took to get to the mission field.

Preparing for the Mission Field

We began asking advice from our pastor and from other Christian leaders whom we knew. I was told that before we left for the mission field, I should seek ordination to Christian ministry. Since I was a university graduate, this meant that I should enroll in a graduate school of theology, namely, a theological seminary. Keep in mind that those were the days when professional ministry was almost entirely in the hands of men. There was no suggestion that Doris should seek ordination as well. Simply put, I was to be the missionary, and her role would be a missionary's wife. Nowadays, it is embarrassing to admit it, but, back then, we simply accepted those gender-specific roles without question. In fact, we had been taught that it was the proper biblical pattern and was theologically correct.

After examining the possibilities with reasonable diligence, we decided that Fuller Theological Seminary in Pasadena, California, would be the best choice. Part of that decision had to do with Doris. Regardless of her formal future role, we knew that she would do better on the mission field with some good biblical training, and Fuller happened to be in the vicinity of the Bible Institute of Los Angeles (Biola), for which she qualified.

During seminary orientation, I was congratulated for choosing Fuller because this relatively new school was determined to offer the finest evangelical theological education in the nation. This built my confidence a great deal because I reasoned that, if I were to be a good missionary, I would need quality preparation for the field. As I went through my three years at Fuller, I felt that I was getting exactly what they had advertised. I graduated with my Master of Divinity degree, I was ordained, and Doris and I ended up on the mission field in rural eastern Bolivia.

Looking Back

This is a book on paradigm shifts. I have tried to explain why my first paradigm for excellence in ministerial training was theological education. This paradigm lasted for a long time. However, before I begin to describe some of the field applications I made with this paradigm, I feel that I must deviate for a moment and fast forward to what I later explain in much more detail in chapter 5, "From Mono-cultural Theology to Cross-cultural Theology."

As I've already written, I enrolled in theological seminary in order to prepare for professional missionary service. However, in three years of study, I was offered only two courses in missions; the first was taught by a professor of church history who had never been on the mission field. The second was reading a series of missionary biographies. This is no reflection on Fuller because it was the accepted pattern in theological seminaries across the board at that time. More relevant academic fields such as cultural anthropology or missiology were not considered in those days.

So what did I do? After I learned Spanish, I was assigned to direct a Bible school for training future ministers. I naturally wanted the very best for the Bolivians who were to pastor the churches that we missionaries were planting in their nation. What was the best? Why, the theological education that I had received in seminary, of course! I had carefully preserved the class notes I took in all my seminary courses, so I built a three-year curriculum for the Eastern Bible Institute (*Instituto Bíblico del Oriente*) around those courses. My class preparation consisted mainly of translating my notes into Spanish, hopefully simplifying things enough so that the students, who had never so much as been to high school, could understand them. Needless to say, I gave them easy exams, and they all eventually passed.

Curriculum

I have just brought up the issue of curriculum. What exactly did we need to know in order to be competent missionaries or pastors of Bolivian churches? The only answer I could give to that question was that they should have theological education, just like I had. I found that this had long been established in the curricula of European universities, with roots even going back to the Middle Ages and later installed in American seminaries like Fuller. The standard curriculum in American seminaries was designed and implemented, with very few exceptions, by academic scholars, not field practitioners. Like begets like. Scholars tend to produce scholars, not hands-on pastors.

Through the years, theology had become known as the queen of the sciences, and the curriculum reflected exactly that. Courses in systematic theology were central. Since it seemed important for future ministers and missionaries to know how theologians had arrived at their conclusions, courses in the history of dogma were required. Biblical courses were focused on exegesis, so learning Greek and Hebrew would be essential. Different ways of interpreting the Bible were covered under hermeneutics. Church history was essential. In order to pass their courses, students were forced to write scholarly research papers with copious footnotes. The few ministry-oriented courses were taught in the department of practical *theology*. Missions courses came basically as an afterthought.

As you would have guessed, when I tried to apply the only ministerial training paradigm I knew to aspiring Bolivian pastors, the results were not far from a disaster. Very few of the students ever ended up in vocational pastoral ministry, and the school eventually disbanded. Before it did, I had transferred from the rural setting of eastern Bolivia to the influential city of Cochabamba, this time assigned to the Emmaus Bible Institute, which had become one of the most respected ministerial training schools in the nation. The curriculum? The same old paradigm of theological education! In fact, I was so deeply programmed with that paradigm that I went one step further. In order to make the school more like Fuller, I changed the name from Emmaus Bible Institute to George Allan Theological Seminary, named after the founder of our mission!

Enough of the old traditional paradigm. Now let's move on to the paradigm shift.

If It's Broke, Fix It!

We have a common vernacular saying: If it ain't broke, don't fix it! The corollary would be, If it *is* broke, fix it. Unfortunately, our traditional paradigm of theological education is broke. How do I know? Let me present some facts.

Researcher Christian Schwartz holds the distinction of having completed the most comprehensive field study of church growth and health ever attempted. He used more than 1,000 churches in 32 nations to build his database. Among other things, here is what he found: "Formal theological training has a negative correlation to both church growth and overall quality of churches."[1] Of the highest-quality and fastest-growing churches, 58 percent of the pastors had never graduated from seminary. Of the lowest-quality and declining churches, a full 85 percent of the pastors had graduated from seminary![2]

I served as Presiding Apostle of the International Coalition of Apostles during the first decade of the 2000s. I surveyed approximately 350 recognized apostles, all of them seasoned Christian leaders, and I found that 60 percent of them had never graduated from theological seminary or even Bible college.

Finally, George Barna, widely recognized as the premier researcher of church affairs in America, has arrived at similar conclusions. He reports, "Most pastors agree that they were inadequately trained for the job of leading the local church. Yet, seminaries continue to forge ahead, providing much of the same irrelevant (and in some cases misleading and harmful) education that has been their forte for the past century."[3] When he tested pastors for a biblical worldview, Barna found that the pastors least likely to have a biblical worldview were those who graduated from seminary (45 percent). On the other hand, 59 percent of pastors who never attended seminary had a biblical worldview.[4]

With this information, it is obvious that a serious paradigm shift is needed.

Theological Education by Extension

My paradigm began to shift soon after I met Ralph Winter, a Presbyterian missionary to Guatemala and later a professor at the Fuller Seminary School of World Mission. While in Guatemala, Winter began noticing a phenomenon, not characteristic of Guatemala alone, but seen throughout all of Latin America. An extraordinary number of Latin American evangelical churches were being pastored by individuals who had been selected from the congregation itself and had never been to seminary or Bible school. Once he pointed it out, I realized that it was definitely true in the area of Bolivia where I was working. Furthermore, their numbers were increasing. Churches were being multiplied much more rapidly than student bodies in our traditional schools.

This new reality led Ralph Winter to design and develop a radical innovation in ministerial training called Theological Education by Extension (TEE). These pastors needed training, but they could not attend our traditional residential schools. They were older people who had families, jobs, financial responsibilities and community involvements, which would not permit them to pack up and go off to school. Winter suggested that instead of expecting the students to come to our schools, we begin taking our schools out to the students, holding classes in regional centers and adjusting the schedules to the needs of the students. TEE spread rapidly throughout Latin America and other parts of the world as well. I incorporated it into our seminary in Bolivia, and enrollment doubled in each of the next two years.

What shifted? It wasn't the whole paradigm. Our curriculum, for example, remained the same. However, TEE brought two very important changes: First, we scrapped our previous assumption that our schools needed to be residential. Students could live at home and still be trained. Second, we began training *in-service* students as well as *pre-service* students. Let me explain the difference in more detail.

I was first introduced to in-service training when I enrolled in the new School of World Mission, founded by Donald McGavran at Fuller Theological Seminary. McGavran's requirements for students were that they must have ministered as missionaries in a second culture, validated by fluency in the vernacular language. This learning environment with mature, experienced field workers was vastly different from my earlier studies in the Fuller School of Theology, where we younger students hadn't been in vocational ministry but were preparing to begin it after our training. Later, when I joined the Fuller faculty, I taught the in-service missions students I have just described plus two kinds of students in the School of Theology, namely, pre-service masters-level students and in-service Doctor of Ministry students, most of whom were practicing pastors. I clearly preferred teaching the in-service students. They were the ones who asked the really significant questions in class.

As an example, I will quote from a recent article by my Fuller colleague Daniel Shaw: "In one course I taught recently, I had forty-two students from thirteen nations, with a combined 313 years of mission experience in forty-six countries. Such prior knowledge of the world generates an expectation of rich classroom participation and dialogue."[5] Traditional pre-service schooling cannot match this kind of teaching and learning environment.

Equipping All the Saints

I have described this paradigm shift as moving from theological education to equipping the saints. The phrase "the equipping of the saints for the work of ministry" is found in Ephesians 4:12. The previous verse lists those who have the assignment of doing the equipping, namely, apostles, prophets, evangelists, pastors and teachers. The new paradigm is an essential component of what now is known as the New Apostolic Reformation, which I will describe in chapter 9.

If we take "the equipping of the saints for the work of ministry" at face value, we find that it has several important implications: One of them is that the people who need to be equipped are the saints, or all the people of God. Another implication is that each individual saint has been assigned a ministry, whether in the church or in the workplace, that requires a particular kind of resourcing. A third is that equipping implies providing whatever resources might be necessary to enable persons to do whatever is required of them.

This undertaking will certainly include schooling, but it cannot stop there. Equipping the saints encompasses a much broader scope than most traditional seminaries and Bible schools have been able to provide. It clearly needs to go beyond the standard curriculum of theological education. While I was teaching in seminary, an energetic debate arose as to whether a seminary was or was not responsible for the spiritual life and character of its students. As I recall, the outcome was a standoff. At least half of the professors believed that focusing on the students' heads, to the exclusion of their hearts, was sufficient.

Now we are in the Second Apostolic Age (see chapter 9 for a description of the Second Apostolic Age). Apostolic leaders are no longer satisfied with a monastic academic model designed to elevate a few clergy to an elite academic level so that they will be qualified to minister to the laity. Rather, their desire is a broad, open, fluid system designed to equip all the saints for the work of the ministry to which they have been assigned. Apostolic training centers are evaluated on their ability to equip God's people on all levels, nothing more and nothing less.

Ordination

Earlier I wrote that I was advised to seek ministerial ordination before I went to the mission field. Without many exceptions, the American public assumes that every church in town is led by an ordained minister. Details of ordination might vary from denomination to denomination, but all have a common assumption that a prescribed course of study is as necessary for ministers as it is for attorneys or physicians. The nature of that training is theological education as I have been describing it. This was all part of my old paradigm.

The new paradigm questions the presumptions of traditional ordination. For one thing, the New Testament does not distinguish between ordained and unordained ministry. In fact, all of the saints—not just selected clergy—are to do the work of ministry according to the varied assignments that they receive from God. Furthermore, the requirements for leaders such as deacons, elders and bishops do not include academic attainments such as theology or church history; rather, the essential components to qualify as a

bishop, a deacon or an elder are character qualities such as blameless, temperate, not greedy for money, the husband of one wife, not
a novice, not self-willed, having a good testimony from those outside, and many more (see 1 Tim. 3:1-7; Titus 1:5-9). Ordination in
the New Apostolic Reformation tends to deemphasize traditional
academics and looks mostly at character and positive performance
in ministry.

What is ordination anyway? Ordination is the public recognition on the part of the body of Christ that a certain believer has received a spiritual gift and has been ministering with that gift
effectively for a period of time. Ordination confers not a gift but an
office. God gives the gift by grace, but the person earns the office by
works, in other words, by displaying the fruit of the gift in his or
her ministry. This applies to pastors, evangelists, apostles, intercessors, deliverance ministers, prophets, teachers, worship leaders, and
many more. There is a predictable increase in spiritual power when
the office is conferred on top of the gift.

Accountability, Not Accreditation

Ordination is only one part of the new paradigm that demands
changing the old patterns of traditional theological education.
What forms are seen in the new educational wineskins? As might
be expected, a wide variety of training methods is now emerging.
Creativity and innovation reign!

This first became clear to me in 1998, when I convened an ad
hoc meeting of 100 educators from a number of apostolic networks.
These educators had all been moving away from the paradigm of
theological education, through which most of them had previously
been schooled, to new paradigms for equipping ministers. However,
no two of them had developed the same design or were using the
same methodologies. As the meeting progressed and the educators
began to feel like kindred spirits, it became obvious that it would
be impossible to agree on an ideal set of standards to which all
would conform. For example, one network was assigned by God to
train leaders for planting churches in university communities, while
another was providing training to godly, gifted people who happened to be illiterate.

One of the first things that became obvious as the discussions progressed was that, for apostolic schools, traditional academic accreditation was a dead-end street. Some had initially attempted it, but most soon abandoned the idea. Conforming to known accreditation associations would be tantamount to deciding to reenter the old wineskin! Rejection of traditional accreditation, as I think back, turned out to be the strongest uniting force of the group. At the end of the day, 40 institutions represented there decided to join together with a covenant of mutual accountability and form the Apostolic Council for Educational Accountability (ACEA) under my leadership. ACEA is a professional society, requiring dues and attendance at the annual meeting. More than 85 schools have been served by ACEA, and it is now in the hands of Apostle Leo Lawson of Raleigh, North Carolina.

In order to implement the concept of uniting under *accountability* rather than *accreditation*, a system of on-site visits has been incorporated. The purpose of these visits is not to evaluate the school according to a set of prescribed standards compiled in an accreditation manual; rather, it is to clarify the exact assignment that God has given to the school in question and then to evaluate, on-site, how well the school is implementing its assignment. This tends to bind ACEA members together, and rather than be competitors, the leaders of these schools become cheerleaders for each other.

Methods Are Changing

As my educational paradigm continued to shift, I transitioned out of Fuller Seminary, where I logged 30 years of teaching, and started Wagner Leadership Institute (WLI), now being led by Apostle Ché Ahn of Pasadena, California. WLI is founded on apostolic principles, some of which are 180-degrees from the traditional theological education mold. The following are some examples:

• *No academic requirements.* Accredited theological seminaries, because they require a college degree for entrance, have eliminated 75 percent of the saints from being equipped in their facilities. Only 25 percent of American adults have college degrees. I wanted to open WLI to all the saints, whether in the church or in the workplace, so I instituted no academic requirements. Academic attainments count, but other considerations are taken into account for placing them in bachelor, master or doctoral levels.

• *Impartation along with information.* In WLI, I instruct my faculty not to focus primarily on transferring a body of knowledge from their heads to the heads of the students, as much as imparting to them tools and anointing for fruitful ministry. As typical WLI students will tell you, they invariably suffer from information overload, but that is secondary to the spiritual growth that comes through impartation by whatever methodology the instructor chooses.

• *No exams or grades.* Because of the focus on impartation, it is impossible to give examinations or letter grades for the courses. Just being in a room and interacting with someone like Chuck Pierce, Cindy Jacobs, Ché Ahn or Bill Hamon for 12 hours is an experience that cannot be graded. Each student writes a self-evaluation paper to bring closure to the course.

• *No resident students or resident faculty.* It is impossible for in-service students to enroll in a residential institution. They have families, homes, jobs, community involvements and ministry assignments wherever they live. The median age in our typical WLI classes is late 40s or early 50s. By using visiting faculty, it is possible to draw on the very best in each field on a time-available basis.

• *Variable delivery systems.* The WLI delivery system of two back-to-back days per course does not fit all ACEA institutions. Some have residence programs. Some offer classes Thursday and Friday nights and all day Saturday. Some have classes one night per week. Some use retreats and conferences. Others will schedule occasional weeklong evening courses. Numerous courses are on CDs and DVDs as well as online, and are available for individual or small-group study.

- *Curriculum.* WLI courses are tailor-made to fit the needs of the students. There are few required courses on the supposition that the saints who are already in ministry know better about what they need in order to be more effective than would a remote school administrator or an accrediting association. The old-wineskin ratio of 80 percent theory and 20 percent practical application is pretty well reversed in apostolic schools.

Moving Ahead

As many of us have gone through this paradigm shift and begun to apply it in real life, it is not surprising that we have received criticism from traditional theological education establishments. Some have condemned our non-accredited schools as being diploma mills. Some say that mutual accountability can never substitute for legitimate accreditation. In fact, when I attempted to advertise WLI in a prominent Christian magazine, I was turned down because WLI wasn't accredited!

Nevertheless, the Second Apostolic Age is here to stay, and paradigm shifts such as the one from theological education to equipping the saints will continue to multiply in order to accommodate the new apostolic wineskin. I do not want to be a spectator as this unfolds; I want to be a player!

Notes
1. Christian A. Schwartz, *Natural Church Development* (Carol Stream, IL: ChurchSmart Resources, 1996), p. 23.
2. Ibid.
3. George Barna, personal communication, 1998.
4. Barna Research Group, "Only Half of Protestant Pastors Have a Biblical Worldview," Barna Research Online, January 12, 2004. http://barna.org/cgibn/PagePressRelease.asp?PressReleaseID=156&Reference=F (accessed February 2004).
5. R. Daniel Shaw, "Beyond Contextualization," *International Bulletin of Missionary Research* (October 2010), p. 208.

4

From **Passive Evangelism** to **Pragmatic Evangelism**

The person who was most influential in renewing my mind concerning the nature of evangelism was Donald McGavran. Let me tell you how I connected with him.

Throughout my 16 years of field missionary experience in Bolivia, I tried to keep track of what was going on among Christian leaders back in the United States as best as I could. I subscribed to a good number of Christian magazines. Using the book review sections of the magazines, I attempted to keep my library up to date by regularly ordering books. Reading all these books was quite a challenge, although the strict rule of siesta while we were in rural eastern Bolivia during our first term helped a great deal. From 12:00 noon until 2:30 in the afternoon, the town completely shut down. Most people took a nap, but I had never accustomed myself to sleeping during the day, so I had two hours every day in my hammock for uninterrupted reading.

Cockroach Food

One siesta, the top book on my stack happened to be *The Bridges of God* by Donald McGavran. I had read a very complimentary review of the book in one of my missions journals, which even suggested that McGavran was putting forth some of the most radical and innovative theories of missiology imaginable. I am embarrassed to admit this now, but as I read these strange ideas of what evangelism and missions should look like, I came to the conclusion that the author of this book must be, to use the vernacular, a missiological quack. What McGavran was advocating was the direct opposite of what I had learned from my seminary professors, the world mission leaders I had met and the fellow field missionaries with whom I was working. I put the book back on the shelf for cockroach food—we lived in the jungle, and cockroaches did chew on some of our books!—and gave McGavran no further thought.

However, a few years later, my alma mater, Fuller Theological Seminary, announced that they were inaugurating a new School of World Mission and that the founding dean was to be none other than Donald McGavran. This certainly aroused my interest, and when the time came for our second furlough, I decided to enroll in the School of World Mission in order to learn a little firsthand about this innovative missiologist. The upshot was that I did not learn a little; I learned a lot. I became a thorough disciple of McGavran; he persuaded me to leave Bolivia and join his faculty; and I ended up McGavran's successor and the first incumbent of the Donald McGavran Chair of Church Growth.

With that background, let's try to understand how McGavran shifted the paradigm of the foreign missions movement in the United States and how I shifted my personal paradigm to become part of it.

My Comfortable Situation

When Doris and I went to Bolivia as field missionaries in 1956, we, like most missionaries of our day, were considered by those who knew us as spiritual heroes. We had left our home, our parents, our brothers and sisters and our comfortable lifestyle to follow the Lord's leading to, for us, an unknown part of the world. Doris and I never personally absorbed the spiritual accolades that came our way, but my point is that, for better or worse, I have described the general attitude of the Christian public toward missionaries. This leads to the conclusion that doing missionary work is a good thing that merits spiritual, personal and financial support.

This was very comfortable for me, and I can speak for most missionaries of my generation. Our public relations organs, largely in the form of missionary prayer letters, were geared toward convincing supporters to approve whatever we happened to be doing. If we could persuade our constituency that we were very busy doing God's work, then they would most likely continue to support us.

One implication of this is that we missionaries, unlike people in most other fields of endeavor, found ourselves virtually exempt from being evaluated on the basis of our performance. Our support-ers never expected the type of information that would enable them to make an independent judgment evaluating what returns they might be getting on their investments. One missionary, reporting his work, said, "This kind of evangelism is a fantastic work for the Lord and produces a rich harvest of souls." Most of the rest of us tended to report our work in that kind of imprecise terminology. We succeeded in communicating the impression that for support-ers to somehow require more precise reporting of missionary en-deavor would be less than spiritual.

The agreed-upon biblical basis for going to the foreign field was to obey Jesus' Great Commission of preaching the gospel to every creature and winning souls. Whatever we did needed to contribute in one way or another to evangelism, and that was ordinarily taken for granted by supporters or leaders of mission boards. We were able to avoid objective evaluation by using this pious-sounding phrase: We leave the results to God. This leveled the playing field so much that it would become impossible, even disreputable, to attempt to distinguish between competent missionaries on the one hand and incompetent missionaries on the other.

Our task, then? Just keep on doing missionary work. Jesus promised that He would always be with us (see Matt. 28:20). Jesus will see that we all accomplish our purpose, and the results will come by the Holy Spirit in His good time.

Do you see what I mean when I say that missionary work was a comfortable occupation?

A New Philosophy of Missions

Now you can understand my reaction to reading Donald Mc-Gavran's *The Bridges of God* when I was in my hammock. He would talk about using scientific principles for missionary evangelism. He distinguished between theoreticians and practitioners. He suggested that missionaries and mission boards be held accountable for their results. He advocated a new philosophy of missions that kept records of production, used graphs to discern trends, and analyzed factors contributing both to successful evangelism and unsuccess-ful evangelism.

This at first sounded very carnal to me. It seemed as if Mc-Gavran was trying to apply worldly principles from business management to the missionary enterprise. I didn't think there was anything in the Bible that told us to be scientific about serving God. I was afraid that sociology, statistics and computers might subtly take the place of the Holy Spirit.

Looking back on all that now, I can see that I definitely needed a paradigm shift!

After meeting McGavran personally, reading more of his material and beginning to take his courses, my paradigm shift came quite quickly. I began to see that my passive approach to evangelism—leaving the results up to God, no matter what I did—was neither a display of heroic spirituality nor even of basic faithfulness to God.

Mission Strategy

In preparation for going to the mission field, I read books and magazines on missions, I attended missionary conferences, I earned a Master of Theology degree from Fuller Seminary, I spent several days in intensive orientation with the General Director of the mission board we had joined, I constantly talked about missions with other believers, and I thought I was fairly well informed. However, after coming into contact with McGavran, I began to realize that none of that pre-service preparation, nor what I subsequently learned after arriving on the mission field, dealt specifically with mission strategy. Yes, we were feverishly doing missionary work, but with what goal in mind other than trusting God to save souls in His good timing?

It was very common among mission boards to assign their new missionaries to fields where there was the most need. The concept of need often was guided by the places where the results of previous missionary work had been negligible. However, when examined according to the principles of a sound mission strategy, the idea of need must not become a criterion for missionary assignment because it bypasses the higher principle of effective use of missionary personnel in order to accomplish certain measureable goals. One of the unfortunate outcomes of assignment according to need has been that some missionaries have spent a lifetime of fruitlessness;

whereas, if they had been more intelligently deployed, the same missionaries could have experienced abundant fruitfulness!

I am speaking in generalities. There are, of course, exceptions to this rule. God does choose certain missionaries to minister to unreceptive people, and I honor that. However, these individuals should go to difficult fields only because they are certain God assigned them there, not because a mission board needed to fill a vacancy.

The Right Goal

The first component of any strategy is the right goal. If there is no goal, there can be no strategy. Why? Strategy is simply the means agreed upon to reach a certain goal. For example, if you need to get from Dallas to Houston, you need a strategy. You have to decide if you are going to fly, take a bus or drive. If you drive, one look at a map will show you there are several routes you can take, so you will need to strategize and choose the one that best accomplishes your goal. Strategy planning is a part of our normal daily lives. Why it had not been applied to missions and evangelism until recently remains a mystery to me.

Furthermore, the goal has to be the *right* goal. The Great Commission talks about making disciples (see Matt. 28:19). Most will agree that the Lord is interested in *disciples* as over against *decisions* for Him. However, the majority of evangelistic reporting counts decisions and not disciples. Take Billy Graham's ministry as an example. For every crusade, we get reports on how many people attended and how many responded to the invitation and made decisions for Christ. Don't get me wrong—I am a dedicated supporter of Billy Graham and his ministry, and I thank God for every decision for Christ. However, we are talking about Great Commission goals.

Because the Graham organization never set up a mechanism to track how many *disciples* were made as a result of each crusade, making disciples apparently was not their goal. It may have been their sincere desire, but desire is not a goal unless a strategy is developed to measure whether or not you accomplish it. I spent many years in personally researching many different scenarios of mass evangelism here at home and abroad. My best conclusion is that a high of 16 percent and a low of 3 percent of first-time decisions actually ended up as church members.

This raises the question of how we define evangelism. Answers to this generally fall into three categories. For the sake of clarity, I have found the terms *presence*, *proclamation* and *persuasion* to be very helpful guidelines. Presence holds that just going to a certain place and living a Christian life among the people and doing good deeds is evangelism, even though you may never verbalize the gospel or the plan of salvation. Not many of my evangelical (charismatic or non-charismatic) readers would agree.

However, where we do find some differences among us is between proclamation evangelism and persuasion evangelism. Some evangelical theologians feel that evangelism should consist simply of making the gospel known, but that it does not require conversion. A good example is J. I. Packer, who wrote, "The way to tell whether in fact you are evangelizing is not to ask whether conversions are known to have resulted from your witness. It is to ask whether you are faithfully making known the gospel message."[1] This is proclamation evangelism.

Persuasion evangelism, which is my view, evaluates the success of evangelism not by how many people hear the gospel or even by how many make decisions, but rather by how many become ongoing disciples of Jesus Christ, ordinarily demonstrated by responsible church membership. This, I believe, is the right goal for evangelistic strategy.

The Right Place at the Right Time

If we have the right goal and if we do make disciples, these disciples become part of what the Bible calls the "fruit" of our labors. "Fruit" is an agricultural term. Inbred in every farmer is what I like to call the vision of the fruit. Whatever strategy the farmer develops is aimed toward harvesting the greatest amount of fruit possible. Likewise, sound evangelistic strategy never loses the vision of the fruit.

Farmers know that, as the seasons progress, they need to be in the right place at the right time. Jesus teaches this to us in the Parable of the Sower (see Mark 4:3-20). You will remember that in this parable a farmer sowed seed on four different parts of his farm, but he got fruit on only one of them.

According to Jesus' interpretation, the variable factor was neither the sower nor the seed (described in verse 14 as "the word") nor the method. It was the soil. Any farmer knows that, no matter how good the seed is, it will not bear fruit on roadways, on rocky soil or among thorns. In order to produce fruit, good seed must be sown in fertile soil.

Applying this to missionary or evangelistic strategy, we then must ensure, as much as possible, that the seed of the Word be planted on fertile soil. At any given time, some peoples of the world are receptive to the gospel and others are resistant. We now have ways of testing the soil in advance. For example, we can examine where disciples are currently being made and then concentrate our resources there. Concentrating our resources on rocky soil is foolish strategy. Farmers who have the vision of the fruit would not make that mistake, but unfortunately, some mission leaders still do.

Fertile soil is the right place. How about the right time? Let's go back to agriculture. The time of the yearly cycle when most workers are needed is the harvest. That's why Jesus told us to pray that the Lord would send workers into His harvest (see Luke 10:2).

Suppose, for example, you owned an apple orchard. In field A, a worker could harvest five bushels in an hour. In field B, it would take five hours just to harvest one bushel. In field C, nothing could be harvested because the apples were still green. If you had 30 workers, where would you send them? I think I would send 29 of them to field A so as not to lose any of that ripened harvest. I would send the other one to field B to harvest anything possible and also to keep an eye on field C. The principal assignment for that worker would be to let me know when those fields were ripe so that I could redeploy my personnel.

Having our missionary and evangelistic workers ready to change when a new harvest presents itself is a key strategy decision. A people group resistant now may suddenly turn receptive five years from now. It is crucial to discern the right time.

The Right Methods

No farmer would take a corn picker into a ripe wheat field nor a potato digger into a peach orchard. The wheat field would get a combine today instead of a reaper and binder, as it would 100 years ago. Likewise, the tools of missions, or the methods used, must be both appropriate and up to date if we are to see abundant fruit.

To give one common example, consider the issue of language. In many cases on record, missionaries thought that preaching in the trade language of the nation would be adequate for making disciples. However, only through switching to the local dialect, the language of the heart, did fruit ordinarily begin to come. If these missionaries had refused to change methods, no amount of otherwise good strategy would have succeeded in making the same number of disciples.

Another rather graphic example of changing methods comes from an Indian friend of mine whom God directed to reach an unreached tribe of naked, fair-skinned people who lived in caves in a remote part of India. They did not know how to cook. They ate fruit, vegetation and wild honey. They never bathed, cut their hair, shaved or cleaned their teeth. My friend assembled a mission team and, after tremendous hardships, finally reached the people. However, all the tribe members ran into their caves and could not be coaxed out. The missionaries regrouped and discussed their methods. The next time, before they approached the settlement, the missionaries stripped almost naked. Sure enough, the people came out, and now there is a thriving church (of properly clothed members!).

The Right Messengers

Having written all this about strategy, I do not want to leave the impression that anyone at all can do the job. God is the one who prepares the fertile soil and brings the harvest to ripeness. However, He chooses qualified Christian people to accomplish the task of reaping, and He is glorified when they bear much fruit.

It is a sad but true fact that some missionaries and evangelists have been victims of carnal motives, laziness, shallow knowledge of the Word, self-centeredness, unwise procedures and lack of flexibility. No matter what strategy they use, their character has disqualified them, and their work has become fruitless.

However, this has never been God's intention. God's intention is that the right messengers are believers filled with the Holy Spirit. They abide in Jesus. They are fully committed. They take up their cross daily and follow their Master. Jesus insisted that His own disciples not begin their missionary work until they were "endued with power from on high" (Luke 24:49). The right messengers, guided by a divinely inspired strategy, will be those who bear abundant fruit.

Playing the Numbers Game

When I finally shifted my paradigm from passive evangelism to pragmatic evangelism, I naively thought that all my friends with whom I shared these new and exciting concepts for fulfilling the Great Commission would change as quickly as I did. Happily, some of them did. But others? Not only didn't they want to change, but also some of them actually turned against me. I did explain in the first chapter that paradigm shifts tend to pull people out of their comfort zones, and this, for me, became exhibit A.

One of the most common ways that many of them attempted to discredit me, and thereby reject my ideas, was to declare, "Wagner is playing the numbers game!" Apparently, the idea behind this form of rebuke was that there is something spiritually reprehensible in using numbers in missionary or evangelistic work. My most extreme condemnation was a public affirmation that I was committing "numerolatry." The literal sense of that word is that I was actually *worshiping* numbers. The intended implication was that I had put numbers and statistical analysis ahead of God. The critics wanted to prove that setting goals, drawing graphs, measuring results and evaluating the performance of individuals was nothing less than taking the place of trusting the Holy Spirit to give increase.

I could only reply that I guess I was, in fact, playing the numbers game—if the numbers represent lost people being saved and coming into the kingdom of God. The only way a shepherd knows that one sheep is missing is to count the number of sheep that are in the fold. When numbers tell the shepherd that one is missing, his task is to find the lost sheep. Jesus commends such a shepherd (see Luke 15:4). When Jesus helped His disciples fish in the Sea of Tiberias, somehow it was important to them to count the fish and find that there were exactly 153 large ones (see John 21:11). It is comforting to know that the Bible commends the numbers game. In fact, a whole book of the Bible is called *Numbers!*

Pragmatism

I have been suggesting that strategy is simply the agreed-upon means to reach a certain goal. When you think about it, this is just another way of asserting that the end justifies the means. What else could possibly determine the best strategy or means other than the desired goal or end? Those who say that the end never justifies the means are usually introducing ethical or moral considerations. If it is a matter of using unethical means to gain even a good end, I would agree. However, when I assert that the end justifies the means in evangelistic strategy planning, I am referring to value-neutral means only, not immoral means. Above all, God's work must be done in God's way.

I am more than aware that this kind of talk causes discomfort, especially among religious leaders. I have been criticized both for numerolatry and for suggesting that the end justifies the means, but perhaps the most serious attempt to discredit this new paradigm has been to cluster my different ideas and call them pragmatism. In fact, just for the fun of it, as I was writing this, I paused and Googled "Peter Wagner pragmatism." I was instantly exposed to a substantial list of sometimes voluminous criticisms of my pragmatism from many different sources. It was fun because telling me that I am pragmatic is like telling a polar bear that it's white!

One of the persons most upset by my pragmatism has been mega-church pastor John MacArthur. In fact, in the early 1990s, he wrote a book called *Ashamed of the Gospel,* which featured me along with researcher George Barna. He argued that we were ashamed of the Gospel because we had succumbed to pragmatism. I thought it would be interesting to conclude this chapter with a quote from me that MacArthur himself chose as a basis for refuting the Church Growth Movement's "inherent pragmatism."[2] It is interesting because it exactly summarizes my new paradigm for evangelism. Here is what I wrote:

> The Church Growth Movement has always stressed pragmatism, and still does even though many have criticized it. It is not the kind of pragmatism that compromises doctrine or ethics or the kind that dehumanizes people by using them as a means toward an end. It is, however, the kind of

consecrated pragmatism which ruthlessly examines traditional methodologies and programs asking the tough questions. If some sort of ministry in the church is not reaching intended goals, consecrated pragmatism says there is something wrong which needs to be corrected.[3]

I wrote this more than 25 years ago, and I don't think I could say it better today!

Notes

1. J. I. Packer, *Evangelism and the Sovereignty of God* (Downers Grove, IL: InterVarsity Press, 1961), p. 41.
2. I think it would be appropriate to mention here that John MacArthur and I have known and respected each other since the 1970s. I commended his church growth leadership in my book *Your Church Can Grow*. We have met with each other one on one to discuss our differences in order to better understand each other. Although we do not keep in close touch, we consider ourselves friends.
3. C. Peter Wagner, *Leading Your Church to Growth* (Ventura, CA: Regal Books, 1984), p. 201.

5

From **Mono-cultural Theology** to **Cross-cultural Theology**

Back in the days when I was working a good bit with denominational executives, I recall a striking statement from the leader of one of America's largest denominations. We were talking about changing times and seasons and the need for churches to be flexible enough to adapt and remain relevant. He said words to this effect: "We are willing to make any changes necessary, except we will never change our doctrine!"

My unexpressed thought was, "Why not?" I happened to know of at least two of their stated doctrines that, in my opinion, definitely needed some change. However, I kept quiet because I realized that, in my friend's mind, considering a change in the theology of his denomination would amount to offending God. If he had drawn his line in the sand on the authority of Scripture rather than on his doctrine, I would have agreed. What's the difference? The difference is that Scripture is inspired by the Holy Spirit, whereas theology is a human endeavor.

What Is Theology?

What am I saying? Let me give you the simple definition of theology that I have been using for a long time: *Theology is a human attempt to explain God's Word and God's works in a reasonable and systematic way*. The phrase "a human attempt" is what separates theology from Scripture. We do not argue with Scripture itself, but when it comes to our *explanations* of Scripture and our *interpretations* of Scripture, the human dimension enters the picture and we begin to formulate theology.

Notice that theology tries to explain two things: (1) God's Word, and (2) God's works. Admittedly, most traditional theologians attempt to confine their theologizing to number one, God's Word, the Bible. Their assumption is that everything that God wanted to reveal to human beings is contained in the Bible. When you think about it, however, this cannot be a valid assumption. Why? For starters, there is nothing in the Bible itself that tells us how many books should be in the Bible. God revealed that to His people later, after the biblical material was written; and it took church leaders hundreds of years to agree that there are 66 books, at least in the Protestant Bible. Catholics are convinced there should be more.

So God continues to give revelation to the church. "He who has an ear, let him hear what the Spirit says to the churches" (Rev. 2:7). The verb "says" is present tense, not past. Of course, one key test for the accuracy of what we think we are hearing from the Spirit is that it will never *contradict* Scripture. Nevertheless, our theology must take what God is now saying and doing into consideration. That is why I include "God's works" in my definition of theology.

Theology and Culture

Every one of us is born and raised in one of the world's cultures. Granted, a few happen to be raised in more than one culture, but these make up a very small percentage of the human race. A simple way of understanding culture is to think of it as the rules of the game. The game, in this case, is human life and relationships. Culture is the set of rules that each particular group of human beings designs and mutually accepts as its own style of life. Culture determines how we think and how we behave. Most people are monocultural, so they think and behave like the others around them. When, for whatever reason, they find themselves among people of another culture, they tend to feel uncomfortable.

This obviously includes theologians. Most theologians are monocultural. The theological culture in our nation could well be described as North Atlantic, because much of American theology has been an importation of ideas originating in Europe. Charles Kraft wrote, "Those whose experience has not taken them beyond the western cultural matrix (and this includes most traditional theologians) have usually not even considered a multitude of problems arising within the other six thousand cultures of the world."[1] This observation is not intended to be a criticism of theologians but rather a simple statement of facts that, of course, implies certain limitations.

I bring this up to explain my own theological formation as a missionary candidate. When I knew that God had called me to serve on the foreign mission field, I wanted the best possible training, so, as I have mentioned before, I enrolled in a theological seminary. The theology I was taught was standard, mono-cultural, North Atlantic theology. Over three years, I absorbed that theology, enjoyed it, passed my exams and received my Master of Theology degree. I felt that I was properly educated to be a missionary.

Soon afterward, I arrived in Bolivia. My first assignment was to lead a Bible school. I quickly learned that, without a traditional faculty of specialists, I myself had to teach just about every course, including theology. For the first time I found myself in a cross-cultural situation. Bolivian culture was substantially different from American culture. Where did theology fit in? I hate to admit it now, but my mindset was that the theology I had learned in seminary was the real, authentic, orthodox theology for any culture in the world. I was a cross-cultural missionary who was programmed with a mono-cultural theology. So, what did I do? I translated my English notes from my theology classes into Spanish and taught the same material to my Bolivian students.

To put it in other terms, I had a North Atlantic theological paradigm, and I taught mono-cultural theology to my Bolivian ministerial students for over 10 years. During that time, it never even occurred to me that there was any other option. My missionary colleagues all approved of what I was doing because they were doing the same thing. I wasn't looking for a paradigm shift.

The Paradigm Shift

However, the paradigm shift did come. I explained in the previous chapter how my enrollment in the Fuller Seminary School of World Mission in the late 1960s sparked a paradigm shift toward pragmatic evangelism. That wasn't the only one. In chapter 3 we saw how my contact with Professor Ralph Winter began my paradigm shift from traditional theological education to equipping the saints. Likewise, the School of World Mission catalyzed this paradigm shift to cross-cultural theology. The reason that all this was happening was that I, as a cross-cultural missionary, found myself for the first time in a school where all the students and faculty had been field missionaries. Not a single professor was mono-cultural. I was fascinated by my first courses in missiology and cultural anthropology.

Donald McGavran, the founding dean, had become known for his advocacy of the radical idea of people movements to Christ. Previously, missionaries had agreed that salvation was a personal thing and that each individual needed to make a commitment to Christ in order to be saved, even against the social tide. However, after years of field research in India, McGavran found that the majority of Indian Christians were coming to Christ, not through individual decisions, but through group decisions, when the leaders of a particular cultural group decided that the whole group would be Christian, which it then did.

According to their worldview, important decisions were community decisions. This would apply to families, extended families, clans, villages and whole tribes. Everyone converted at once, and the quality of the churches that subsequently developed was at least comparable to the quality of the churches resulting from individual conversions, and in some cases higher. How about theology? Did these newly converted people groups, sometimes counting tens of thousands, need my mono-cultural North Atlantic theology in order to please God? Obviously not! In due time, they would explain God's Word and God's works in ways that were relevant to their culture.

A corollary of McGavran's people movement theory has become known as the homogeneous unit principle. His observation was that people like to become Christians without crossing racial, linguistic or class barriers. Conversion should occur with a minimum of social dislocation. Most people already know this and practice it, but, particularly in America, church leaders tend to become very insecure at the thought of it. They know that most Koreans are won to Christ in Korean churches, most Hispanics are won to Christ in Hispanic churches, and most blacks are won to Christ in black churches, but they don't believe it *should* be that way. They are embarrassed that, as they put it, "Sunday morning is the most segregated time of the week in America." They think this is outright unethical. They would prefer that everybody melt together and adhere to the same mono-cultural theology and church lifestyle.

The controversy over the homogeneous unit principle became so heated that I, after I had joined the School of World Mission faculty, decided to do a Ph.D. in social ethics at the University of Southern California and write my dissertation on the ethical issues surrounding the homogeneous unit principle. When I finished, I thought that I had successfully defended its ethical integrity, and I published it in a book, *Our Kind of People*. This stirred up a hornet's nest of opposition. Paradigm shifts definitely pull people out of their comfort zones. One Christian magazine published an article against me called "Where Church Growth Fails the Gospel." An article-length critical review of my book was entitled "Evangelism Without the Gospel." I lost count of the number of public rebukes I had to endure as I taught these things across the country.

Flunking a Tenure Exam

The conflict between mono-cultural theology and cross-cultural theology came very close to home when I flunked a Fuller Seminary tenure exam. One of the perks for academic faculty is that they are awarded tenure after teaching a period of time. When my turn came, I was teaching on the missions faculty, but according to school rules, I had to be examined by members of the theology faculty in order to qualify for tenure. This means that my cross-cultural theological paradigm was to be scrutinized by mono-cultural theologians.

Things seemed to be going well during the exam until one of the professors asked me, "What do you think of systematic theology?" My honest answer was, "I think we should rephrase the question and ask what I think of systematic *theologies*, plural." Please recall that, as I mentioned before, mono-cultural theologians are convinced that their theology is true and valid for any culture of the world.

When I began to suggest that theologians in other cultures might develop systematic theologies that are also true and valid but come to different theological conclusions than theirs, my examiners became visibly uncomfortable. Then I brought up Muslims who honestly think that Christians are polytheists. That is not true. We, of course, are pure monotheists. I suggested that possibly our systematic theologians could consider restating our doctrine of the Trinity so that Muslims could understand our true position. From that point on, things quickly went downhill, and the committee decided that I should not be awarded tenure at that time.

The theology faculty later invited me back for another tenure examination in which I wisely avoided all cross-cultural issues and, consequently, passed with flying colors.

This also brings to mind a theological examination for a new faculty member for our School of World Mission. Another rule of the seminary was that new faculty had to be examined by theology faculty before they could be hired. School of World Mission professors could sit in on the meeting, but they were not allowed to speak. This time our new professor was a Chinese-American scholar, Dr. Tan. One of the first routine questions was, "What do you think of the Fuller statement of faith?" The anticipated answer would almost always be, "I agree with the statement, and I like it very much." However, Tan replied, "I think it is a seriously incomplete statement. It would not be adequate for a Chinese seminary!"

This, as you can imagine, precipitated one of the liveliest theological examinations on record. Tan's objection? The Fuller statement of faith said nothing about supernatural power, the evil works of Satan and his demons, or of angelic activity. The balance of the interview focused on these and related issues, and Dr. Tan finally passed. Some of the mono-cultural theologians apparently began to give credence to Tan's cross-cultural perspective.

Contextualization

Back when I first went to seminary to prepare for the mission field, there were no courses in missiology because missiology had not yet become a recognized academic discipline. In fact, it wasn't until the 1970s, after Donald McGavran founded the School of World Mission, that it did become widely recognized. By then, new missiological terminology, such as "contextualization," was being introduced.

Contextualization is fitting Christian beliefs and practices into the behavior patterns and worldviews of other cultures. Skilled missiologists were learning how to do this without compromising the essence of the Christian faith or the integrity of Scripture. An awareness of contextualization obviously ends discussion of theology in the singular, as if there were some universal Christian theology that could apply to all peoples at all times.

In the introduction, I brought up the paradigm shift that James of Jerusalem went through, concerning the circumcision of Gentiles. Now, with your permission, I would like to tell the story once again, this time emphasizing the process of contextualization.

The New Testament gives us an excellent illustration of contextualization. With some exceptions, such as the Samaritan woman and her friends (see John 4:39-42) and Cornelius's household (see Acts 10), all of the early believers were immersed in Hebrew culture. By necessity, the beliefs and practices of the churches were contextualized to fit Hebrew culture. The only Scriptures that the Jewish believers had were the Old Testament, so many Old Testament practices, such as circumcision, dietary requirements, Sabbath observance and others, were preserved. Church services were largely patterned after synagogue services. Theology, as would be expected, was mono-cultural.

Even outreach and missions were mono-cultural to begin with. The first significant missionary thrust was forced on the church by the persecution that arose after Stephen was killed, when many of the believers were driven out of Jerusalem. We are told in Acts 11 that they scattered out to many parts of the Roman Empire, including Antioch, but they "preached the word to no one but *the Jews only*" (Acts 11:19, emphasis added). We need to be reminded that in those days segregated housing was the norm in cities like Antioch, so the Jews lived together in their "Jewish quarter." Therefore, even though the missionaries had traveled geographically, they were still mono-cultural.

Provoking "Judaizers"

Then things changed. Ten years later some new missionaries were sent to Antioch from Cyprus and Cyrene who targeted the Hellenists, or the Gentiles. These are the ones who later sent out Paul and Barnabas. Paul and Barnabas ministered in synagogues, where some Jews believed, but they soon found that the most receptive people were Gentile God-fearers. At one point they even said that now "we turn to the Gentiles" (Acts 13:46). As we know, Paul eventually became the apostle to the uncircumcised, meaning the Gentiles (see Gal. 2:7-8). One of Paul's tasks, then, became contextualizing theology and practice to the Gentile culture, which he did. As a cross-cultural theologian, Paul decided to cut slack on the Jewish dietary laws and also on circumcision.

When word of this got back to Jerusalem, the tensions began to erupt. James, the brother of Jesus, was a chief apostolic leader in the Jerusalem church. His mono-cultural theology told him that Paul was violating Mosaic Law and that his teaching should be corrected. He sent emissaries, later called Judaizers, to visit the churches that Paul had planted and tell the believers that, in order to be true believers, they needed to be circumcised (meaning, essentially, that they should convert to Judaism). Paul, who was very upset, then wrote his letter to the Galatians, to be circulated among those churches. In it he tells that he rebuked Peter by asking, "Why do you compel Gentiles to live as Jews?" (Gal. 2:14). Later he warns the Gentile believers, "If you become circumcised, Christ will profit you nothing" (Gal. 5:2).

This conflict between mono-cultural theologians and cross-cultural theologians was what brought about the famous Council of Jerusalem in AD 50. The upshot was that James himself opened up to contextualization. After the full debate had been held, James, the leader of the Council, said, "Therefore I judge that we should not trouble those from among the Gentiles who are turning to God" (Acts 15:19). This, in my opinion, was the most important theological decision this side of the cross.

Jesus, the Son of God

To conclude, let me flash back to my first tenure exam. One of my mistakes was bringing up the issue of the Muslims' misunderstanding of our theology of the Trinity, concluding that we must be polytheists, believing in three Gods. My mono-cultural examiners were stymied, so they flunked me. That was 35 years prior to this writing. Since then, missiology has gained a widespread respect and reputation as a legitimate discipline in academic circles. Consequently, this has opened new doors for some theologians, not all to be sure, to actually begin wrestling with possible attempts at restating Christian truths in ways that might better communicate the gospel to Muslims without compromising sound doctrine.

To avoid repeating my tenure-exam mistake, let me affirm that I myself have not yet made up my mind regarding the outcome of current discussions on the issue. However, my personal paradigm of cross-cultural theology draws me to the debate with great interest. Let's face it: Our efforts to evangelize Muslims have not borne fruit 30-, 60- and 100-fold as has our evangelization of some other people groups. I, for one, am inclined to ask the question why. I would like to encourage some exploration, possibly even thinking outside of the box. That is why I am bringing this up in a chapter on cross-cultural theology.

The Bible reveals that Jesus is the Son of God. As the Apostles' Creed states, "I believe in God, the Father almighty, . . . and in Jesus Christ His only begotten Son, conceived by the Holy Spirit, born of the Virgin Mary." I imagine you believe that as well. Because Mary was a virgin when Jesus was born, we entertain no thoughts that He could have been conceived through sexual intercourse, the way the demonic gods of Greek mythology were supposed to have conceived offspring.

Is It Blasphemy?

So far, so good. However, let's go cross-culturally. When sincere, unevangelized Muslims hear that Jesus is the Son of God, they are driven to the conclusion that God must have had sex with Mary, and they cannot stand the thought! To them it is blasphemy! This builds a barrier in their minds to receiving and understanding anything else that Jesus might have said or done. Can anything be done about this?

Rick Brown of Wycliffe Bible Translators, who is both a biblical scholar and a missiologist, thinks there is. Cross-cultural theology has become second nature to him. His scholarly focus is on the Muslim world. He feels so strongly against using a literal translation of "Son of God" for Muslim readers that he writes:

It is not our fault, of course, if people stumble over the truth, but if they stumble because of our stubbornness, because we insist on using a phrase that evokes the wrong meaning and is deemed insulting to God, then it might be better if a millstone were hung around our necks and we were thrown into the depths of the sea (Luke 17:2).[2]

What are the other options? One suggestion is "beloved Son who comes from God"; another is "spiritual Son of God." In Arabic, these alternatives reportedly avoid the biological connotation of "Son of God." However, not everyone agrees that these changes should me made, as you could imagine. *Christianity Today* magazine reports, "A dispute over the most faithful and effective way to render the common biblical phrase 'Son of God' is dividing missionary from missionary, scholar from scholar, in a time of evident mistrust between Western Christians and Muslims."[3] The opponents of Rick Brown and others who advocate radically new translations "charge their colleagues with compromise that undermines belief in Jesus Christ as the pre-existent, only begotten Son of God."[4]

Welcome to the world of cross-cultural theology. The issues can get to be quite complex, as you can see, and conclusions can even influence the spread of the gospel in one way or another. As I have said, I have not made up my mind on how "Son of God" should be translated. Have you?

Conclusion

My choice of a key Muslim issue as an illustration of the differences between mono-cultural theology and cross-cultural theology might raise some American eyebrows, but I hope no one has lost my main point: The Bible is inspired by God, but theology is not. All theology is influenced by the effects of a particular culture on the theologians who are articulating it. Theology should be malleable, not set in concrete. I regret the years that I tried to impose my mono-cultural American theology on my Bolivian students, but I am thankful that, eventually, I was open to renewing my mind and going through a paradigm shift to cross-cultural theology. Now I hope that I can help others from making the same mistakes that I made.

As we have seen, applying cross-cultural theology is not always easy. However, let me once again bring up the Council of Jerusalem.

There the leaders of the early church proved that, even though the theological disagreements might be severe, they can be settled under the guidance of the Holy Spirit, and the church can move forward in advancing the kingdom of God.

Notes

1. Charles H. Kraft, *Christianity in Culture: A Study in Dynamic Biblical Theologizing in Cross-Cultural Perspective* (Maryknoll, NY: Orbis Books, 1979), p. 11.
2. Rick Brown, "Explaining the Biblical Term 'Son(s) of God' in Muslim Contexts," *International Journal of Frontier Missions* (Fall 2005), p. 93.
3. Collin Hansen, "The Son and the Crescent," *Christianity Today* (February 2011), p. 20.
4. Ibid.

6

From **Programmed Evangelism** to **Power Evangelism**

As you might surmise by now, my central assignment from God since the day I was converted in 1950 has been to do my part to fulfill the Great Commission: "Go into all the world and preach the gospel to every creature" (Mark 16:15). This calling placed evangelism (winning souls and multiplying churches) front and center in my life and ministry. It was the motivating force that took me to the mission field in Bolivia and later to a 30-year teaching career in the Fuller Seminary School of World Mission.

Learning Programmed Evangelism

In order to prepare myself for what lay ahead, I spent three years as a student in Fuller Theological Seminary in the early 1950s, earning my Master of Theology degree. Courses in evangelism and missions weren't as plentiful as they are today, but I'm sure my professors taught me the state of the art, as they understood it. Since Fuller was in the Los Angeles area, the ripple effects of Billy Graham's famous Los Angeles Crusade of 1949 were still strong in the seminary, and I learned a good deal about how Graham and his staff organized and executed citywide evangelistic events. The Billy Graham Evangelistic Association was decidedly the bellwether of public evangelism at the time.

When Fuller Seminary first opened in 1945, a successful businessman named Bill Bright had just been converted at Hollywood Presbyterian Church, and he enrolled at Fuller to prepare for ministry. While there, he began witnessing to students at UCLA, which led to the formation of Campus Crusade for Christ. His movement ended up growing so rapidly that he decided to leave seminary before graduation, but his presence there left a notable impact on my Fuller professors, and he became a model for personal evangelism. Bright had written the "Four Spiritual Laws," and I memorized them well. I learned Graham's public evangelism and Bright's personal evangelism.

However, attempting to implement these evangelistic methodologies when we arrived in Bolivia was quite futile. We landed in a pre-Vatican II, Roman Catholic-dominated nation where Protestants, called evangelicals (*evangélicos*), were at best marginalized and at worst openly persecuted. We found ourselves in the jungle, so we had no cities to evangelize like Billy Graham nor college campuses to evangelize like Bill Bright. However, what remained in my mind was that evangelism was something that needed to be planned and executed, using the right structures, the right strategies and the right tools. I have since called it programmed evangelism.

Evangelism in Depth

A bright and shining evangelistic star began to rise over Latin America in 1960. It was more than welcome because the prevailing mood among missionaries had been quite gloomy. With some exceptions, the fruit produced by evangelistic missionary work throughout the continent had been sparse. The name of the new star was Evangelism in Depth, and it sprung forth from Costa Rica under Latin America Mission leader Kenneth Strachan. Exciting news began spreading among mission leaders of what a powerful impact Evangelism in Depth had been making in Nicaragua, Honduras, Guatemala, and other countries. Bolivia's turn came in 1965, much to the excitement of us all. By then I had moved from the jungles to the city of Cochabamba, which became the national headquarters of the movement, so I personally was very much involved in helping to provide the leadership.

Evangelism in Depth was the epitome of programmed evangelism. The team that was sent from Costa Rica to Bolivia insisted ahead of time that we pledge to follow their established pattern, which we did. The program was 12 months long. Unity was a key. The Strachan Theorem, upon which the initiative was based, stated, "The expansion of any movement is in direct proportion to its success in mobilizing its total membership in continuous propagation of its beliefs."[1] In order to demonstrate our unity, I was put in charge of the first Bolivian national pastors' retreat. I recruited World Vision to sponsor it, and they paid the budget to bring together no fewer than 1,000 pastors from every nook and cranny of Bolivia for a week. It was a joyous expression of unity never previously dreamed of!

This kicked off the most historic year up to then in Bolivian Protestant history. The flurry of activities over the 12 months was breathtaking. Local committees were formed, national assemblies gathered, prayer cells multiplied, and special congresses for youth, women and ethnic groups held. An intensive training course in personal evangelism was designed to mobilize every believer for his or her evangelistic responsibility. A national periodical was published and distributed. We launched a national radio program. High-profile parades marched through towns and cities. A national song, "We shall win our homeland for Jesus," was on the lips of believers and unbelievers alike. Then, through mass evangelism campaigns, some 20,000 decisions for Christ were recorded, just under the total number of evangelicals in the whole nation! This lifted the gloom from missionaries and national church leaders alike!

The Rest of the Story

However, we need to look realistically at the rest of the story. In order to do so responsibly, we must be pragmatic, as I argued in chapter 4, and play the numbers game in the right way. The Evangelism in Depth leaders in Costa Rica publicized their excitement about the positive results of their program. One wrote, "During the year of Evangelism in Depth more conversions occur than in any other year in the entire history of Christian work in that country."[2] Another claimed that the success of the Bolivian initiative "is evidenced in the marked growth of the 750 cooperating churches during the year, in the nearly 20,000 professions of faith in Christ."[3] Most of us who were in Bolivia throughout the event would have agreed that this demonstration of programmed evangelism substantially increased the evangelical community in Bolivia.

However, we turned out to be wrong! At the end of the 1960s, I earned my Master of Arts in Missiology under Donald McGavran at the Fuller School of World Mission. My thesis was *The Protestant Movement in Bolivia,* and as a part of my research I carefully researched the Evangelism in Depth initiative of 1965. My reluctant conclusion was that "the percent of annual increase was greater during the year preceding Evangelism in Depth than in any of the following three years."[4] What this means, simply put, is there likely would have been more evangelicals in Bolivia four years later if Evangelism in Depth had never come! Subsequent research by others in Central America and Colombia came to similar conclusions.[5]

In 1973, Evangelism in Depth came to America under the name Key '73. It caused excitement among participating churches similar to what we experienced in Bolivia. Unfortunately, the result, in the form of subsequent growth of American churches, was likewise disappointing. As I mentioned previously, my research on mass evangelism in America, including Billy Graham Crusades, found that among first-time decisions for Christ, a low of 3 percent and a high of 16 percent of them became church members over the next two years. Not an enviable track record!

I am sharing these reports so that you can see how I began having second thoughts about my commitment to programmed evangelism. *However,* I wondered, *was there any other option?*

Anti-Pentecostal!

When I went to Bolivia, I was anti-Pentecostal! Why? My training in Fuller Seminary taught me to be a cessationist. I was taught that some of the spiritual gifts that we read about in the Bible, such as healing, miracles, tongues, prophecy and others, ceased after the first century or two and were no longer in effect today.

I can recall some of my professors making reference to faith healers as if they should be included in the lunatic fringe. The idea was planted in my mind that the reason we read about Jesus and the apostles healing the sick was that medical science had not yet been developed, so miracles were more useful then than they are now. Now that we have doctors, hospitals and pharmacies, we have much better ways to heal the sick.

In the late 1800s and early 1900s, one of the most highly respected conservative Christian theologians was Benjamin Warfield of Princeton Seminary. When I was in Fuller, my professors leaned heavily on Warfield for their view of miraculous gifts, so this is what I learned:

> The power of working miracles was not extended beyond the disciples upon whom the Apostles conferred it by the imposition of their hands. As the number of these disciples gradually diminished, the instances of the exercise of miraculous powers became continually less frequent, and ceased entirely at the death of the last individual on whom the hands of the Apostles had been laid.[6]

Do you see that word "ceased" in Warfield's quote? That is the root word from which the term "cessationism" is derived. As I've already written, I was a cessationist, and in Bolivia I preached openly against the Pentecostal idea that God does miraculous healings today. Consequently, I alienated myself from the leaders of the Pentecostal churches in Bolivia. This closed my mind to the idea that supernatural power could have anything to do with effective evangelism.

Chilean Pentecostals

The beginning of my paradigm shift came when I studied church growth under Donald McGavran at the School of World Mission. He taught us that, in order to research the growth of the churches in any given area, you have to ask four questions: (1) Why does the blessing of God rest where it does? (2) Churches are not equal. Why are some churches more blessed than others at certain times? (3) Can any pattern of divine blessing be discerned? (4) If so, what are the common characteristics of those churches? Fair enough. I came back to Bolivia in 1968 with these questions. Much to my consternation, I honestly had to conclude that the blessing of God was resting most strongly on the Pentecostal churches that I had been preaching against!

Since my personal relationships with the Bolivian Pentecostal leaders was not the best, I decided to fly over the Andes to Chile and take a firsthand look at the highly publicized Pentecostal Movement there. To my surprise, the miraculous gifts that Warfield declared had ceased were actually in full operation among Chilean

Pentecostal churches. I interviewed the leaders, and they went on to convince me of the integrity of their underlying theology.

From that moment on, I was no longer anti-Pentecostal. I returned to Bolivia, made friends with the Pentecostal leaders, and we moved on from there. After I returned to America and began teaching at Fuller, my first book was *Look Out! The Pentecostals Are Coming.* In it I showed that the Pentecostal Movement was the fastest growing Christian movement in the world and that it was not growing because of programmed evangelism but because of power evangelism.

John Wimber

I became a believer in power evangelism, but not a practitioner. I had the faith but not the works. This began to change when I became connected with John Wimber. We first met when John, pastor of a church in nearby Orange County, enrolled in one of my Doctor of Ministry church growth courses at Fuller. By the end of the course, I recognized that he had one of the most brilliant minds for church growth that I had encountered, so I persuaded him to leave his pastorate and come work for me as a church consultant in the Fuller Evangelistic Association. After a few years, John felt led by God to leave Fuller and plant a new church, which eventually became the renowned Anaheim Vineyard mega-church.

From the beginning, John set out to preach slowly through the Gospel of Luke. As he did, he taught about Jesus' healings and wondered why we weren't seeing such things today. John began praying for the sick. It took 10 months of praying before the first sick person was healed. From then on, the supernatural power and the growth of the church were exponential, and the whole Vineyard Movement spread across the nation and into many other countries of the world. After seeing the amazing results, Wimber wrote his best-selling book *Power Evangelism.*

What does that have to do with me? All through this process, I had been inviting John to team-teach with me in my advanced church growth courses. At one point, he introduced, with my permission, a lecture entitled "Signs, Wonders and Church Growth." This was historic because, as I have mentioned, most of the Fuller theologians were still cessationists. John's teaching became so popular that we began to offer a whole course on the subject in the School of World Mission, and I was the official professor of record. During his first course, I changed from a spectator to a participant in the healing ministry. In class, I was healed from high blood pressure, and then I saw some people for whom I prayed instantly, supernaturally healed, especially when they had problems with their back and legs.

This completed my paradigm shift. I became so involved that I soon wrote my books *Signs and Wonders Today* and *How to Have a Healing Ministry in Any Church*. With all of this, I became more and more convinced that evangelism accompanied by supernatural power, consisting of healing, miracles and casting out demons, needed to take precedence over programmed evangelism.

Power Evangelism in the Bible

After all, the manifestation of supernatural power through believers is biblical. Jesus consistently preached the gospel of the Kingdom. Matthew puts it this way: "Jesus went about all Galilee, teaching in their synagogues, preaching the gospel of the kingdom, and healing all kinds of sickness and all kinds of disease among the people" (Matt. 4:23). Jesus' miraculous works led to conversions, so it could rightly be called power evangelism. "Many believed in His name when they saw the signs which He did" (John 2:23). Then, when Jesus first sent out the twelve disciples, He "gave them power and authority over all demons, and to cure diseases. He sent them to preach the gospel of the kingdom of God and to heal the sick" (Luke 9:1-2). This soon expanded, and Jesus sent out seventy, directing them to "heal the sick there, and say to them, 'The kingdom of God has come near to you'" (Luke 10:9).

The only person in the Bible identified specifically as an evangelist was Philip (see Acts 21:8). How did he evangelize? With power evangelism. He went to Samaria and "the multitudes with one accord heeded the things spoken by Philip" (Acts 8:6). What brought these positive results? He cast out demons and healed the sick (see v. 7), preaching "the things concerning the kingdom of God" (v. 12).

Even the famous apostle Paul, toward the end of his career, looked back and described his fruitful ministry as what we would call "power evangelism." Here is what he wrote to the Romans:

I will not dare to speak of any of those things which Christ has not accomplished through me, in word and deed, to make the Gentiles obedient—in mighty signs and wonders, by the power of the Spirit of God, so that from Jerusalem and round about to Illyricum I have fully preached the gospel of Christ (Rom. 15:18-19).

Power evangelism is definitely biblical!

Power Evangelism in the Field

When I first began changing my paradigm toward power evangelism, I was greatly encouraged by the well-known Korean pastor David Yonggi Cho. Since I was a church growth professor and he had built the largest church in the world, Yoido Full Gospel Church, we connected and became friends. Over the years that I studied how his church exploded and multiplied in Korea through power evangelism, I became permanently impressed. Cho's book *The Fourth Dimension* is very important because it takes us beyond the three dimensions of the physical and material world into the fourth dimension of the power of the Holy Spirit. Although he doesn't use the terms, he sees the difference between programmed evangelism and power evangelism like this:

I cannot carry out my ministry of winning souls by simply knocking on doors, struggling and working myself to death. I use the way of faith . . . and am not constantly striving in my flesh to bring to pass those things that the Holy Spirit can easily do. . . . The church is growing by leaps and bounds.[7]

The greatest harvest of souls in one nation that history has ever recorded is happening in China. It began in 1975, when the stifling Cultural Revolution came to an end, and continues today. It is reported that 30,000 people, give or take, are being born again there every day! I have heard estimates of 140 million Christians, which would mean that over 10 percent of Chinese are believers. This could not have happened through programmed evangelism, because the government of China has and still does oppose the Christian religion and deals out heavy doses of persecution. What has been the secret? Carl Lawrence reports:

> The single spark that started this prairie fire [in China] were signs, wonders, and miracles. A report from the conservative Lutheran China Study Center in Tao Fung Shan, Hong Kong, concludes that 80 to 90 percent of Christians in rural China are the result of a miracle, casting out of evil spirits, or divine intervention, and of first-hand witness' testimonies.[8]

One of the greatest revivals of all time swept Argentina during the 1980s and 1990s. Again, the focal point was power evangelism, but in Argentina, evangelists like Omar Cabrera and Carlos Annacondia were able to wrap power evangelism in a package of programmed evangelism with great success. The key was that the program for both of them was not only for saving souls but also for healing, miracles and casting out demons. When I was traveling with Omar Cabrera, who was preaching in sports arenas, I saw dental miracles for the first time. People were having rotten teeth filled, old bridges repaired and new teeth appearing where there were none before. Not long afterward, dental miracles became so common that you could hardly find a local church of any stripe in Argentina in which at least one person could not show you a supernatural filling.

Carlos Annacondia would secure large urban vacant lots for his programmed meetings, which typically would be held nightly, from 8:00 to 12:00, for 30 consecutive nights. He would lead and minister in each meeting, which wasn't easy because he was also the owner and CEO of a busy hardware factory. Every night there was a time when he would provoke the demons there to manifest; then the afflicted would be ushered to a 120-foot-long tent where deliverance teams would minister to them for as long as it took—at times until daybreak! There was another time each night when Annacondia would pray for healing, and many were supernaturally healed. Some of those who were healed would come forward and give public testimony, which produced a strong atmosphere of faith. Dental miracles were so common that Carlos made a rule that people who had only one or two teeth healed couldn't give testimony. Only those who had three or more teeth healed could do so!

We have seen examples of power evangelism from Asia (Korea and China) and Latin America (Argentina), but how about Africa? My experiences in Africa have left me with the impression that power evangelism has become so embedded in the lives, ministries and experiences of God's people that it is not even a common theme of conversation among believers.

Asking someone whether they have seen a supernatural healing recently is almost like asking what they had for breakfast this morning. Not a vital topic! I recall that I was once conversing with a grassroots African evangelist—I think it was in Nigeria. I asked him whether, in his evangelistic ministry, he ever saw signs and wonders. After giving me a rather curious look, he said, "Of course!" I then probed deeper and asked, "Have you seen anyone raised from the dead?" "Oh, yes!" he replied. Trying to disguise my surprise, I went on, "How many?" He scratched his head and said, "I really don't know—I've never counted them!" I concluded that African power evangelism has reached quite admirable heights!

The Big Picture

As would be expected, the segment of world Christianity that is growing the fastest is the segment that regularly practices power evangelism. Researcher David Barrett calls that segment Pentecostals/Charismatics/Neocharismatics. Let me give you some numbers. In 1900 this power evangelism segment counted 981,000 adherents. By 2000 it had reached 483 million, and by 2010 there were 614 million! The annual growth rate is 2.42 percent, compared to 0.14 percent for all Christians and 1.82 percent for Muslims.[9] The kingdom of God is definitely advancing!

Arguably, the most astute observer of world Christianity at this writing is Philip Jenkins, a professor of history at Penn State University. Jenkins's book *The New Christendom* opened the eyes of the academic world to the astounding growth of Christianity in what he calls the Global South, meaning Africa, Asia and Latin America. In this book and its successor, *The New Faces of Christianity*, we have a high-level scholarly verification of the effectiveness of power evangelism (although he does not use the term).

Consider these statements by Jenkins. In *The New Christendom,* he writes:

> Southern Christians retain a very strong supernatural orientation.... They preach messages that, to a Westerner, appear simplistically charismatic, visionary, and apocalyptic. In this thought-world, prophecy is an everyday reality, while faith-healing, exorcism, and dream-visions are all basic components of religious sensibility.[10]

In *The New Faces of Christianity,* Jenkins writes:

> Across the global South, healing ministries have been critical to the modern expansion of Christianity, much as they were during the conversion of Western Europe following the collapse of the Roman Empire.... Their testimonies often refer to God healing the sick, raising the dead, granting special wisdom of direction, communicating through dreams, visions, or prophetic messages, providing boldness for witness, or granting miraculous strength and protection.[11]

This is the kind of Christianity that I want to believe, practice and preach because this describes God's preferred methodology for the propagation of the gospel of the Kingdom.

Notes

1. R. Kenneth Strachan, *The Inescapable Calling* (Grand Rapids, MI: Wm B. Eerdmans Publishing Company, 1968), p. 108.
2. Rubén Lores, "Evangelism in Depth," in *One Race, One Gospel, One Task,* edited by Carl F. H. Henry and Stanley Mooneyham (Minneapolis, MN: World Wide Publishers, 1967), vol. 2, p. 497.
3. W. Dayton Roberts, *Revolution in Evangelism: The Story of Evangelism in Depth in Latin America* (Chicago: Moody Press, 1967), p. 112.
4. C. Peter Wagner, *The Protestant Movement in Bolivia* (South Pasadena, CA: William Carey Library, 1970), p. 167.

5. See C. Peter Wagner, *Frontiers in Missionary Strategy* (Chicago: Moody Press, 1971), pp. 142-145.

6. Benjamin Breckenridge Warfield, *Miracles Yesterday and Today: Real and Counterfeit* (Grand Rapids, MI: William B. Eerdmans Publishing Company, 1965), pp. 23-24.

7. Paul Yonggi Cho, *The Fourth Dimension* (Plainfield, NJ: Logos International, 1979), p. 49.

8. Carl Lawrence, *The Coming Influence of China* (Gresham, OR: Vision House, 1996), p. 67.

9. David B. Barrett, "Status of Global Mission," *International Bulletin of Missionary Research* (January 2010), p. 36.

10. Philip Jenkins, *The Next Christendom: The Coming of Global Christianity* (New York: Oxford University Press, 2002), pp. 7-8.

11. Philip Jenkins, *The New Faces of Christianity: Believing the Bible in the Global South* (New York: Oxford University Press, 2006), p. 114.

7

From **Tolerating Satan** to a **Declaration** of **War**

As I wrote in the last chapter, I began my ministry as a convinced cessationist. More than anyone else, John Wimber helped me shift my paradigm into receiving and ministering in the power of the Holy Spirit. Healings, miracles, prophecy and deliverance were part of my new paradigm. However, beginning to apply the power of the Holy Spirit to spiritual warfare on higher levels caused some people, including John himself, to draw a line. Try as I might, I could not persuade him to embrace spiritual warfare on any level higher than casting demons out of individuals.

Fundamental Beliefs vs. Operational Concerns

When I started my ministry, if anyone asked me whether I believed in Satan, I would say, "Of course!" The Bible teaches about Satan going into the Garden of Eden and deceiving Adam and Eve. Throughout Scripture, Satan, or the devil, is described as the perpetrator of evil and the enemy of God. I had no doubt that he was a created being, that he was cast down from heaven and that ultimately he would be thrown into the lake of fire. However, beyond those kinds of fundamental beliefs, I had no operational concerns about dealing with Satan directly.

During the time I was a missionary in Bolivia, I was with a group that was privileged to have an audience with one of Brazil's most renowned Christian leaders. He was the pastor of a mega-church, and he was a high profile evangelist who held massive crusades. For some reason, I remember clearly that a member of our group asked him how he managed to deal with all the attacks that Satan must launch against him. He smiled and said that it was of no concern. Long ago he had made a deal with Satan. If Satan didn't bother him, he wouldn't bother Satan! As I look back now, I am rather appalled at myself because I thought that he gave us a quite sensible answer. My assumption—which I have since corrected—was that Satan plays fair.

I was not alone. I had identified with a stream of Christianity that had decided not to confront Satan but simply to tolerate him. At best, the devil was just a nuisance. I cannot recall any of my seminary professors making more than passing mentions of the devil in class. An underlying assumption was that when Jesus shed His blood on the cross, it all but nullified Satan's power. I heard the devil referred to as a "toothless lion." Some likened him to the Wizard of Oz, who, when the bravado was stripped away, turned out to be a powerless wimp.

This point of view is immortalized in the prestigious *Global Dictionary of Theology*, where P. J. Gilbert writes, "Demons are real, but their reality is mere illusion in the presence of the ontological absoluteness of God. . . . Since demons are separated from God, the only power they can possibly have is the power human beings mistakenly and naively attribute to them."[1]

John Wimber helped me to take my first steps toward a paradigm shift. He believed that Satan was a real enemy and that demons were powerful beings that could be cast out of people, and he demonstrated the reality of that in our Fuller Seminary classes. However, I found that a full paradigm shift would require further steps.

Lausanne II in Manila

The process involving these new steps began in the historic Congress on World Evangelization, commonly referred to as Lausanne II. In 1989 the Lausanne Committee for World Evangelization (LCWE) invited 4,500 leaders from all over the world to gather in Manila. At that event, no fewer than five speakers chose to address a topic heretofore absent from the radar screens of the majority of delegates, namely, the subject of territorial spirits. I happened to be one of the five, sharing some concepts that I had picked up after traveling with Omar Cabrera of Argentina.

In Manila the five of us suggested that the church should begin to do whatever is necessary to implement what Paul describes as "[wrestling] against principalities, against powers, against the rulers of the darkness of this age, against spiritual hosts of wickedness in the heavenly places" (Eph. 6:12). We felt that, to reach the unreached peoples of the world, such "air war" was necessary to pave the way for the ground troops of evangelists, church planters and humanitarian agencies.

Some speakers postulated that there might be demonic principalities assigned by Satan to attempt to keep certain geographic territories in spiritual darkness. In the book of Daniel, for example, we read about the "prince of Persia" and the "prince of Greece" (Dan. 10:20). Could similar demonic forces be in operation today, attempting to deter the advance of God's kingdom in specific regions? Many delegates heard questions like this for the first time. By the time they left, they began wondering whether God might have given them the authority to engage and neutralize such powers of darkness in their home regions.

Before I left Manila, I clearly heard the voice of God say, "Son, I want you to take leadership in the area of territorial spirits." For someone who was a novice in understanding the demonic world, this was a surprising assignment. Nevertheless, I welcomed it, because my life had been dedicated to fulfilling the Great Commission and I was anxious to do whatever was necessary to speed the process; so I went into action.

Since I am a scholar, my first step was to do extensive research in an attempt to uncover material in which others had addressed this subject. Much to my amazement, I found a good bit. I selected what I thought was the best and compiled it into a book that was released as *Engaging the Enemy* in the United States and *Territorial Spirits* in the United Kingdom. Among the 19 contributors were well-known figures such as Jack Hayford, Yonggi Cho, John Dawson, Ed Silvoso, Michael Green, and even respected theologian Oscar Cullmann. It was very encouraging to find that the five of us in Manila were not alone.

The Spiritual Warfare Network

I then convened a think tank, bringing together leaders who were at least somewhat acquainted with the subject of what we were then calling territorial spirits so we could learn from each other and perhaps form a critical mass of spokespersons who would communicate these relatively new ideas to the body of Christ in general. The group of 25 or so met together several times in the early 1990s and adopted the name Spiritual Warfare Network (SWN). It was then that we agreed to standardize the terminology: "ground-level spiritual warfare" (casting out demons or personal deliverance); "occult-level spiritual warfare" (confronting organized forces of wickedness, such as Satanism, witchcraft, New Age, Freemasonry, voodoo, Eastern religions, and the like); and "strategic-level spiritual warfare" (engaging high-ranking principalities of darkness, such as territorial spirits).[2]

While all this was going on, I, of course, continued teaching at Fuller Seminary. I had recently been through the signs and wonders controversies that I wrote about in the previous chapter, and I hoped that things would be calming down. However, it was not to be. When the theologians began to hear that I was now dealing with such things as supposed territorial spirits and what some caricatured as "demons behind every bush," I found myself in trouble again. Conducting healing services in seminary classrooms was suspect enough, but when I began teaching that there might be demonic principalities over whole cities like Pasadena, California, it sounded to some professors more like science fiction than serious, theological seminary material. The situation further deteriorated when secular news media began reporting activities of the Spiritual Warfare Network, causing certain influential donors to begin asking questions about the direction the seminary might be headed.

No one ever said that shifting paradigms is easy!

My trouble came in the form of a summons to appear before the Faculty Senate and to give an account of what was perceived to be my devious behavior. I tried to explain why I thought that researching and teaching on the subject of strategic-level spiritual warfare could measurably advance the cause of fulfilling the Great Commission, but I was not successful. The hostility in the room was thick. One of my disadvantages was that I was still very much in a learning mode, and I did not have ready responses to all the questions they were asking. My grilling felt almost like a heresy trial. Fortunately for me, the seminary statement of faith said so little about such things that I could not be found in violation of any written seminary doctrinal standard.

The upshot was that I received a letter from the president saying that the Faculty Senate was not satisfied that I had taken their concerns seriously enough and that further steps would be coming. However, these steps somehow never materialized, and we were able to coexist as faculty colleagues for many more years.

An Antiwar Movement

One of the things I discovered through this intense learning process was the surprising fact that a subtle anti-spiritual warfare movement exists within the church. This is not something new. In fact, it undoubtedly dates back at least to the Enlightenment of the eighteenth century, when a lot of the plain facts of the Bible started being questioned by rationalists.

I recall that, when I was a seminary student before going to Bolivia, my professors, with a knowing look in their eyes, would flash a wry smile when they would report the famous incident of Martin Luther's throwing an inkwell at a demon in his study. Poor Luther—he was pre-Enlightenment. He was a child of his times. Unlike today's professors, Luther had been deprived of the benefits emerging from the age of human reason. If Luther only knew what we know today, he would have ignored what he thought was a demon and would not have bothered to take overt action against it. Back then, I had no grounds on which to question my professors'—what I now consider *un-enlightened*—attitude.

One of the most pernicious rulers of darkness that Satan has unleashed is a powerful corporate spirit of religion. Its main assignment, the best I can discern, is to prevent God's people from moving into whatever new times and seasons God desires for His church. The spirit of religion is an inveterate preserver of the status quo. It devises ways and means to make the old wineskin so appealing that Christian leaders are either oblivious to God's new wineskin or they know about it and actively oppose it. It causes its victims to believe that the old is the will of God. This demon does what it can to prevent paradigm shifts.

If such is the case, it makes sense that promoting a Christian antiwar movement would be a predictable strategy for the corporate spirit of religion. The Second Apostolic Age is characterized by a heightened awareness of the serious warfare involved in the kingdom of God pushing back the kingdom of Satan. This is a byproduct of the activation of apostles in our Second Apostolic Age. Previously, pastors and theologians dominated corporate Christianity and set an agenda that did not usually prioritize war. The unfolding situation has required nothing less than apostles to bring forth the new aggressive Kingdom agenda, and, predictably, such apostles would be opposed by the corporate spirit of religion, which attempts to maintain the pastoral, antiwar past.

Apostolic Warfare

For those who may be hesitant to believe that the recent activation of apostles is behind an escalation of the awareness of spiritual warfare in our times, let me quote three of our more prominent contemporary apostles. Look carefully at what they say.

John Eckhardt of Crusaders Ministry, Chicago, Illinois, writes:

> Apostolic ministry is a ministry of warfare. It entails commanding, mobilizing, rallying and gathering the army of God to challenge and pull down the strongholds of the enemy. The apostolic invades new territories and breaks through. It has the ability to go first. It is the first to encounter the spiritual resistance of the powers of darkness and the first to penetrate the barriers they erect.[3]

Chuck Pierce of Global Spheres, Inc., in Corinth, Texas, writes:

> Through the resurgence of the prophetic and the apostolic, we are destroying the demonic structures in the second heaven that have been holding both the church and the unsaved world captive. God is teaching us methods and strategies that will rip the blinders off the eyes of whole territories of people. This new warring anointing will cause us to reap a great and bountiful harvest of souls![4]

John Kelly of the International Coalition of Apostles, in Fort Worth, Texas, writes:

Warfare is the number one role of the apostle. Prophets will woo you with the word of the Lord; teachers will educate you; pastors will help you through your problems and hurts; evangelists will get folks saved; but it is the apostle who will declare war on the enemy and lead the church into war. The apostle is the one who will unify the church into a fighting force. The apostle is the one who will bring all past and present truth and every past and present move of God to bear against the enemy.[5]

If what Eckhardt, Pierce and Kelly say is true, it is not difficult to imagine why the spirit of religion would be giving high priority to promoting a Christian antiwar movement. With the help of modern technology, the people of God worldwide are now being mobilized and equipped as never before. The kingdom of Satan is suffering severe setbacks with the advance of the kingdom of God. God is speaking to more and more of His people about aggressive spiritual warfare.

It Takes War to Make Peace

Peace is ideal, but it takes war to make peace. I have been blessed by living most of my life in a world of relative peace. What allowed this to happen was the last war the United States Congress officially declared, namely, World War II. I was a teenager during World War II, so I know what real war is—and I don't like it. However, I do like the 50 years of peace that it produced.

Some younger people who might not remember World War II are likely to remember the Vietnam War, the first war that America lost. There were some dramatic differences between the two wars. For one thing, Congress never declared war on Vietnam. Consequently, it turned out to be a halfhearted effort, characterized by antiwar movements across the country. I don't recall a single antiwar demonstration during World War II. It never occurred to us to criticize our leaders or to complain about the personal sacrifices that war required. Sugar was rationed; we needed government stamps to buy shoes; we couldn't fill our gas tanks or take pleasure drives; we saved paper and scrap metal; we bought savings bonds; and we said goodbye to our relatives, many of whom we never saw again.

Jesus is known as the Prince of Peace (see Isa. 9:6). However, look at the words that He spoke: "Do not think that I came to bring peace on earth. I did not come to bring peace but a sword" (Matt. 10:34). One reason Jesus said this is that the main reason He came to earth was to invade the kingdom of Satan. Jesus said, "From the days of John the Baptist until now, the kingdom of heaven has been forcefully advancing, and forceful men lay hold of it" (Matt. 11:12, *NIV*).

Apostles take Jesus' words literally, and they take seriously their role as generals, leading the church into war. They know that peace will eventually come, but not without war.

Know Your Enemy

One of the first rules of warfare is to know your enemy. If that is the case, how is the spirit of religion operating? As a starter, it seems to be attempting to orchestrate the Christian antiwar movement on three fronts.

The first front relates to a considerable number of church leaders who do not believe that Satan or demons really exist. In their minds, the notion of demons might be useful to describe evil influences produced by unrighteous people or unjust social structures, but demons are not to be regarded as personalities who could be confronted, engaged and dealt with. Naturally, the spirit of religion desires to preserve this convenient status quo, and the task is relatively simple. This group is characterized by a relatively low view of biblical authority and a typical indifference to the person and work of the Holy Spirit. Such leaders see little need to declare war against what is considered a figment of the imagination.

The second front of the Christian antiwar movement is directed toward Bible believers who have concluded that Jesus has given us only limited authority to deal with the invisible world. They do not question whether Satan or demons are real. They believe in spiritual warfare, but only to a point. Yes, we have authority to cast out demons, but we have no authority above ground-level warfare. We step out of bounds if we attempt to confront principalities or powers or territorial spirits. They contend that, if we do this, we run the risk of becoming needless casualties of war. This antiwar movement discourages believers from engaging in occult-level or strategic-level spiritual warfare. It has actually succeeded in instilling a spirit of fear into a significant number of believers, much to the devil's delight.

The third front is an attempt to neutralize God's forces by convincing some believers that Christians cannot be demonized. Unfortunately, there are whole denominations that adhere to this principle, and their leaders oppose deliverance ministry in their churches. Obviously, warring against Satan on any level is not on their agendas. This is regrettable because it causes these believers to declare themselves conscientious objectors and to leave the battle against the enemy to others.

Invading Satan's Kingdom

Despite these attempts of the enemy to prevent God's people from warring against Satan and his forces of darkness, the body of Christ is awakening to the imperative to advance the kingdom of God by force. It is time to go to war! We are not to *tolerate* the kingdom of Satan; rather, we are to *invade* it! Let's reject the antiwar movement in our midst and move aggressively into the battle. I can say these things so directly because it is what the Bible teaches us to do. Let's look at this more closely.

Our Mandate

Our mandate is clear. Jesus left heaven and came to earth "to seek and to save that which was lost" (Luke 19:10). When He went back to heaven, He left us with the mandate to "preach the gospel to every creature" (Mark 16:15) and to "make disciples of all the nations" (Matt. 28:19).

When we preach the gospel, the good news of salvation, to lost people and they do not respond, something is wrong. The gospel is the best news they could ever hear, so why don't they accept it? Here is the reason: "If our gospel is veiled, it is veiled to those who are perishing, *whose minds the god of this age has blinded*" (2 Cor. 4:3-4, emphasis added). The god of this age is Satan. His power to prevent the spread of the gospel must be confronted and bound. This is built into our mandate to fulfill the Great Commission.

Our Assignment

Our assignment is to attack aggressively. Now is not the time for passivity! Sitting back and hoping against hope that God will save the world without us is misguided thinking. God never said, "I will evangelize the world." He said, "You will evangelize the world."

God is sending us into the invisible world to do hand-to-hand combat. Paul used the word "wrestle" to describe this combat. Wrestling was the closest and most intense contact sport in the Roman Empire. Paul wrote, "We do not wrestle against flesh and blood, but against principalities, against powers, against the rulers of the darkness of this age, against spiritual hosts of wickedness in the heavenly places" (Eph. 6:12). We must not back off from our assignment.

Our Weapons

Our weapons of warfare come from the arsenal of heaven. The Bible reads, "For though we walk in the flesh, we do not war according to the flesh" (2 Cor. 10:3). This does not say, "We do not war." Just the opposite is true! As believers we certainly war, but not in our own strength. "The weapons of our warfare are not carnal but mighty in God for pulling down strongholds" (2 Cor. 10:4). There can be no doubt that, as long as we depend on God's weapons, we have the ways and means to overcome the power of the enemy.

Our Authority

Our authority is unlimited. When Jesus sent His disciples out to war, He said, "Behold, I give you the authority to trample on serpents and scorpions, and over all the power of the enemy, and nothing shall by any means hurt you" (Luke 10:19). Jesus did not say that He gave His disciples authority over *some* of the power of the enemy, but over *all* the power of the enemy. This means that we are not limited to ground-level spiritual warfare as some might say. No, we have divine authority to do occult-level spiritual warfare and strategic-level spiritual warfare as well.

Our Responsibility

Our responsibility is to confront forces of spiritual wickedness on all levels by declaring to them the intention of God to extend His kingdom throughout the earth as it is in heaven. The Bible says that "the manifold wisdom of God might be made known by the *church* to the principalities and powers in the heavenly places" (Eph. 3:10, emphasis added). We are the church, so God expects us to be explicit as we confront high-ranking spirits of wickedness.

Conclusion

Since Jesus died on the cross and rose from the dead, the kingdom of heaven has been advancing. However, the rate has greatly accelerated in recent times, and the advent of the Second Apostolic Age is speeding it up greatly. More and more of God's people are renewing their minds and growing in their understanding of the intense spiritual warfare that is involved in taking the Kingdom by force. I am delighted that so many are joining me in this paradigm shift. We are agreeing that we will no longer tolerate Satan. We are declaring war!

Notes

1. P. J. Gilbert, "Spiritual Warfare," *Global Dictionary of Theology,* edited by William A. Dyrness and Veli-Matti Karkkainen (Downers Grove, IL: IVP Academic, 2008), p. 850.
2. See chapter 12, where I describe these terms in greater detail.
3. John Eckhardt, *Moving in the Apostolic* (Ventura, CA: Renew Books, 1999), p. 64.
4. Chuck D. Pierce and Rebecca Wagner Sytsema, *The Future War of the Church* (Ventura, CA: Renew Books, 2001), p. 95.
5. John Kelly with Paul Costa, *End-Time Warriors* (Ventura, CA: Renew Books, 1999), p. 54.

8

From **Reformed Sanctification** to **Wesleyan Holiness**

When I was saved at age 19, it was one of those abrupt, 180-degree life changes. I had been living a lifestyle of habitual sin, which, I'm glad to say, ended immediately. Granted, it took a few months to clean up some of the more deeply embedded patterns of thinking and acting (such as my barnyard language), but I accomplished my goal over time and began living a reasonably godly life. I tried to follow the examples of more mature Christians. I paid attention to my pastor's sermons on Sunday, I read the Bible for the first time, and I determined to do what the Bible said. Whenever I had the choice between right and wrong, I made my best effort to choose the right.

I soon recognized that there were fellow Christians who were obviously living a more godly life than I. I read biographies of Praying Hyde, George Mueller, Hudson Taylor, and the like, and I suspected that I would never reach the level of spiritual exploits that characterized their lives and others like them. To be honest, for some reason, deep down, I never really had much desire to achieve the five-star spirituality of such heroes of the faith. Nevertheless, I definitely wanted to establish an ongoing lifestyle of acceptable Christian conduct, which, by and large, I think I did.

At the time, I was a spiritual tabula rasa. Whatever I heard and read from Christian leaders, I tended to believe. Since I had no religious background, I had no reason to question what I was learning. In fact, I naively thought that just about all Christians would believe the same things, so what I was hearing must be right and agreeable to all. Among other things, I learned that the Bible says that no matter how we behave, we can never be free from sin. This puzzled me, but only a little bit. No big deal!

The Reformed Doctrine of Sanctification

During my three years in seminary, I received and absorbed some theological explanations of our human struggle of dealing with sin in our lives. First, let me say that the seminary I attended identified itself as adhering to Reformed theology. Reformed theology emerged during the Protestant Reformation of the sixteenth century, led by Martin Luther, John Calvin and others. This doctrine, often referred to as Calvinism, characterized most of evangelicalism, the stream in which I found myself located as a new believer at that time.

A primary tenet of Calvinism is total depravity. This means that every human being since Adam is contaminated from birth with a sinful nature, continuing both before and after salvation. The difference is that when we're saved our sins are forgiven, and we then have the indwelling presence of Christ to help us deal with our depraved nature on an ongoing basis. The more we mature in Christ, the more effectively we can reduce the effects of our inbred sinful nature and display the fruit of the Spirit rather than the works of the flesh. However, our flesh will continue to be with us throughout our life, which prevents us from ever reaching the goal of personal holiness. This point of view is frequently labeled the Reformed doctrine of sanctification.

I recall writing a rather disturbing exegesis paper on the Greek text of Romans 7:15, where Paul writes that he is a wretched man because what he wants to do he doesn't do and what he does do he doesn't want to do. He seems to be in a constant struggle with his sinful nature, even losing the battle a good bit of the time. In Romans 8, Paul goes on to write that there is relief from this in Christ, but this relief must be attained through repentance, confession and appropriating the divine presence. I got an A on the paper, but as I look back, I now find myself glad to be free from such an ongoing struggle toward sanctification without clear victory in sight.

To illustrate what I am saying, I have some friends who actually ask God to forgive their sins every time they say grace before meals. What does this mean? It must mean that they assume that, if God answers their prayer and forgives them at breakfast, they inevitably will sin again before lunch and need to be forgiven once more. Many fear that if they don't commit an outward sin, they still must be committing sins of omission, sins of which they may not be aware but which nevertheless would bring them under the judgment of God before their next meal. Life, then, is a never-ending battle against the sin nature and carnality. In my current opinion, this belief system can easily develop into a spiritual malady of hyper-repentance.

Babies in Heaven?

Before I explain my paradigm shift away from Reformed sanctification, let me raise an interesting, related theological question. Do babies who are stillborn or aborted go to heaven? They are conceived with original sin inherited from Adam and have a depraved nature, but they never have a chance to accept Christ as their Savior and be born again. John 3:3 says that unless you are born again, you cannot see the kingdom of God. In spite of this, just about everyone I know believes that innocent babies who die do, indeed, go to heaven. I agree, and here is the reason: Jesus died to make atonement for *actual* sin, not *original* sin. This, I realize, requires an explanation.

When you think about it, Jesus didn't have to die for original sin, simply because "the wages of sin is death" (Rom. 6:23). God told Adam that if he ate the forbidden fruit, he would die. If that were the case, the converse must have been true. If Adam did not eat the fruit, he would not die. This means that because of the way God created Adam, it was possible for him to die (in other words, be mortal), and it was also possible for him not to die and to end up immortal. Adam's choice to commit the original sin caused him to die, and each one of us today eventually also dies, thus paying the price for our own original sin. Since the babies in question actually died, they paid the price for their original sin and consequently go to heaven. They never had a chance to commit an actual sin, which, if they did, could only be pardoned through the blood of Jesus and the new birth. Just a thought!

Eradication

Now let's get back to those of us who have committed, and unfortunately still do commit, actual sins. Yes, when we're born again, all

of our past sins are forgiven; but our sinful nature, caused by original sin, has not been eradicated. Therefore, we need to learn how to
deal with our present and future sins. That word, "eradicated," is an
interesting word, because there happens to be a certain line of doctrine that *does* teach eradication of the sinful nature. It is a subset of
what is commonly known as the Holiness Movement.

Later on, I am going to explain my paradigm shift to Wesleyan
holiness, meaning that my current view of holiness coincides with
that of much of the historic Holiness Movement. Meanwhile, one of
the reasons that it took me so long to change goes back to my seminary days in the 1950s. As a new believer I was so sheltered that I
knew nothing of holiness teaching. My professors may have mas-
tered Reformed theology, but, looking back, I now realize that they
were unsympathetic, even negative, toward the Holiness Movement.
In class, the Wesleyan doctrine of holiness was never presented as a
viable alternative to Reformed sanctification. It was mostly caricatured as an aberrant form of Christianity, practiced by some who
supposedly were victims of a rather unsophisticated theology.

To emphasize their point, my professors would typically choose
the doctrine of eradication, which some holiness people actually
taught. The idea revolved around a second blessing. The first blessing was being born again. Subsequent to that, believers were taught
to seek and expect a sudden filling of the Holy Spirit, which would
then result in their sanctification. Many taught that this second
blessing would eradicate the sinful nature and that, consequently,
a sanctified person could no longer sin. The public testimonies of
holiness believers would almost invariably contain two dates, one
when they were saved and another when they were sanctified. Since
I could not accept the idea that our sinful human nature is ever totally eradicated, I concluded that it would be best to keep my dis-
tance from holiness doctrine. As you know, I now believe in holiness,
but I still cannot embrace eradication. Unfortunately, I catch myself sinning from time to time, proving, at least to me, that I still
have a sinful nature.

I am now convinced that there is a way to deal with this sinful
nature more effectively than either what is taught in the Reformed
doctrine of sanctification or what is taught in eradication. I'll explain how I went through my paradigm shift.

Holes in the Armor

In the previous chapter I told about how I became involved in strategic-level spiritual warfare and also how risky it could be if we deviate from God's prescribed rules of engagement. The individual who mentored me the most as I began to move into the paradigm of spiritual warfare was Cindy Jacobs of Generals International. She emphatically underscored the intensity of the struggle involved in wrestling with principalities and powers and the concomitant danger of casualties.

As would be expected, Cindy went to Ephesians 6 and stressed that, before going into strategic-level spiritual warfare, we must put on the full armor of God (see v. 11). This was common Christian teaching. However, she went on from there to add something I have never forgotten. She said that we can put on the full armor of God, but if we do not have a pure heart under that armor, we will have holes in our armor! Obviously, the one who knew where those holes were would be the devil, and he would aim his fiery darts toward those very holes in order to take us down.

The more I processed this, the more I realized that my long-held Reformed doctrine of sanctification could not assure me that I could either achieve or maintain a pure heart under the armor. By then I knew that John Wesley, regarded as the father of the Holiness Movement, had taught that believers could and in fact should be holy and actually live an ongoing holy life. I had connected personally with enough of the leaders of the Church of the Nazarene, Church of God (Anderson), Pentecostal Holiness, Salvation Army, and the like, to know that their theology could not casually be dismissed as unsophisticated. The more I was exposed to holiness theology, the more I became convinced that I needed to renew my mind and embrace it.

Wesley's chief and ongoing contribution to Christian theology was his doctrine of Christian perfection. By this he meant that a Christian could live a life in thought, word and deed that met God's principles and desires. However, he distinguished this from sinless perfection, which would necessarily lead to eradication, as I explained previously. While we could live a life without sin, he taught, we could never get to the place where sin is no longer a possibility in our lives. Yes, we could be holy, but we could never be holy enough. Holiness is dynamic, not static.

Embracing Holiness

In order to embrace Wesleyan holiness, I did not join a Methodist, Wesleyan or Nazarene church. I just went back to the Scriptures to study as much as I could about having a pure heart. A starting point became 1 Peter 1:15: "As He who called you is holy, you also be holy in all your conduct." When I began to think back, I realized that those who espouse the Reformed doctrine of sanctification tend to stress the first part of that text, namely, the holiness of God. Since no one disputes the holiness of God, it is safe ground. In fact, dealing with God's holiness is much easier than dealing with personal holiness.

For example, if you would ask a traditional church music director to do a song about holiness, he or she would likely select the famous hymn "Holy, Holy, Holy! Lord God Almighty." Notice that the lyrics focus on the holiness of God, not on our personal holiness. In fact, the song contains a line that actually reflects the Reformed doctrine of sanctification, namely, "Only Thou art holy." Suppose we take that statement literally. If we do, it would mean that since God is the *only* being who truly is holy, neither you nor I could ever hope to become holy, because we cannot become God.

Now I believe that we must give as much consideration to the second part of 1 Peter 1:15, "you also be holy in all your conduct," as the first part. If we do, we must conclude that you and I can actually be holy simply because the Bible says that we can be. God would never ask us to do something that was impossible for us. The phrase "in all your conduct" gives us a measuring stick. There is obviously conduct that is holy and conduct that is not holy.

Making the Right Choices

The book of James has a good bit to say about holiness. In James 4:7-8, we find four active verbs that point us toward holiness:

- "Submit to God"
- "Draw near to God"
- "Cleanse your hands"
- "Purify your hearts"

The first two of these actions, submitting to God and drawing near to Him, have to do with our relationship to God. The second two, cleansing our hands and purifying our hearts, have to do with our own behavior, or "conduct," as we see in 1 Peter 1:15.

How do we go about being holy in our daily lives? Obviously, our personal relationship with God is the starting point, but by itself it is not enough. Our attitude is important as well, but attitude alone will not make us holy. Some think that the presence of God will make us holy. Granted, we need God's presence, but that does not suffice. To understand this, take Adam and Eve as an example. There was a time when they were holy, and then there was a time when they were no longer holy. However, God was present with them during both.

What, then, could be the key factor at play for Adam and Eve? It was nothing less than their personal choice as to whether to adhere to God's standards or not. Unfortunately, they chose to disobey. Holiness, then, must go beyond the mere presence of God to our choice to obey Him.

Living Faith

Faith is obviously an essential prerequisite for holiness. However, it is important to understand the fact that faith can be dead. What, then, brings faith to life? It is our behavior. The Bible teaches that faith without works is dead (see Jas. 2:17-18). No one else can do our works for us, so the choice is ours. Let's move forward with living faith!

I know that this is strong teaching. Many will not like it. Martin Luther, for one, couldn't stand it. At one point he was so upset that he declared James to be an epistle of straw. He would have preferred a Bible that did not include the book of James! I will admit, however, that we do need to cut some slack for Luther. He was battling the Catholic Church, which taught salvation by works instead of justification by faith, so he had some substantially different issues concerning faith and works to deal with.

Holiness Is Countercultural

Bringing it closer to home, let me tell you about my 120 Fellowship Sunday School class in which I taught around 100 adults for 13 years. The members cared deeply for one another, and we felt like we were family—that is, until I taught on holiness for three months.

Before the three months were over, we had lost no fewer than five families from the class, two of them the most influential families we had! The idea that personal holiness depended on our decision to live according to God's standards was, apparently, too much for them. In their minds, relationships always trumped conduct. They wanted to hear about God's mercy but not His judgment.

The families who left our Sunday School class had chosen to flow with the American culture of the time. They regarded biblical holiness as countercultural, and it disturbed them. To help explain this, let's go to researcher George Barna. His studies have uncovered some rather startling sociological facts. Barna concludes:

> The Bible clearly states that true believers should be readily distinguished from nonbelievers by the way they live. Yet, the evidence undeniably suggests that most American Christians today do not live in a way that is quantifiably different from their non-Christian peers, in spite of the fact that they profess to believe in a set of principles that should clearly set them apart.[1]

That is not good news!

Kadosh and Hagios

Please notice Barna's final words: "set them apart." With this, he goes right to the heart of biblical holiness. The Old Testament Hebrew word for "holy" is *kadosh*, meaning "special" or "elevated above the ordinary." The New Testament Greek word *hagios* means "set apart," as Barna wrote.

In the broadest arena, the first step toward being special, or set apart, is to be born again into the family of God. John Wesley taught that sanctification begins with regeneration. Those who are born again are set apart from those who are born only once. This is the reason that the Bible considers all true believers to be holy. If you are a believer, you are set apart—you are holy. However, this is only the first step.

In the area of everyday life, the designation "special," or "set apart," obviously includes two further aspects: One is what we are set apart *to*; the other is what we are set apart *from*. Interestingly enough, every major New Testament passage on holiness contains a list of explicit standards, reflecting what aspects of our conduct God considers holy. They tell us what we must be set apart *to* and also what we must be set apart *from* if we are legitimately holy.

Take, for example, Colossians 3, one of the major New Testament passages on holiness. In verse 12 the apostle Paul addresses "the elect of God, *holy* and beloved" (emphasis added). Within the preceding 11 verses, Paul lists 12 areas of conduct that, if we are holy, we are to be set apart *from* (fornication, evil desire, idolatry, filthy language, and so on). In the following verses, he lists another 12 areas of conduct that, if we are holy, we are to be set apart *to* (meekness, forgiveness, love, husbands loving wives, wives submitted to husbands, and so on). God's standards for holiness are not vague; they are quite specific. They obviously require certain observable patterns of behavior.

The Pitfall of Legalism

See that phrase "observable patterns of behavior"? Unfortunately, a generation or two ago, some advocates of the Holiness Movement decided to go beyond the stated biblical standards for holiness and add to them a humanly devised list of do's and don'ts against which they thought they could more easily measure the holiness of individuals. This turned out to be a compilation of carnal regulations that degenerated into an unbiblical code of legalism. Some went so far as to require for church membership such things as these: women weren't able to wear make-up or have certain hair styles, and they had to wear skirts and sleeves of a certain length; men weren't able to shave their beards or chew tobacco; and no believers were allowed to go to movies, play cards, drink any alcohol, use electricity or telephones in their homes, and the list goes on.

How wrong is this? To answer that, we need look no further than what the apostle Paul wrote in his letter to the Colossians. He warns against those who say, "'Do not touch, do not taste, do not handle,' which all concern things which perish with the using—according to the commandments and doctrines of men" (Col. 2:21-22). These religious, legalistic requirements had little to do with adhering to the holy standards of God. In fact, they had the opposite effect.

What do I mean by that? I mean that some believers who saw through this legalistic façade ended up turning against the Holiness Movement in general. This concerns me because I count myself among the adherents of Wesleyan holiness but without the trappings of legalism that Wesley himself would have rejected. I hope there is a way in which we can be holy in all of our conduct (remember 1 Peter 1:15?) without falling victim to the trap of legalism. The good news is that, at least in my personal observation, unbiblical legalism is not as much of a stumbling block to biblical holiness today as it was some years ago. I think we are in a new season of understanding, and this puts us in a better place!

Let's Be Holy!

If, in the final analysis, our holiness depends on our personal choices, then where do we get the power to make the right ones? We can't generate that power ourselves because we have sinful natures. The power only comes from being filled with the Holy Spirit.

I believe it is important to ask God to fill us with His Holy Spirit every morning. Jesus said, "If a son asks for bread from any father among you, will he give him a stone? How much more will your heavenly Father give the Holy Spirit to those who ask Him!" (Luke 11:11,13). The filling of the Holy Spirit brings many wonderful blessings to God's people, but keep in mind that one of the major roles of the Holy Spirit is to convict us of sin, righteousness and judgment (see John 16:8). What does this mean? It means that when we step out of bounds and do something that does not please God, we will definitely know it because the Holy Spirit will make sure that we do!

I am saying this in an attempt to build our confidence that each one of us can, indeed, be holy in all our conduct. May I be personal? I happen to be writing this paragraph in the afternoon. So far today, I have not sinned! I say "so far" because I don't believe I could ever get to the place where sin could not possibly enter my life before the day is over. However, I fully plan to live the rest of the day without sinning. I realize that this is a rather bold statement, so let me try to explain where my expectation comes from.

Many, many years ago I developed the habit of praying the Lord's Prayer (see Matt. 6:9-13) every morning. Let me stress that I *pray* it; I do not just *say* it. When I come to the part "forgive my sins as I forgive those who sin against me" (see v. 12), I do a mental review of the past 24 hours to see if I have any sin that needs to be confessed. This morning when I prayed, it so happened that I had nothing to confess. How could I be sure of this? It was because I was filled with the Holy Spirit and He brought no sin to my mind.

Sometimes, of course, He does. When this happens, I know exactly what to do about it, and you undoubtedly know this as well. I confess my sin, and He is faithful and just to forgive my sin and cleanse me from all unrighteousness (see 1 John 1:9). This wipes my slate clean. My sin is now as far from me as the east is from the west (see Ps. 103:12). I'm ready to move into a new day, and I do not have to confess that sin again.

No sin yesterday? How about today? This morning I also prayed, "Lead me not into temptation" (see Matt. 6:13), and I expected the Lord to answer that prayer all day long. If I am not tempted, I will not sin. Then, just to make sure, I pray, "Deliver me from the evil one" (v. 13). If Satan, the one who does the tempting, can't touch me, then I will not be tempted to sin.

My conclusion is that if I can go for one day without sinning, then I can go another day and any number of days. I can live a holy life! I know that I must keep praying and staying filled with the Holy Spirit because at any time sin can invade my life. When that happens— not *if* that happens!—I deal with it immediately and get back on track.

Keeping the Armor Intact

When people learn about some of the fairly high-level leadership assignments that God has given me through the years to advance His kingdom, they occasionally ask, "What do you do to survive all the spiritual warfare that the devil throws up against you? You must be near the top of his hit list!"

I reply that, day in and day out, year in and year out, I do not personally experience many attacks of spiritual warfare. I attribute that rather enviable situation to two things. The first and most important is that God has brought into my life a small group of personal intercessors who build and maintain a prayer shield around me, my wife and my ministry.[2] They are out on the front lines taking the hits from the realm of darkness that were intended for me.

Second, when some of those attacks do get through, they find that I have put on the full armor of God. That would not be enough, however, if I harbored an impure heart under the armor. I would then have holes in my armor. However, thanks to the paradigm shift I made to Wesleyan holiness, I believe my heart is spiritually healthy, and consequently holes in my armor are few and far between. I hope that this chapter helps you to move into that kind of a victorious spiritual life as well!

Notes

1. George Barna, *The Second Coming of the Church* (Nashville, TN: Word Publishing, 1998), pp. 120-121.
2. For details see C. Peter Wagner, *Prayer Shield* (Ventura, CA: Regal Books, 1992).

9

From **Denominational Government** to **Apostolic Government**

When I became a believer in the middle of the twentieth century, most American Christians belonged to churches that belonged to denominations. Denominations were as much a part of the Christian landscape as church pews and offering plates. Since I had no previous Christian background, I just assumed that denominations and denominational government had always been around.

State Churches

In due time, however, I learned that my assumption was incorrect. In fact, denominations as we know them actually started only about the time the Pilgrims came over to America, less than 400 years ago. Before that, most Christians belonged to what were called state churches. Church and state were closely connected. The religion of the king automatically determined the religion of all of his subjects in the territory that he ruled.

Not only did the people have no choice, but also they never even desired to make their own choice because, according to their paradigm, that is the way things were supposed to be. The Roman Catholic Church was the only option in places like Italy, France and Spain. The Orthodox Church was taken for granted in places like Russia and Greece. When the Protestant Reformation came along, Sweden, for example, was still a Catholic nation, but the decision of King Gustavus Vasa to become a Lutheran meant that all Swedish Christians would also be Lutherans from that day on. Likewise, when King Henry VIII of England decided one day that he didn't want to be a Catholic anymore, he established the Church of

England (the Anglican Church), which would then be the only acceptable form of Christianity in his territory.

The Beginning of Denominations

Although some state churches still exist, two things happened to reduce their dominance. The first was the migration of Europeans to the American colonies. The Europeans came from many different countries, and the Christians among them brought their particular state church affiliation with them.

Most of them found themselves settling in regions that also hosted Christians with different state church connections. There were no kings on site to rule territories and dictate what the religion of the territory should be. Then, when America became a nation and wrote a constitution, the new government was prohibited from establishing a religion and thereby creating a state church as the Europeans had done. Christians of different affiliations learned to live with one another in the same territory without government support. Those of like mind tended to cluster together and form what came to be known as denominations.

The second historical development that reduced the dominance of state churches was the Modern Missionary Movement, beginning in the late 1700s with William Carey. European state churches began sending missionaries, many to nations that were not Christian and therefore had no desire for a state church. Frequently, missionaries from more than one European country would arrive on the same mission field, so, as was the case in America, they needed to learn to live together in the same territory. Thus, the denominational pattern rather than the state church pattern became common in many parts of the world.

Denominational Government

Inherent in the American social environment, in which denominations were initially formed, was the political ideal of democracy. Consequently, most denominations were established on the premise that democratic rule needed to be incorporated into their legal structure. Contrary to what some denominational leaders even think today, the introduction of democracy into church government came largely from the culture of the time rather than from drawing on biblical principles.

Democratic procedures were established on all levels of church life. This meant that decisions affecting local churches were made by votes taken in church boards or sessions or vestries, boards of elders, congregations or the like. On state or regional levels, decisions were to be made by votes taken in presbyteries, synods, district councils or state conventions. Nationally, general assemblies, national conventions or general councils would make the determining decisions. The key thing to notice in what I have just described is that throughout the whole system, important church decisions are always to be made by *groups* of some kind rather than by *individuals*.

This paradigm of denominational government was virtually unquestioned for hundreds of years. When I became a Christian, I personally had no reason to reject it. The churches that I joined used it. I was taught how to work with democratic processes in my classes in seminary. When I arrived on the mission field, the missionaries were busy introducing this model into the new churches they were planting, and I joined in with them. My paradigm was clearly one of denominational government.

No longer! I have now renewed my mind and shifted my paradigm to apostolic government. What is the main difference? It is moving from the assumption that *groups* of people need to make the important decisions in church life rather than *individuals*. I will explain the details as I go along, but at this point, let me say that two sets of factors forced me into the paradigm shift: (1) field data on the growth and vitality of newer churches, and (2) a reconsideration of pertinent biblical material.

Learning from Church Growth

My role on the faculty of the Fuller School of World Mission was to teach church growth. In order to do so, I needed to spend considerable time in researching the growth of churches in America and around the world. Naturally, the churches that were growing the fastest tended to attract my attention. I was responsible not only to track and record their growth but also to analyze what factors might have contributed to the obvious vitality of such churches.

It was during the 1990s that three prominent, rapidly growing world movements became known to missiologists in general:

1. *African Independent Churches.* The first churches that were planted by Western missionaries throughout Africa closely resembled the state churches or the denominational churches back home. They looked and functioned much like the German Lutherans, the British Anglicans, the Swiss Reformed or the New England Congregationalists. As the second generation of Christian believers in these African churches matured, however, many of them became aware of the lack of contextualization in the teachings coming from the pulpit. The churches they belonged to did not seem to be very African. For example, most of the missionaries would not even allow drums in their churches. Consequently, a number of believers decided to separate from the mission churches of their parents and birth new churches and networks of churches that were more rooted in African culture. Before long the membership of these African Independent Churches far outnumbered that of the traditional mission churches across the continent, and they still do.

2. *Chinese House Churches.* The phenomenal Chinese House Church Movement began when Chairman Mao's Cultural Revolution ended in 1975. Since then, this movement has generated the most voluminous national harvest of souls in the history of the world. For 25 years it was largely a rural phenomenon, but more recently a parallel Urban House Church Movement has arisen, seeing influential people in business, government, education and the arts following Christ. Some researchers estimate that up to 10 percent of Chinese people are now Christian believers despite a government that has been expressly anti-Christian.

3. *Latin American Grassroots Churches.* Evangelical missionaries had been preaching the gospel and multiplying
churches in largely Roman Catholic Latin America for
over 100 years with fair, but not vigorous, growth. A
change came around 1980 with the emergence of what
researchers have called Latin American Grassroots
Churches in most Latin American metropolitan areas.
Individuals who for the most part have had no personal
mentoring from foreign missionaries lead these mega-
churches, which typically consist of thousands or even
tens of thousands in the central congregation plus numerous branch churches. Many of these individuals have
never attended a seminary or Bible school. Some were
called by God to plant a church while they held positions in the business world. These dynamically growing
churches are permeated with authentic Latin American
cultural forms, functions and behavioral patterns.
Largely because of these churches, some countries, such
as Guatemala, count more than 50 percent of their population as evangelicals. In Brazil, more people now attend
evangelical services on a Sunday than Catholic mass.

As I said, by the late 1990s these three movements were common
knowledge among those of us who were missiologists. However, during the mid-1980s I received an assignment to research and write a
major article on church growth for a volume called *Dictionary of Pentecostal and Charismatic Movements.* By that time most Pentecostal
churches had adopted the standard American denominational government, but an offshoot of classic Pentecostalism, independent
charismatic churches, had begun to flourish around 1970. By the
time I finished my two-year research project, it became clear that
these charismatic churches had become the fastest growing segment
of American Christianity.[1]

Triggering the Shift

Why do I bring up these four notable moves of the Holy Spirit in
our days? It is because my missiological research became the major

factor in triggering my paradigm shift from denominational government to apostolic government. As I studied these movements I began to notice several characteristics that they had in common, including the governmental structures of the churches.

Surprisingly, at least to me at the time, these churches, by and large, did not govern themselves on democratic principles. Typically, they were founded by a strong leader who was in charge of the church. Those affiliated with the church who liked the leader and perceived that he or she was called, gifted and anointed by God for the responsibility of leading the church stayed with the congregation and supported the pastor in every way. Those who did not simply left the church to seek other affiliations.

Be sure to notice that the church—traditionally represented by boards of elders or pastoral search committees, denominational executives or congregations—did not hire these pastors I have just described. God assigned them to the church. In this dynamic, all the top-level, important and determinative decisions concerning church life are made by the pastor—one individual—not by groups of people as in traditional denominations. This is one of the main characteristics of apostolic government. I do not mean to imply that all such pastors are apostles per se, but I do mean that they are all *apostolic* by nature.

Do you see how this frees pastors to be true leaders? They don't have to be worried that something they might do or say would cause them to be reprimanded or fired. They can freely cast the vision for the church, set the direction and make policy decisions. If an individual parishioner or a group of them might come up with a serious complaint against pastors of this nature, they simply find themselves invited to leave the church and choose another one that they like better. Part of the paradigm shift is moving from bureaucratic authority to personal authority; from legal structure to relational structure; from control to coordination; and from rational leadership to charismatic leadership.

The Guiding Assumptions

In order to clarify all that is involved in this paradigm shift, let me list the guiding assumptions of both forms of church government.

For years, these were my assumptions concerning the role of the pastor in the traditional denominational structure:

- Pastors are employees of the church.
- Pastors can come and go. For example, the average pastoral tenure among Southern Baptists is less than three years.
- Pastors are enablers. Their responsibility is to implement the vision of the congregation.
- Pastors are, to use anthropological terminology, the medicine men of the church rather than the tribal chiefs. They are expected to do the religious things around the church, but not to lead.
- Pastors are subject to performance reviews. They can be fired at will.

Now that I have renewed my mind and made my shift to favor apostolic government, these are my assumptions:

- Pastors—not the congregations—cast the vision for the church.
- Pastors major in leadership and minor in management.
- Pastors make top-level policy decisions and delegate the rest to others.
- Pastors build a solid management team of both elders and staff. Pastors are not subject to the authority of this team but rather the team serves at the pleasure of the pastors. Staff members are employees of their pastor, not of the church.
- Pastors are called for life, and they choose their successors.

Do All Agree?

As we have seen, paradigm shifts tend to pull some out of their comfort zones. You can imagine the reaction of many American denominational leaders to these new suggestions for church government. Sad to say, but democracy, in the minds of certain denominational leaders, has risen virtually to the status of a religious doctrine. It is almost as sacred a belief to some as the deity of Christ. To imply that a different form of government, especially one that tends to be more authoritarian, is as biblical or even more biblical than democracy tends to cause considerable consternation. Some denominational leaders label it dictatorship. To them it is a major threat to the status quo to even consider the introduction of apostles who would not see themselves as subject to their entrenched American democratic processes.

To make this more concrete, let me use as a real-life example one of America's largest and fastest growing denominations, the Assemblies of God. Why the Assemblies of God? The reason I have chosen them and not Methodists, Congregationalists, Christian and Missionary Alliance, Lutherans or any number of others that I might well have chosen is because the Assemblies of God top leadership in Springfield, Missouri, has, at least to my knowledge, been the most outspoken against apostolic government.

The first apostles in modern times appeared right after World War II in several movements called, among other labels, the healing evangelists, the Restoration Movement, the Shepherding Movement, and arguably the strongest unit among them was the Latter Rain. They advocated apostolic government, but, for a number of reasons that I am not going to enumerate at this moment, they made only a minor impact and did not flourish. However, I will say that one of these reasons was the strong, public opposition of the Assemblies of God. In 1949, the Assemblies of God published an official denominational white paper stating in part, "The teaching that the Church is built on the foundation of present-day apostles and prophets [is] erroneous."[2]

Nevertheless, the apostolic movement surfaced again when what I call the New Apostolic Reformation began to be recognized in the 1990s. I say "recognized" because the roots of the New Apostolic Reformation can be traced back to the initial emergence of the African Independent Churches around 1900. They were subsequently joined by the Chinese house church movement, the Latin American grassroots church movement, and the American Independent charismatic movement to constitute what I like to call the most radical change in the way of doing church since the Protestant Reformation. As one of the first missiologists to recognize this new form of the church, I felt a label was needed. After wrestling with several alternative terms,

I finally decided on the New Apostolic Reformation, and the term seemed to stick. When this became public in the mid-1990s, true to form, the Assemblies of God published another denominational white paper in 2000, stating that the "teaching that present-day offices of apostles and prophets should govern church ministry" is "a departure from Scripture and a deviant teaching."[3]

The following year, George Wood, now the denomination's General Superintendent, circulated a theological essay arguing his view that the New Testament's references to apostles and prophets had in view the role of these offices only in the first century or two as the Bible was being written and compiled, but that there are no longer New Testament-type apostles and prophets today. Unlike what happened in the post-World War II era, however, this type of public opposition has no longer deterred the vigorous growth of the current apostolic movement as we have seen in Africa, China, Latin America and many other places, including the United States.

Apostolic Denominational Leaders

Even certain denominational leaders have come to function in an apostolic manner. Don't forget that the major issue is whether the pastor is an *employee* of the church or whether the pastor *leads* the church. For example, almost all of the pastors whom you see weekly on television with their Sunday morning services are truly apostolic leaders even though they belong to democratically oriented denominations.

At this writing, one of the highest visibility pastors in America is Rick Warren of Saddleback Church in Southern California. Rick is a personal friend, and he helped me teach my church planting classes when I was on the Fuller Seminary faculty, probably more than 20 years ago. Rick is clearly one of today's most outstanding apostles, even though he personally would not accept the title. Nevertheless, he leads his church apostolically.

As a Southern Baptist, he adheres to congregational government and thereby is required to convene a congregational business meeting at least once a year to make important church decisions, such as finances, and to cast the vision for the following year. However, I remember Rick, with a smile on his face, telling my students that he schedules the annual congregational meeting at the most inconvenient time possible, and he has no trouble persuading the few who attend to approve whatever he presents to them. Is this apostolic or what?

Apostolic Authority

One of the strongest concerns that denomination-oriented leaders have about apostolic government is that, if you trust the Holy Spirit to work through the life and leadership of a single individual rather than through the consensus of a group, it can open the way to authoritarianism and the abuse of power. I share their concern, and, sadly enough, I need to admit that records show far too many real-life examples of how such leadership arrogance has actually harmed churches and church members.

As mentioned previously, I led the International Coalition of Apostles during the first decade of the 2000s, and I had to apply discipline to some members who allowed themselves to fall into this trap. However, my observation of the lives and ministries of hundreds of apostles in many countries allows me to affirm with considerable confidence that the abuse of power is clearly the exception to the rule. Most apostles are humble men and women who use the gifts that God has given them more for the benefit of those who follow them than for their own personal gain.

In any case, apostles do possess extraordinary spiritual authority. Where does this authority come from? This is such a key question that I think it would be well to answer it as fully as possible. First, apostles have authority because it comes along, part and parcel, with the spiritual gift of apostle. Spiritual gifts come only from God. "God has set the members, each one of them, in the body just as He pleased" (1 Cor. 12:18). God chooses the ones to whom He gives any spiritual gift, and therefore those who end up with the gift of apostle have received it, first and foremost, because God has chosen them. True apostles are not self-appointed, as some critics like to suggest; instead they are God-appointed. If any doubt that "apostle" is one of the spiritual gifts, they have only to check with 1 Corinthians 12:29-30, where apostle is part of a list that also includes obvious spiritual gifts such as prophecy, teaching, miracles, healings, tongues and interpretation of tongues.

Second, apostles have authority because they have an assignment, or call, from God. First Corinthians 12:4-6 tells us that there are different gifts, different ministries and different activities, but they are all assigned by "the same God who works all in all." Experienced apostles know that not only their gift but also their apostolic assignment have come from God, and that gives them personal confidence along with a good measure of authority.

Third, apostles have extraordinary character. Why do I call it extraordinary? It is because, contrary to what many people think, God has a double standard of judgment. He reveals it in James 3:1: "My brethren, let not many of you become teachers, knowing that we shall receive a stricter judgment." Obviously, there is one standard for teachers and another for those who are not teachers. However, if we read 1 Corinthians 12:28, we can imagine that apostles would expect an even higher standard than teachers. Here is how it reads: "And God has appointed these in the church: first apostles, second prophets, third teachers."

The apostles whom I know, with a few unfortunate exceptions, live up to the biblical standards of leadership. One of these standards is to be "blameless" (1 Tim. 3:2). The apostle Paul claimed that he met this high standard when he wrote, "I know of nothing against myself" (1 Cor. 4:4). Paul's display of extraordinary character qualified him to go on to say, "Therefore I urge you, imitate me" (v. 16). Today's apostles take Paul's yardstick very seriously and live accordingly. It should go without saying that extraordinary character carries with it great authority.

Fourth, apostles have followers. Simply put, no followers, no apostle! Those who are aligned with apostles and who follow their example and their leadership are characterized by two attitudes: Their submission is both *voluntary* and *grateful*. It is voluntary because nothing requires them to continue following the apostle's leadership. The reason they choose to keep following is because they are grateful for the spiritual alignment, the protection and the camaraderie they receive from the apostle that allow them continually to attain new levels in the ministry to which God has called them.

The driving motivation within an apostle regarding his or her followers is, *How can I help this person be all that God wants them to be?* Furthermore, the grateful follower is affirming: "This apostle adds value to my life and ministry, and I will gladly submit to this apostolic authority." With such a combination, everybody wins, and no one has reason to question the divinely granted authority of the apostle.

Spheres Limit Authority

While apostles are distinguished by their authority in the church, this authority is also limited by the apostolic sphere or spheres of ministry to which God has assigned the apostle. Paul writes to the Corinthians, "If I am not an apostle to others, yet doubtless I am to you" (1 Cor. 9:2). Here he openly admits that his apostolic authority has boundaries. There is no such thing as an apostle to the whole church. Paul, for example, was not an apostle to the church in Alexandria, in Jerusalem, in Rome or in other such places. However, he certainly was in Corinth—and we could add Ephesus, Philippi, Thessalonica, Galatia and other spheres to which he was assigned by God.

When he later wrote to the same Corinthians, Paul saw fit to boast about his authority: "For even if I should boast somewhat more about our authority, which the Lord gave us for edification and not for your destruction, I shall not be ashamed" (2 Cor. 10:8). However, he quickly added that his authority was limited: "We, however, will not boast beyond measure, but within the limits of the *sphere* which God has appointed us—a *sphere* which especially includes you" (v. 13, emphasis added).

Apostolic spheres can be *ecclesiastical*, such as would be seen in the ministry of apostle Paul. It is very common to find apostles who oversee a number of churches in their apostolic network. Some spheres are *territorial*. Certain apostles have authority within a city, a region or a nation. Others are *functional*. Apostles of prayer and apostles in the workplace have authority within this sphere. Yet some spheres can be *ethnic*. As an example, Peter was an apostle to the circumcision (Jews) while Paul was an apostle to the uncircumcised (Gentiles).

The Second Apostolic Age

As I have been attempting to observe the flow of the stream of the Holy Spirit in our day, I have come to believe that we now live in the

Second Apostolic Age and that this new season began in 2001. The First Apostolic Age took place during the initial two or three centuries of the Christian movement. Then, for perhaps 1,800 years, the church functioned and even expanded without affirming the biblical gift and office of apostle. However, things have changed. Although the changes are not so noticeable in Europe, the United States, Canada and other western nations, they undeniably are in what historian Philip Jenkins calls the Global South, where Christianity is exploding as never before.

Apostolic government is a new wineskin for the church today. Some 400 years ago denominational government began as a new wineskin and served the church well, sending missionaries to the far corners of the earth. I was one of those missionaries who went to the field under denominational government, so I honor it and respect it. However, as history moves forward, denominational government has now become an old wineskin. Yesterday teaches us valuable lessons, but I have always been one who leans toward focusing on tomorrow, namely, the future. That is why I am grateful that God has permitted me to renew my mind and change my paradigm from denominational government to the new wineskin of apostolic government.

Notes

1. See C. Peter Wagner, "Church Growth," *Dictionary of Pentecostal and Charismatic Movements,* edited by Stanley M. Burgess and Gary B. McGee, (Grand Rapids, MI: Zondervan Publishing House, 1988), pp. 180-195.
2. 1949 Minutes of the General Council of the Assemblies of God, Resolution 7: "The New Order of the Latter Rain." Available from the Assemblies of God; 1445 Boonville Ave., Springfield, MO 65802.
3. General Presbytery of the General Council of the Assemblies of God, "Endtime Revival—Spirit-Led and Spirit-Controlled: A Response Paper to Resolution 16" (August 11, 2000), p. 2.

10

From a **Greek Mindset** to a **Hebrew Mindset**

This chapter is going to be a bit different from the rest. The whole book is about paradigm shifts, but I can't honestly say that moving from a Greek mindset to a Hebrew mindset has been exactly a full *shift*. It is probably more like a paradigm *tweak*.

Why would I say this?

The Pervasive Infusion of Culture

When we equate paradigm shifts to the biblical phrase "renewing of your mind" (Rom. 12:2), it immediately causes us to examine the way we *think* about certain things. This has been my approach in every other chapter, but this time I am going to discuss a matter that, though it does include the way we think, goes far beyond that. It deals with things like who we are and how we live out, day by day, our destiny here on earth.

My favorite book on this subject is Charles Kraft's *Christianity in Culture*. The definition of culture that he likes the best is "the integrated system of learned behavior patterns which are characteristic of the members of a society and which are not the result of biological inheritance."[1] Humans are related to culture like fish are related to water. Every one of us is "totally, inextricably immersed in culture."[2] Kraft goes on to explain, "Each of us is shaped in the non-biological portion of our being by the culture into which we are born. We are shaped by a culture transmitted to us by the adults in our life."[3] And when we talk about paradigm shifts, we need to keep in mind that "our mental behavior is likewise pervasively influenced by our culture. Our culture shapes both our acting and our *thinking*" (emphasis added).[4]

I am a product of Western culture, being born in the United States in the early twentieth century. The word "Western" has nothing to do with the American Wild West, as some might think, but rather with the world before the Americas were discovered. In those days, what we now know as Asia was considered the East and what became Europe was considered the West. Western nations today generally include Europe, the United States, Canada, Australia, New Zealand and other areas strongly influenced by European culture. I know that I am greatly oversimplifying this, but no more details are necessary to understand why a total paradigm shift would be all but impossible for me.

Historians of Western culture generally trace its origin to the Greek Empire, best known by Alexander the Great. Some famous Greek philosophers, such as Plato, Aristotle, Socrates and many others, became so influential that most of us in Western nations are still strongly influenced by them. The Greek Empire, of course, stood on the shoulders of others, such as the Medo-Persian Empire, the Babylonian Empire, the Egyptian Empire, and so on. However, the paradigm for *thinking*, which the Greek philosophers developed, launched a new season in world history, at least for the segment of the earth's population into which I was born. My parents, my friends, my teachers, the media and all the rest of American culture were shaped by the paradigms of the Greek mindset, and I was also.

This pervasive influence of culture is the reason why I cannot claim a paradigm *shift* from a Greek mindset to a Hebrew mindset, so I would rather call it a paradigm *tweak*.

Greek Thinking

What is it that the Greek philosophers introduced? A full answer to this question would require a whole book, which I have no credentials to write. Besides, every respectable library will offer many volumes already published on the subject. Instead, my interest is on whatever portion or portions of the Greek mindset would obviously be regarded as clearly at odds with the revelation of God in the Bible, which, as we know, was written from a Hebrew mindset.

The Greek philosophers were not students of Moses, Isaiah or Ezekiel. From their perspective, human beings were supreme, not

God. As far as God was concerned, they did have an underlying sense that something must have caused the universe to start moving, so they came up with concepts like Aristotle's Unmoved Mover. The Unmoved Mover is not a God who is a divine person who communicates with human beings, but rather an unavoidable philosophical category, conceived by the human mind. It is accurate to say that Greek philosophy was human-centered, not God-centered, as was the Hebrew mindset. Today we describe this as humanism, which, unfortunately, is the predominant cultural orientation of most unsaved Americans today.

If humans are the center, then a logical conclusion has to be moral relativism. The Hebrews believed in moral absolutes laid down by God, but not the Greeks. You might remember that Socrates, one of history's most distinguished teachers, used what is called the dialectical method. Instead of telling his students what they should believe, Socrates liked to lead them into figuring out what they themselves chose to believe. When they disagreed with each other, he did not suggest that one was right and one was wrong; rather, he encouraged them to live by their own personal conclusions. For moral issues, each one had to make up his or her own mind about what is right and what is wrong, while respecting what others thought. Again, it is too bad that this moral relativism persists and is a growing mindset among more and more Americans today.

Both humanism and moral relativism are huge components of the Greek mindset that differentiate it from the Hebrew mindset. However, I believe that another significant part of Greek thinking could actually be the most disturbing difference of all. What is that? It is dualism.

Dualism

Plato, who lived 400 years before Christ, is considered to be the chief advocate of understanding the world by dividing it into two categories, thus the term "dualism." One category is the ordinary, natural world that we see, touch and interact with on a daily basis. This is the lower level of existence, which, according to Plato's conclusions, is not the real world. The higher level of existence, the real world, is to be found in the unseen realm of ideas, unfettered by space, time, things and people. This is where perfection can be attained. This is the spiritual and eternal sphere, where truth can be found and where we can discover the real meaning of life. The two realms are disconnected from each other.

I know that this sounds very philosophical, but, after all, Plato was a philosopher. The problem that we have with it today is that, through our Western, Greek-mindset culture, these ideas have seeped into the church. In fact, two of the most respected Christian theologians in history, namely, Augustine of the fifth century and Thomas Aquinas of the thirteenth century, each attempted to blend Christian theology with the Greek mindset, and they, along with their followers, have had tremendous influence on the church until today.

As an example of dualism, consider the supposed difference between the sacred and the secular. According to the Greek mindset, selected sacred things and people touched the real world on a higher level, whereas most people and most of everyday life would be secular, doing things that were relatively unimportant because they were just temporal. This leads to the separation between clergy and laity. Clergy would be those in touch with true spirituality, while others, such as pharmacists, truck drivers or computer programmers, would exist on a lower plane.

In fact, through much of church history and even in some churches today, laity are not expected to have direct touch with God. In order to connect with God, they need to go through an ordained priest. Under the Greek mindset, the ideal for those lay people who truly wanted to serve God would be to quit their secular jobs and go into full-time ministry. To be a pastor or a missionary would please God much more than someone who is a mere businessperson, a schoolteacher or a mom who homeschools her children.

The Flaw of the Excluded Middle

One of the individuals who most helped me reexamine my inbred, Western, Greek mindset was Paul Hiebert, a former missionary to India and one of my colleagues on the faculty of the Fuller School of World Mission. In 1982, Hiebert wrote a very open and transparent essay confessing how his Western culture actually hindered his ministry among the people of non-Western India. He reflected on how Jesus ministered by demonstrating His power to cure the sick and cast out evil spirits. Then Hiebert wrpte, "As a Westerner, I was used to presenting Christ on the basis of rational arguments, not by evidences of his power in the lives of people who were sick, possessed, and destitute."[5]

Paul Hiebert was different from most in that he was a trained social scientist specializing in anthropology, as well as a trained theologian and an ordained minister. On that basis, he saw reality, like Plato did, in two tiers. The lower tier was "secular" science, dealing with sight and experience, natural order and this-world problems. The "sacred" upper tier was religion, dealing with faith, miracles and other-world problems. However, the two were disconnected. Hiebert wrote, "As a scientist I had been trained to deal with the empirical world in naturalistic terms. As a theologian, I was taught to answer ultimate questions in theistic terms. For me the middle zone did not really exist."[6] He admits that he had no answers to the questions that the Indian villagers would raise about evil spirits.

How bad can this get? Hiebert wrote, "It should be apparent why many missionaries trained in the West had no answers to the problems of the middle level—they often did not even see it. When tribal people spoke of fear of evil spirits, they denied the existence of the spirits rather than claim the power of Christ over them."[7] Hiebert then goes on to make a most amazing statement. Agreeing with other missiologists, he affirms, "Western Christian missions have been one of the greatest secularizing forces in history."[8]

The underlying root of this startling observation? Our Greek mindset! This, as you can imagine, was a wake-up call for me!

The Hebrew Mindset

Why would we Christian believers desire to move, as much as we can, from a Greek mindset toward a Hebrew mindset? It is because the inscripturated revelation of God, the Bible, is written from a Hebrew point of view. The Old Testament was written in the Hebrew language. God chose Abraham to become the progenitor of the whole Hebrew culture through which He would make Himself known. The New Testament was written in Greek because it was the trade language of the Roman Empire at the time; but it was written by Hebrews, with the possible exception of Luke, whom most scholars identify as a Gentile, although some think he might have been a Hellenized Jew.

Remember what I wrote about culture earlier on? Most of us who have been born and reared in Western culture have unwittingly tended to superimpose our worldview on our understanding of the Scriptures, which we take as the Word of God. We can't help it. The good news is that to the degree that we become conscious of this, we can make certain mid-course corrections in the way that we live our Christian lives, carry on the ministry of our churches and understand the nature of God Himself. We can't become Hebrews, which is why I don't believe it is possible to make a paradigm *shift* from a Greek mindset to a Hebrew mindset, but at best a paradigm *tweak*.

While the Greek mindset is human-centered, resulting in humanism, the Hebrew mindset is God-centered, resulting in theism. Truth, for Hebrews, does not emerge from human reason but from the revelation of God. Greeks stress knowledge, or proper thinking, while Hebrews stress practice, or proper living. Have you noticed how much squabbling there is among Christians over correct doctrine? Some even think that what you believe is more important than what you do. This comes from our Western culture. Jews tend not to separate the two. A proper belief in God cannot be separated from following God's moral and ethical principles. This clearly reflects what the New Testament teaches.

Greeks like to analyze things in clearly defined categories. We have seen, for example, that from Plato on, their dualism separates existence into two levels: the lower one of the physical world and the upper one of the spiritual world. Hebrews would not do this. The only upper layer that they have is God, and everything else is intertwined as part of His creation. The spiritual is part of the physical, and the physical is part of the spiritual. The supernatural constantly works in with the natural. There is no flaw of the excluded middle. To the degree that we can appreciate this, we can begin to take the Bible more at face value. When the Bible talks about things like evil spirits, miracles and resurrection from the dead, we should have no reason to question those things or, worse yet, ignore them.

The Jewish Advantage

When I think about the Hebrew mindset, I find it very interesting to review the statistics of the American Jewish community. Jews make up only 2 percent of the American population. Nevertheless, look at these figures:

- 45 percent of the top 40 of the Forbes richest Americans are Jewish.
- 33 percent of American multimillionaires are tallied as Jewish.
- 20 percent of professors at leading universities are Jewish.
- 40 percent of partners in the leading law firms in New York and Washington are Jewish.
- 30 percent of American Nobel Prize winners in science are Jewish.
- 25 percent of all American Nobel Prize winners are Jewish.[9]

Even a brief glance at these rather amazing facts raises the obvious question: What makes Jews more successful than other Americans? My response, which I hope does not sound flippant, is that they think like God! By this I do not mean that Jews are necessarily more religious than other Americans; many of them are not. I do mean, however, that they were born and raised in Jewish households. Their mothers and fathers instilled in them a Hebrew mindset. God, of course, is not bound by human culture, but for some presumably good reason He chose the Hebrew culture through which to reveal His being and His thoughts to the human race. Jews born in America have been provided with an innate cultural buffer zone to protect them from falling uncritically into the Greek mindset that surrounds them.

Close, but Not Quite

I want to conclude this chapter by repeating that I am only personally able to *tweak* my Greek mindset paradigm, not *shift* it. In order to do this, let me give you a negative example and then some positive ones.

It is natural for the Greek mindset to analyze and categorize theological concepts, ending up with what is commonly called systematic theology. I studied systematic theology, I taught systematic theology, I own books on systematic theology, and I am comfortable with systematic theology. Having said that, I will quote Brad Young's pointed observations:

> The Hebrew mind viewed God quite differently from the systematic theological thinking of the West, which defines God and his work with creation in a linear manner. The Western-style treatment of the divine character attempts to explain inconsistencies and harmonize contradictions systematically. The Hebrew mind was filled with wonder at the mystery of God. The vastness of God and his inscrutable ways left them awestruck. Inconsistencies and contradictions are intimately related to human, finite understandings of the infinite God. He is beyond human comprehension.[10]

When I read this, I know for sure that I am not a Hebrew—I still prefer systematic theology! Why pretend to be something that I am not?

However, I think I have made some progress. For example, when I look over the table of contents of this book, I see paradigm shift after paradigm shift that I do not believe I could have made if I had not developed some appreciation for the non-Western, Hebrew mindset. Without going into detail, I would like to list some of them.

- *Power evangelism* (chapter 6). Cessationism, the belief that some of the spiritual gifts ceased after the first couple of centuries, comes from a Greek mindset. It separates the supernatural from the natural, something that Hebrews would not do.

- *A declaration of war* (chapter 7). For those who have an excluded middle, spiritual warfare makes no sense. However, the Hebrews have no problem in integrating all of God's creation, making the confrontation with evil spirits an imperative part of life.

- *Open theism* (chapter 11). When the Bible says in Jeremiah 18:7-10 that God changes His mind, Hebrews simply accept it. This causes serious problems for Greeks, who see contradictions with their philosophical constructs of the nature of God.

- *A Kingdom vision* (chapter 12). "Your kingdom come. Your will be done on earth as it is in heaven" (Matt. 6:10) makes sense to the Hebrew mindset. God's kingdom isn't something far off: it can be right here.

- *Ministry in the workplace* (chapter 13). For Hebrews, the church is not something sacred, where ministry is done, while the workplace is secular. They are blended, and ministry is done in both places.

- *Reforming society* (chapter 14). Separating evangelism from social reformation is a Greek exercise because the Greek mindset tended to dichotomize reality. Evangelism would seem like a spiritual exercise, while social reformation would be relegated to a lower level or natural undertaking. Hebrews would feel that the gospel is for all of God's creation, including discipling whole nations.

- *Victorious eschatology* (chapter 16). The solution to the world's problems is not for the representatives of God to be raptured out and taken to a more blessed home in heaven, which a Greek mindset entertains, but rather to buckle down and incorporate God's blessings here on earth, as Hebrews would encourage.

- *A spirit of prosperity* (chapter 17). The Greek mindset would tend to relegate wealth or money as secular or unspiritual, not a respectable spiritual goal. On the other hand, Steven Silbiger reports: "For Jews wealth is a good thing, a worthy and respectable goal to strive toward. What's more, once you earn it, it is tragic to lose it. Judaism has never considered poverty a virtue."[11]

As I review that list, I become more and more convinced that I could never be where I am now by relying solely on the Western culture in which I was raised. Thank you, Abraham, Isaac and Jacob! I know I am not yet one of you, but I am certainly one of your great admirers!

Notes

1. Charles H. Kraft, *Christianity in Culture* (Maryknoll, NY: Orbis books, 1979), p. 46.
2. Ibid.
3. Ibid., p. 47.
4. Ibid.
5. Paul G. Hiebert, "The Flaw of the Excluded Middle," *Missiology: An International Review* (January 1982), p. 35.
6. Ibid., p. 43.
7. Ibid., p. 44.
8. Ibid.
9. Steven Silbiger, *The Jewish Phenomenon* (Atlanta, GA: Longstreet Press, 2000), p. 4.
10. Brad H. Young, *Paul the Jewish Theologian: A Pharisee Among Christians, Jews, and Gentiles* (Peabody, MA: Hendrickson Publishers, 1997), p. 25.
11. Silbiger, *The Jewish Phenomenon*, p. 15.

From **Classical Theism** to **Open Theism**

Through most of the years that I have served God as an ordained minister, I was bothered by the nagging question, Does what I do really matter? In other words, God is God! He is the great creator and ruler of the universe. He has everything in order. He knows the end from the beginning. Doesn't God have everything planned no matter what I do or what I don't do? What difference do I make?

Fortunately, this question didn't interrupt my service to God as a missionary or a seminary professor because I had an overriding desire to obey the Lord and to serve Him as faithfully as I could in whatever assignment He might give me at the moment. If I did what I could, I assumed that God would take care of the rest. I lived a happy life and felt fulfilled; nevertheless, I couldn't completely shake that question. Take prayer, for example. When I prayed, I knew that God heard me, but I wondered, *Did any of my prayers cause God to do something that He wouldn't have done without my prayer?* I doubted it, but I still kept praying.

Classical Theism

The seminary in which I was trained chose to be known to the public as a Reformed seminary. "Reformed" means adhering to the theology that was established during the Protestant Reformation of the sixteenth century. The two leading theologians were Martin Luther and John Calvin. Luther's theology, as would be expected, was ingrained into the Lutheran Church. Calvin's theology influenced the Reformed Church, the Presbyterian Church and others. My professors favored John Calvin, so, over three years, I was indoctrinated into Calvinism.

Calvinism is frequently characterized by the acronym TULIP. Here is what it means:

T   *Total depravity:* Human beings are completely corrupted by sin and therefore cannot by themselves do any righteous acts.

U   *Unconditional election:* God, through His own personal choice, elects some to be saved, and those who are not elected are lost forever.

L   *Limited atonement:* Jesus did not die for all people, but just for those whom God has elected to be saved.

I   *Irresistible grace:* Those whom God elects to be saved can do nothing to prevent this from happening.

P   *Perseverance of the saints:* Once someone is saved, he or she is always saved.

I know that most of you who are reading this book would look at those five points of Calvinism with some serious questions. One of them, I imagine, would relate to the unavoidable observation that it looks as if we human beings have no real choice. Remember my first question: Does what I do really matter?

However, that wasn't all. On top of that I learned the five classical attributes of God:

1. *Omnipotence*: God is all-powerful and has sovereignty over all things.
2. *Omnipresence*: God is present everywhere and at all times.
3. *Omniscience*: God knows everything, past, present and future.
4. *Impassibility*: Nothing ever happens *to* God; He takes the initiative in all things.
5. *Immutability*: God never changes, including changing His mind.

At one point in my career I memorized the Westminster Shorter Catechism, which provides the doctrinal basis for the Presbyterian Church. Here is their definition of God: "God is a spirit, infinite, eternal, and unchangeable in His being, wisdom, power, holiness, justice, goodness and truth." The most important word in that definition, at least for my purposes in this chapter, is "unchangeable." I believed that nothing could change what God had already predetermined. Another word for this is "predestination," meaning that God ordained everything that will happen in the future, including who will be saved. Furthermore, since God predestined everything, He knew ahead of time what would happen; this is called foreknowledge.

Seminary Discussions

I realize that I have unloaded a considerable amount of theology in the last few paragraphs. Some may feel that it is very boring, which it might be until you pause a moment to think about it. I remember back in seminary, groups of us students would get fixed on coffee and stay up until the wee hours of the morning debating these concepts. As I recall those conversations, one of the main issues to us was that what our professors were teaching us, and what we had to memorize to pass exams, did not always seem to correspond with reality, to say nothing of what we were reading in the Bible. The net impact of believing that God is in full control of everything is to place doubts in our minds that what we do can possibly have any influence on what might happen or what might not happen in the future.

Let's look at an example. As an ordained minister, I was naturally expected to minister to the sick. When I did, I would pause to wonder why they might be sick. I knew God was omnipotent, so if He wanted to, He could have kept them from falling ill. For some reason, however, He chose not to. This could well mean that being sick could be part of God's long-range plan for those people, possibly teaching them something through the sickness that they might not have learned otherwise.

With this Calvinistic mindset, how would I minister to sick people? I would tell them how sorry I was that they were sick. I would comfort them and reassure them that they would get better. I would remind them that God loved them and that He knew what was best for them. I would read an uplifting portion of Scripture. In addition, I would pray that God would give them grace to endure what they were going through and that His will would be done. In these kinds of situations, I had no thoughts that anything I said or did could possibly change what God had already predestined for these sick people.

Doubts Begin Surfacing

Having a type A personality, I always seemed to have plenty to do. I was goal-driven and active. Through much of my career, I rarely paused long enough to take inventory of my theological presuppositions. Besides, I didn't really know of any viable alternatives to classical theism. All my friends and associates had a Calvinistic orientation as well, and once those night-long discussions in seminary were over, I never had the desire to go around that mountain again.

Looking back, however, I think the first crack in my Calvinism came at the point of limited atonement. The Bible seemed so clear to me that Jesus died for the sins of the whole world that I became a bit uncomfortable imagining that He died only for the elect. Once I began doubting limited atonement, I then began harboring some questions about unconditional election and irresistible grace; but I must admit that I was too busy with other things to allow these feelings to surface. I was happy just coasting along theologically and trusting God to work things out. I was in a comfort zone and not looking for a paradigm shift. Classical theism was all right with me!

Roots of the Shift

The roots of my paradigm shift go back to the 1980s and the 1990s. In chapter 6 I wrote about my shift to power evangelism and healing the sick. That was in the 1980s. In chapter 7 I wrote about my shift to spiritual warfare and dealing with the demonic. That was in the 1990s. As I became a part of national and international leadership in both of those fields, I began to realize more and more that what we did really mattered.

Among other things that were happening around that time, I discovered that God had given me a gift of healing. After experimenting for a long time, it became clear to me that my most consistent healing results came when I prayed for people with back ailments that were frequently connected to short legs. When opportunity presented itself, I would often see 10, 20 or more serious back problems healed in one night. Quite often, all of those who requested prayer on a certain occasion were supernaturally healed. People from out of town would make appointments to see me and leave with healed backs, some after years of constant pain. Before long, I was convinced that many, if not most, of those healed through my ministry would still have had back pain the next morning had I not prayed for them. It's true that God could have used someone else to do it, but in these cases He happened to use me. What I did apparently made a difference. In the minds of the people healed, a *big* difference!

I could not help but to begin to think theologically about what must have been going on. With my Calvinistic mindset I used to pray for the sick, not really expecting they would get well, and most of them didn't. Now things were different. Almost everyone I prayed for got well. What was happening? As a starter, it is important to keep in mind that I myself never healed anyone. God was the only one who ever did the healing.

Let's imagine a woman who is a faithful believer, who goes to church, who is raising a nice Christian family, and who has had back pain for 12 years. God certainly knew about the pain all the time, but it wasn't healed. Then one day she asks me to pray for her back. I spend 5 to 10 minutes with her, I take authority over what is causing the pain, I command it to be healed in the name of Jesus, and the pain leaves and does not return. When you think about it, there must have been some cause and effect relationship between my prayer and God's decision to heal our sister right then, rather than at any other time during the 12 years. As I began to analyze many cases just like the one I described, I could not help but begin to imagine that God was open to hearing and visibly answering my prayers. One result was that I began to realize that I probably had to make some changes to my classical-theistic paradigm.

How I Became an Open Theist

I think that for many years I knew down deep that I couldn't have been a real Calvinist, but I kept it quiet because I still didn't know what I really was. I knew the negative all right, but not the positive. I was acquainted with Arminianism, which left some room for human free will to operate in salvation, but Arminianism also argued that God, by His foreknowledge, knew ahead of time who would believe in Him and who would not. This was not the direction I wanted to go. I knew of no other alternatives, so for a long time I existed in what might be called a theological limbo.

I have always been a subscriber to several key Christian periodicals in order to try to keep up with what is going on in my religious world. Toward the end of the 1990s, I began to notice the mention of names like John Sanders, Greg Boyd and Clark Pinnock in relationship to certain new theological ideas relating to the "openness of God." At first I didn't pay a lot of attention to them because I had several much more demanding items on my plate. However, suddenly the May 21, 2001, issue of *Christianity Today* took me by surprise and helped me begin to change my theological paradigm. It featured the first part of a two-part article titled "Does God Know Your Next Move?" In it, two professors of religion debated open theism. Christopher Hall argued for classical theism, and John Sanders argued for open theism. I devoured those articles because I strongly suspected that I was finally discovering my new theological anchor.

Just about that time, Gregory Boyd published *God of the Possible*. I had already learned to respect Greg because I knew him personally and I regarded his previous book, *God at War*, as the best theology of spiritual warfare that we have. On the cover of *God of the Possible* is this crucial question: Does God ever change His mind? Classical theists, of course, would say, "No, God is unchangeable." Boyd, on the other hand, says yes. His book became the tipping point for my paradigm shift. By the time I had finished it, I had become an unapologetic open theist![1]

Open Theism

What, then, is involved in the open view of God? Let me begin by taking us back to the Garden of Eden. When God created Adam and

Eve on the sixth day, they were to have dominion over the rest of His creation (see Gen. 1:28). However, this did not happen as planned. Instead, as we know the story, Satan entered the Garden and succeeded in usurping Adam's authority.

I will elaborate on this substantially in chapter 14. Meanwhile, let me point out one thing here. God, if He so desired, could have done it differently. He could have kept Satan out of the Garden altogether, but why didn't He? He didn't do it because Adam would never have been an authentic human being if he were not a free moral agent. He had to make his own decision whether he would fully obey God. God wanted Adam to love Him, but true love must be the choice of the individual concerned. True love is never forced. The choice had to be Adam's, and, as we now know, he made the wrong choice.

Let's go one step further. Did God know ahead of time what Adam's decision would be, or could it be that God chose not to allow Himself to know what Adam would end up deciding? What I am doing is raising one of the most crucial theological differences between classical theism and open theism, namely, the foreknowledge of God. Classical theists would say that part of God's very nature is that He knows all things that would ever happen anywhere. Consequently, before He created Adam, He knew that Adam would fall into sin. I cannot agree with this. To put it in plain language, this means that God would have been saying to Himself something like, *I know that Adam is going to eat the apple, but I'm going to order him not to eat it anyway.* I don't think so.

God Is Sovereign

How do open theists explain this? Both sides agree that God is sovereign. He created the earth and everything in it, and He can do whatever He wants to. However, each side sees God's sovereignty a bit differently. I like the distinction that Harold Eberle makes between Calvin's view (classical theism) and the biblical view (open theism). He explains that for classical theists, sovereignty means that "God controls all things, and therefore all things are predestined." On the other hand, for open theists, sovereignty means that "God does whatever he chooses and consequently some things are predestined."[2]

Open theists contend that God is sovereign enough to limit His own sovereignty, including His foreknowledge, if He so desires. Here is how John Sanders describes this crucial point: "God has, in *sovereign freedom*, decided to make some of his actions contingent on our requests and actions. God elicits our free collaboration in his plans. Hence, God can be influenced by what we do and pray for, and God truly responds to what we do."[3] Applying this to Adam, God presumably chose not to know ahead of time what decision Adam would make. When Adam made the wrong choice, God was sorry that the human being He made would not follow His plans, so He needed to go to a Plan B for the human race.

It may sound strange to say that God could be sorry about something He did, but the Bible does describe God as having emotions. As a starter, we know that He loves certain things (see 2 Cor. 9:7) and that He hates other things (see Prov. 6:16-19). Humans can please Him (see Heb. 11:6). He gets angry (Nahum 1:3). After Adam's fall, the whole human race went downhill so badly that God became upset: "Then the LORD saw that the wickedness of man was great in the earth, and that every intent of the thoughts of his heart was only evil continually" (Gen. 6:5). What was God's reaction? "And the LORD was sorry that He had made man on the earth" (Gen. 6:6). The implication of this is that God was unpleasantly surprised with the way things turned out. To imagine that God knew that all of this would happen before He even created Adam leaves no logical room for Him to be surprised or to be sorry like the Bible says He was.

Not only is God sometimes surprised, but He also can change His mind. Take, for example, the well-known story of King Hezekiah's extra 15 years. King Hezekiah, one of the good kings, was ill, and God sent the prophet Isaiah to let him know the future. God's word to Hezekiah was "Set your house in order, for you shall die, and not live" (2 Kings 20:1). Nothing could be clearer. Still, when Hezekiah heard this, he turned to God and implored God with tears that he would not die. What happened? God then said, "I have heard your prayer, I have seen your tears; surely I will heal you. . . . And I will add to your days fifteen years" (2 Kings 20:5-6).

The best way to make sense of this, I think, is to assume that Hezekiah's prayer mattered to God and actually caused Him to change His mind. It wouldn't make much sense to turn it around and suppose that God would tell Hezekiah that he was going to die if He already knew ahead of time that he would not die but would have 15 more years of life. This story is encouraging because it helps give us an answer to the lead question for this chapter: Does what I do really matter? Hezekiah discovered the answer.

"I Will Think Twice"

To take this a bit further, God Himself tells us that He can and does change His mind. For example, "At any moment I may decide to pull up a people or a country by the roots and get rid of them. But if they repent of their wicked lives, I will think twice and start over with them. At another time I might decide to plant a people or country, but if they don't cooperate and won't listen to me, I will think again and give up the plans I had for them" (Jer. 18:7-10, *THE MESSAGE*).

Classical theists, of course, are aware of these accounts from 2 Kings and Jeremiah and many others like them. Their explanation is that they must be considered anthropomorphisms. This means that the writers of the Bible needed to use the language of human attributes in order to explain God in such a way that their readers would understand. Classical theists tell us that this accommodating language should not be taken at face value. Under their assumption that God is unchangeable, they say that we must not allow ourselves to take literally what the Bible says about God's changing His mind, having emotions or other human things like that. On the other hand, open theists like to think that the Bible means just what it says.

A good number of my friends are classical theists. I understand their point of view because I was one of them before my paradigm shift. In this chapter, I am trying to explain that I now think open theism is a better way of understanding God and His revelation, but I am also trying not to show disrespect for those who disagree with me. Many of the best apostles, prophets, evangelists, pastors and teachers through the centuries have held to classical theism. God has blessed them, and so do I.

A Heresy?

Although I am unaware of any research on the subject, I would think that we open theists are still in the minority. As such, we are, of course, susceptible to criticism. We tend to pull some people out of their comfort zones. One reason that I like the *Christianity Today* article debating open theism and its subsequent expansion into the book *Does God Have a Future?* is that, while Hall and Sanders both vigorously defend their opposite positions, the two like each other and respect each other. Some critics, however, are on the hostile side. In more than one posting on the Internet, I am called a heretic because I agree with the open view of God. Heresy, by the way, is a most serious allegation, and I certainly do not want to be branded as a heretic.

The question then becomes, Is open theism really a heresy? I contend that it is not. Let me explain why. First of all, *Christianity Today* is a journal of high Christian integrity. As such, they decided to run the articles giving open theism equal exposure to classical theism. I don't think that they would have done this if they had thought that open theism was a heresy. In fact, their fair treatment of both sides was a major factor in beginning my paradigm shift.

Even more important was the process that unfolded within the Evangelical Theological Society (ETS). It so happened that all three of the pioneer proponents of the open view of God—Greg Boyd, John Sanders and Clark Pinnock—were members of ETS in good standing when they began going public with their ideas. Predictably, some of the classical theists in ETS soon began to cry foul, and then some of them attempted to prove to the whole organization that open theism was a heresy.

In 2001 they succeeded in presenting an official resolution to the ETS to the effect that God had complete foreknowledge of everything. However, 107 members (one-third) would not approve the resolution. *Christianity Today* reported that the following year "more members spoke against the motion than in favor."[4] Undoubtedly, some ETS members had begun to shift their paradigm. Finally, the classical theists became so outraged that they attempted to have the open theists dismissed from ETS, and they failed with that tactic as well.

Through the whole scenario, ETS as a group decided that, while they were certainly dealing with strong differences of opinion, open theism did not deserve the label of heresy. This opinion has since prevailed, Internet bloggers notwithstanding.

Prayer Matters!

It is safe to say that every believer prays and has an underlying assumption that God hears their prayers. But what does God do with the prayers that He hears? I was taught in seminary that God knows everything that will ever happen and that He is unchangeable. Consequently, it would be wrong to imagine that our prayers would ever change what God already knows will happen, much less affect God Himself. No, I learned that through our prayers God changes *us* so that we can more readily adapt to whatever He has already planned. What does this lead to? Greg Boyd writes, "The problem, I believe, is that despite all the pious talk about how God wants and even needs us to pray, many Christians have an understanding of divine sovereignty in which the urgency of prayer simply doesn't make much sense."[5]

I was one of those whom Boyd describes, but things are different now. I have written a series of six books called *The Prayer Warrior Series*. I agree with Walter Wink, who writes, "History belongs to the intercessors."[6] Richard Foster puts it this way: "Certain things will happen in history if we pray rightly."[7] The underlying thought is that, if we pray, God will do certain things that He wouldn't do without our prayers. This is open theism. Jack Hayford likes to say, "If we don't, He won't."[8] It's not that God *can't*—He can do anything. However, His nature is to choose not to know all that will happen in the future so that He can decide what the future will be, based, to whatever degree He chooses, on our prayers and our actions. Earlier in this chapter I used my healing ministry as an example. I'm quite sure that if I hadn't prayed for certain people on a given night, they would still have had their back pain the next morning. If I didn't, He wouldn't have!

Please notice that I said that God chooses "not to know *all* that will happen." Let's not fall into the trap of imagining that God has no foreknowledge whatsoever. He is sovereign. He chooses what of the future to know and what not to know. For example, when He sent Jesus to earth, He knew that Jesus would die on the cross for our sins, and nothing would have changed His mind. Jesus Himself in Gethsemane briefly attempted to persuade the Father to change His mind, but to no avail (see Matt. 26:39). John Sanders writes, "Sometimes God alone decides how to accomplish his goals. Usually, however, God elicits human cooperation in such a way that it is both God and humanity who decide what the future will be."[9] It can go both ways.

Open theism builds my faith in God. I now believe that God loves me so much that He allows me to work along with Him to make a better world. Serving God is exponentially more exciting! Yes, what I do really matters!

Notes

1. For any who desire to read more about open theism than this chapter provides, I suggest first *Who Is God?* by Harold R. Eberle. This is the clearest, most direct book I know of on the topic. Second, I suggest *God of the Possible* by Gregory A. Boyd, which has more theological content but is still very easy reading. Then, for those who might want to go to the graduate level, I recommend *Does God Have a Future?* by Christopher A. Hall and John Sanders. This is an expansion of the *Christianity Today* articles I referred to, and it goes into as much theological detail as most people could possibly digest.

2. Harold R. Eberle, *Who Is God?* (Yakima, WA: Worldcast Publishing, 2008), p. 72.

3. Christopher A. Hall and John Sanders, *Does God Have a Future?* (Grand Rapids, MI: Baker Academic, 2003), p. 12. Emphasis in the original.

4. Doug Koop, "Closing the Door on Open Theists?" *Christianity Today* (January 2003), p. 25.

5. Gregory A. Boyd, *God of the Possible* (Grand Rapids, MI: Baker Books, 2000), p. 95.

6. Walter Wink, *Engaging the Powers* (Minneapolis, MN: Fortress Press, 1993), p. 298.

7. Richard Foster, *Celebration of Discipline* (San Francisco: HarperSanFrancisco, 1988), p. 35.

8. Jack Hayford, *Prayer Is Invading the Impossible* (Orlando FL: Bridge/Logos Publishers, 1977), p. 71.

9. Hall and Sanders, *Does God Have a Future?* p. 12.

12

From a **Church Vision** to a **Kingdom Vision**

Many people know me mostly as a church person, a professor of church growth. One of the reasons that Jesus came was to build His church (see Matt. 16:18). I was dedicated to the kind of evangelism that not only won people to Christ but also incorporated the converts into the church. The church was the center of gravity for the Christian life. I thought that one good measurement of a person's spiritual life was the degree of their responsible involvement in the life of a local church.

In my mind, all Christian ministry was to be done in relationship with a local church or possibly with a parachurch organization of some kind. God gave spiritual gifts to build up the body of Christ, which was the church. In fact, if a believer was not personally involved in a church, I suggested that their salvation itself might be questioned. To preserve my integrity as a role model, I was always a member of a local church, confirmed, among other things, by paying my tithe to that church.

The Church Manifests the Kingdom

Being a Bible reader, I was well aware of the kingdom of God. However, I thought that the body of Christ was supposed to be the visible manifestation of God's kingdom in the world today. Church leaders were to do Kingdom work, but that work was done primarily through the local church. Local church pastors should focus their efforts on the growth and health of their congregations. Denominational leaders should focus their efforts on the particular cluster of churches under their jurisdiction. This, in my mind, would be their Kingdom work.

If whatever we did for God resulted in building and multiplying churches, then we were supposedly on the right track. I taught that the best way to measure your effectiveness for God was to measure the growth of your church or churches. You may recall that I elaborated on my church growth pragmatism in chapter 4. As I was writing that chapter, I constantly had to discipline myself to avoid moving beyond the church to the Kingdom in order to most accurately reflect my unfortunate absence of Kingdom vision back in those days. My task in this chapter, on the other hand, is to show how my vision for the church eventually became transformed to a vision for the Kingdom.

The Cultural Mandate

I must confess that, during the 16 years that I served as a missionary to Bolivia, I regretfully paid no appropriate attention to the kingdom of God. It was only after I joined the faculty of the Fuller School of World Mission in 1971 that things began to change. One of my colleagues, Arthur F. Glasser, was the first to plant some seeds. He constantly affirmed that the Bible contained two mandates: the *evangelistic* mandate and the *cultural* mandate. Admittedly, I previously was paying attention only to the evangelistic mandate. As I listened to Glasser, I found that while I had no reason to doubt what he was saying, neither did I sense any particular inclination to change my way of thinking.

I probably should admit that it was comforting to know I was not alone. It is safe to say that the majority of evangelical leaders back in 1970 adhered strictly to the evangelistic mandate and had a church vision. Back in the 1960s a few evangelical leaders like Arthur Glasser began opening their minds to the cultural mandate, which would lead to a Kingdom vision. Several of my Latin American friends were also among the first to move in this direction, but I let them know that I thought they were headed in the wrong direction. I am embarrassed to admit it now, but my friends were really hearing what the Spirit was saying to the churches more clearly than I was. My problem was that I could not get past my passionate commitment to church growth. I was locked into a church mindset.

By the way, chapter 14, which explains my paradigm shift to re-forming society, is closely related to this chapter. They both have to do with accepting the cultural mandate alongside the evangelistic mandate. Here I am dealing specifically with the concept of the king-dom of God, while the other chapter will draw out principles for im-plementation. Here I lean toward theory, and there I lean toward practice. I like to regard them as two different paradigm shifts for me.

The Final Nudge

By the time I had finished my Ph.D. in Social Ethics in 1977, I had begun moving toward a more biblical understanding of the king-dom of God. My paradigm was shifting, but I needed a final nudge. I was fortunate enough to have my Ph.D. dissertation published in 1979 under the title *Our Kind of People: The Ethical Dimensions of Church Growth in America*. I, of course, had invested huge amounts of time in research and writing, and I was pleased with the book and the at-tention it had attracted among leaders, both positive and negative.

My surprise came when my friend Ray Bakke, then professor at Northern Baptist Seminary, wrote a review of the book in 1980. The review was, much to my relief, generally affirming, but one pithy comment he made caught my attention: "It's been a long time since I read a significant work on ecclesiology or missiology that never mentioned the kingdom."[1] I was shocked! I hoped he was wrong, but I checked it out and he wasn't! That jolt from my friend com-pleted my paradigm shift, and my books since then have been King-dom-oriented books.

Jesus Came as King

When we have a Kingdom mindset, we look back and see Jesus com-ing not only as a Savior, "the Lamb of God who takes away the sins of the world" (John 1:29), but also as a King. The shepherds received the first part: "There is born to you this day in the city of David a Savior, who is Christ the Lord" (Luke 2:11).

The three wise men received the second part. These were very in-telligent and prestigious men who were occult practitioners and who could read the heavens. They followed the star, came to Jerusalem and asked, "Where is He who has been born King of the Jews?" (Matt.

2:2). Unlike the shepherds, they knew that something very significant had transpired in the invisible world. They knew that history itself had changed. Indeed, it had. How big was the change? For one thing, the history of the human race since then has been divided between BC and AD.

What was new? The kingdom of God! Jesus came as a King, and He brought a new Kingdom. When John the Baptist preached, he exclaimed, "Repent, for the kingdom of heaven is at hand!" (Matt. 3:2). When the proper time had come, Jesus received baptism from John, resisted the devil's temptation in the wilderness, went to Capernaum and began His three years of public ministry.

What was His initial message? Matthew reports, "From that time, Jesus began to preach and to say, 'Repent, for the kingdom of heaven is at hand'" (Matt. 4:17). He taught His disciples to pray, "Your kingdom come" (Matt. 6:10). He explained the Kingdom in a series of parables, likening it to a sower, a grain of mustard seed, leaven, a hidden treasure, a pearl of great price and a dragnet (see Matt. 13). When He sent the twelve apostles on their first mission, He instructed them to "preach, saying, 'The kingdom of heaven is at hand'" (Matt. 10:7). When He later sent out seventy, He told them to "heal the sick there, and say to them, 'The kingdom of God has come near to you'" (Luke 10:9).

The kingdom of God was a prominent theme after the resurrection as well. During the 40 days between the time Jesus was raised from the dead and His ascension, He spoke to His apostles of "the things pertaining to the kingdom of God" (Acts 1:3). When Philip evangelized Samaria, he was preaching "the things concerning the kingdom of God" (Acts 8:12). Paul preached the kingdom of God in Ephesus (see Acts 19:8), and the very last thing we know about him is that he was in Rome "preaching the kingdom of God" (Acts 28:31). Paul, James, Peter and the author of Hebrews all mention the Kingdom in their epistles. For them, Jesus was the King.

Thinking About the Kingdom

It embarrasses me as I write about the Kingdom because (1) as we have seen, the Kingdom is so prominent in Scripture; and (2) for so many years of my career as a professional, ordained minister, I didn't catch on. Jesus never sent His disciples out to preach the gospel of the church. He never sent them to preach the gospel of salvation. He consistently sent them to preach the gospel of the Kingdom, which, by the way, includes both the church and salvation.

Let's think about the kingdom of God for a bit. This is not a kingdom of this world. It does not have territorial boundaries. It cannot issue passports or join the United Nations. It will exist wherever there are individuals for whom Jesus is their King! If Jesus is your King, you take the kingdom of God wherever you go. That's why Jesus said, "The kingdom of God is within you" (Luke 17:21).

When Jesus said to Peter, "On this rock I will build My church" (Matt. 16:18), He had a bigger picture in mind. He next said, "I will give you the keys" (v. 19). However, they weren't keys of the church; they were "keys of the kingdom" (v. 19). The church is wonderful—it is the bride of Christ. Nevertheless, it is only a part of the kingdom of God. That is why Jesus tried to instill in His disciples a kingdom vision.

I like what my friend Bruce Cook frequently says. He imagines that Christian believers can be located on one of three rungs of a Kingdom ladder. The first rung is focus on self. Most believers are there. Ask them why they go to church, and they will generally say, "To get a blessing." Church does something for them. The second rung is focus on the church, and a smaller percentage is there. They attend all meetings, they volunteer whenever necessary, they pay their tithe to the church, and they are satisfied if their church is healthy and growing. Most pastors, by the way, find themselves on the second rung of the ladder. The third and top rung of the ladder is focus on the Kingdom. Unfortunately, very few are there, but my observation is that a significant shift has begun and that more and more believers are becoming Kingdom-minded.

Jesus said, "Seek first the kingdom of God and His righteousness, and all these things shall be added to you" (Matt. 6:33). What are some of "these things"? Your personal needs and the needs of the church—the first two rungs of the ladder.

The Kingdom Was an Invasion

When Jesus came and brought the Kingdom, it was a D-Day type of invasion into the kingdom of Satan. I will give many more details on this in chapter 14; meanwhile, suffice it to say that before Jesus came, Satan's rule had gone virtually unchallenged for who knows how many millennia. This is not to question whether God is the ultimate owner of the whole world; "The earth is the LORD's, and all its fullness" (Ps. 24:1). Satan's kingdom consists in the control he possesses over people who inhabit the earth, and he maintains that control by securing their allegiance through various means, known as "the wiles of the devil" (Eph. 6:11).

Before Jesus came, virtually every person on the face of the earth had pledged allegiance to Satan, usually in the form of one of his deceptive adaptations that people would label their gods. The exception was the relatively small group of descendants of Abraham called the people of God, the Jewish people. However, even they were not immune to serious problems affecting their spiritual allegiance.

When Jesus came, the situation changed permanently, and Satan was the first to realize its full significance. Jesus contrasted the Old Testament era with the New Testament era when He told His disciples that they were particularly privileged to see what they were seeing at the time. Jesus said, "I tell you that many prophets and kings [representing the Old Testament period] have desired to see what you see, and have not seen it" (Luke 10:24). To what was Jesus referring? He was referring to the experience His disciples had just enjoyed, causing them to report enthusiastically, "Lord, even the demons are subject to us in Your name" (Luke 10:17).

We read no such report in the Old Testament. Why? No such direct threat had ever been made to Satan's dominion before Jesus came. That was one of the reasons why Jesus said that although there was no greater prophet than John the Baptist, who was symbolically the last representative of the pre-Jesus era, "he who is least in the kingdom of God is greater than he" (Luke 7:28). The difference between BC and AD is enormous.

Satan Is Losing

No wonder Satan did everything he possibly could do (and continues to do everything he can do) to prevent the spread of the kingdom of God. He lusts for people's allegiance and their worship, but he is ultimately defeated, and he is losing. Satan has incredible power, but it can never match the power of God. For 2,000 years the kingdom of God has been pushing back the spiritual boundaries of the kingdom of Satan, and the rate of advance is accelerating incrementally, especially in that part of the world known as the Global South. Over the last 20 years, God has been giving His people access to powerful weapons of spiritual warfare in response to our fervent prayer, "Your kingdom come!"

Jesus is often referred to as the Prince of Peace (see Isa. 9:6). That is a biblical title. However, here is what Jesus Himself said, "Do not think that I came to bring peace on earth. I did not come to bring peace but a sword" (Matt. 10:34). How do these two things fit together? I believe it is relatively simple. Peace comes after you win the war. I lived through World War II, and I enjoyed an extended season of peace in America after we had won the war. One day there will be peace on the whole earth, but it will come only after God's kingdom is sufficiently extended through spiritual warfare against Satan's kingdom.

Jesus went on to say, "From the days of John the Baptist until now the kingdom of heaven suffers violence, and the violent take it by force" (Matt. 11:12). It is unfortunate that in parts of the church today we find an anti-war movement that opposes all-out spiritual warfare. I wish these people would shift their paradigm to a Kingdom vision. When Jesus the King came, He declared war! Furthermore, He delegated the responsibility of fighting and winning the war to His people, the body of Christ. It is my hope that the whole church will become the army of God to push the enemy back and allow God's kingdom to come across the earth sooner rather than later.

To see this more clearly, let's go back to Matthew 16. After Jesus told His disciples that He would build His church and then gave them keys to the kingdom of God, He went on to say, "Whatever you bind on earth will be bound in heaven, and whatever you loose on earth will be loosed in heaven" (Matt. 16:19). This puts the initiative for winning the war squarely with us human believers, not with Jesus. We have choices to make in order for God to act, though God will only act according to His purposes. Actually, a more literal translation of this Bible verse is, "Whatever you bind on earth *will have been bound* in heaven and whatever you loose on earth *will have been loosed* in heaven," meaning that God first decides what is to be bound or loosed. We need to do here on earth only what we discern the Father is doing. This still leaves the action up to us, but before we act we need to be sure that we are doing God's will.

The Three Strategic Theaters

Most wars are fought in more than one theater. In World War II, Americans were fighting both in the European theater and in the Pacific theater. This is the same with spiritual warfare.

To give a bit of history, starting in 1989 I began to organize what became the Spiritual Warfare Network (SWN). It was a group of 20 to 25 recognized Christian leaders who had done some thinking, praying and ministering in areas of spiritual warfare. Cindy Jacobs, Jack Hayford, John Dawson, Gwen Shaw, Ed Silvoso, Frank Hammond and others were part of the SWN. As we met regularly over a few years, we agreed that one of our first tasks would be to identify and name the principal theaters of spiritual warfare, which we proceeded to do. We agreed that we should settle on three chief areas of spiritual warfare: ground-level, occult-level and strategic-level.

Ground-Level Spiritual Warfare

Ground-level spiritual warfare includes the ministry of casting out demons, commonly known as deliverance ministry. Mark, for example, chooses to begin his story of Jesus' ministry with the familiar story of a man, oppressed by a demon, shouting out in the synagogue at Capernaum: "Let us alone! What have we to do with You, Jesus of Nazareth?" (Mark 1:24). Jesus commanded the spirit to come out, there was a manifestation, and the man was delivered. Everyone who saw it was amazed because they had never seen anything like it before. They exclaimed, "With authority He commands even the unclean spirits, and they obey Him" (Mark 1:27). This is an example of ground-level spiritual warfare. It is a visible sign of the arrival of the kingdom of God.

When Jesus sent out His disciples to spread the gospel of the Kingdom, He first "gave them power over unclean spirits, to cast them out" (Matt. 10:1), which they used. Since then, ground-level spiritual warfare has been the most common form of deliverance ministry. Most members of the International Society of Deliverance Ministers, which Doris and I founded in the late 1990s, do ground-level spiritual warfare. The books on ground-level warfare that I recommend the most are *How to Cast Out Demons* by Doris Wagner, *Breaking the Bonds of Evil* by Rebecca Greenwood, and *So Free* by Bill Sudduth.

Occult-Level Spiritual Warfare

Occult-level spiritual warfare deals with a more complex grouping of demonic forces, often affecting not only individuals but also certain social networks in which they become involved. Some of the better-known examples would be witchcraft, New Age, occult practice, Freemasonry, satanism, voodoo, Santería, shamanism, Eastern religions, wicca, and the like. The demonic power at work here is much more sophisticated and powerful than we usually find in ground-level demons. Consequently, we end up with fewer occult-level deliverance ministers than ground-level ministers. The book with the best overall view of occult-level spiritual warfare is *Deliver Us from Evil* by Cindy Jacobs.

Strategic-Level Spiritual Warfare

Strategic-level spiritual warfare is what the apostle Paul references when he wrote, "We do not wrestle against flesh and blood, but against principalities [and] powers" (Eph. 6:12). The principalities and powers are high-ranking demons who serve the kingdom of Satan by taking authority over territories. Some of these are identified by Daniel's experience with delayed answers to prayer. In response to Daniel's prayer and fasting, God sent the angel Gabriel to visit him, but Gabriel was delayed 21 days by the "prince of the kingdom of Persia" (Dan. 10:13), obviously a territorial spirit over Persia. Then, when the angel was ready to leave, he said, "I must return to fight with the prince of Persia; and when I have gone forth, indeed the prince of Greece will come" (v. 20). Spirits like this have continued their evil domination of nations until today.

Not surprisingly, relatively few believers are called to enter into this higher level of spiritual warfare. Those who are will be mature, experienced, deeply spiritual, highly gifted team players. I say "team players" because one of the key rules of engagement is never to attempt strategic-level spiritual warfare alone. These are God's special forces. They know the rules of engagement and do not violate them. They are on the cutting edge of extending the kingdom of God today. Some of the best guidebooks for strategic-level spiritual warfare are *Possessing the Gates of the Enemy* by Cindy Jacobs, *Authority to Tread* by Rebecca Greenwood, and my books *Warfare Prayer* and *Spiritual Warfare Strategy*.

I'm sure that if I had read things like this before my paradigm shift from a church vision to a Kingdom vision, my mind would be full of cautions at this point. The Bible says that "the violent take [the Kingdom] by force" (Matt. 11:12). Those who are still on the first two rungs of the Kingdom ladder may well be doubting if they want to go to the third rung after all. Yes, a Kingdom vision inevitably involves spiritual warfare. The enemy has "great wrath, because he knows that he has a short time" (Rev. 12:12). Keep in mind that he is angrier today than he has ever been because his time is shorter than ever before, and he does not hesitate to direct that escalating wrath against those who are on the front lines of Kingdom advance. However, greater is He that is within us than he that is in the world!

Paul, the Practitioner

For those of you who would like a bit more assurance that these different kinds of Kingdom spiritual warfare are biblical, I thought it would be good to close by taking another look at the story of Paul's missionary work in Ephesus. This is the last account of Paul's assignment to extend the kingdom of God geographically into a new territory, and it is also the most fruitful. Acts 19:10 reads, "This [Paul's ministry] continued for two years, so that all who dwelt in Asia heard the word of the Lord Jesus, both Jews and Greeks." It is easy to skip over this incredible statement unless you know that the city of Ephesus had around 400,000 people and the population of Asia Minor was some 15 million, by far the largest province in the Roman Empire at the time. In two years they *all* heard the gospel of the Kingdom!

In order to enable this to happen, Paul first of all taught "the things of the kingdom of God" (Acts 19:8). That was kingdom *teach-*

ing. He followed it, however, with kingdom *action,* doing spiritual warfare in all three theaters.

Paul engaged in *ground-level spiritual warfare.* Verses 11 and 12 read, "Now God worked unusual miracles by the hands of Paul, so that even handkerchiefs or aprons were brought from his body to the sick, and the diseases left them and the evil spirits went out of them." Demons were cast out by handkerchiefs taken from Paul, carried unknown distances, and touched by those who were afflicted! This was unusual, as it says. However, I have heard through credible witnesses that similar things happen from time to time today, especially in the Global South.

Paul also engaged in *occult-level spiritual warfare.* Ephesus was the center of magic for the whole Roman Empire. The city had the best training schools for magicians, so large numbers of them were in the city at any time. What happened? "Many of those who had practiced magic brought their books together and burned them in the sight of all. And they counted up the value of them, and it totaled fifty thousand pieces of silver" (v. 19). In today's economy, the value of the destroyed occult articles would be $4 million. Reading between the lines, it must have taken a huge amount of warfare to snatch so many practicing magicians from the hand of Satan.

Finally, Paul engaged in *strategic-level spiritual warfare.* The territorial spirit ruling over Ephesus and Asia Minor was Diana of the Ephesians. Her temple was one of the seven wonders of the ancient world. In fact, some scholars say that she probably was the most worshiped deity in the Roman Empire. Paul never went into Diana's temple or confronted her directly one on one. However, we read later in Acts 19 that she began losing so much power because demons were being cast out and magicians were getting saved that the silversmiths could no longer market her occult idols. They rioted against Paul because they knew that Paul's God was causing their economic crisis.

It gets better. While Paul did not take on Diana directly, the apostle John did. The evidence for this does not come from the Bible but rather from history. Ramsay MacMullen of Yale University, one of America's most respected historians, published a book called *Christianizing the Roman Empire.* In it we learn that the apostle John succeeded Paul in Ephesus, and he eventually went into the temple of Diana and entered into confrontational strategic-level spiritual warfare. MacMullen quotes John's prayer: "O God . . . at whose name every idol takes flight and every demon and every unclean power: now let the demon that is here take flight at thy name!"[2] When John prayed, the altar of Diana split in many pieces, and half the temple fell down. The spectators were dumbfounded, and those who were unsaved were converted on the spot.

I know that some will doubt this, but MacMullen puts his integrity as a historian on the line and writes, "I don't think the explanatory force of this scene should be discounted on the grounds that it cannot have happened, that it is fiction, that no one was meant to believe it. . . . Such wonderful stories were most reliably reported."[3] Why not take Ramsay MacMullen's word for it and rejoice together that the kingdom of God spread so powerfully in Ephesus through Paul and John? In fact, Ephesus then became the center of world Christianity for the next 200 years.

This leaves us with an interesting question. Why did John confront Diana, but not Paul? They were both apostles. They were both filled with the Holy Spirit. They both had authority over the demonic spirits. The underlying difference was obviously God's timing. Another one of the rules of engagement when battling principalities and powers is to seek God for the proper timing. I believe that if Paul had attempted it, he would have been shattered instead of Diana's altar, because he would have been outside of God's timing.

Conclusion

As you can see, a Kingdom vision is much greater than a church vision. I want to be among those who seek first the kingdom of God, because I know that if I do, all the other necessary things will be added supernaturally!

Notes

1. Raymond J. Bakke, "Our Kind of People," *Evangelical Missions Quarterly* (April 1980), p. 127.
2. Ramsay MacMullen, *Christianizing the Roman Empire AD 100-400* (New Haven, CT: Yale University Press, 1984), p. 26.
3. Ibid.

13

From **Ministry** in the **Church** to **Ministry** in the **Workplace**

In the previous chapter I confessed that for too long a time I had a church vision but not a Kingdom vision. One of the unfortunate ways that this played out was that I believed and even taught that all bona fide Christian ministry was supposed to be done in the context of the local church.

Spiritual Gifts

The starting point for developing the old paradigm that I call "ministry in the church" was my understanding of spiritual gifts. As you might recall from chapter 2, researching, writing and teaching on spiritual gifts has been a central theme in my ministry since I was ordained in 1955. My first book on the subject was *Your Spiritual Gifts Can Help Your Church Grow*. It has remained in print for over 30 years, and it is by far my best-selling book.

Here is my definition of a spiritual gift: "A spiritual gift is a special attribute given by the Holy Spirit to every member of the Body of Christ, according to God's grace, for use within the context of the Body."[1] Look at the phrase "within the context of the Body." That's the same as saying "within the context of the church." A few years ago, after I had shifted my paradigm, I found it necessary to revise the book at some of these crucial points. However, before I did, I taught that ministering with spiritual gifts was supposed to be in the local church or in its various outreach ministries. I supported my point of view by quoting Jack MacGorman, who writes, "Not only are the gifts *functional*, but they are also *congregational*."[2]

I would frequently be challenged by individuals in my audience when I was teaching this. One schoolteacher, for example, asked me,

"If I have a spiritual gift, can't I use it in my class in public school?" My answer was, "No, because that is not the body of Christ." To my way of thinking, if it were a *Christian* school, it would be different because the Christian school is an extension of the church, so that would be "in the context of the church." In my book I wrote, "Most of the things God does in the world today are done through believers who are working together in community, complementing each other with their gifts in their local congregations."[3]

Turning the Corner

It was back in 2001 when some friends from the Twin Cities invited me to fly up and address a group of Christian business people who had been convening once a month for some time. This was not one of those invitations that was easy to respond to because it would pull me out of my comfort zone. Most of my ministry had been training and equipping church leaders, and I had no personal experience in the business world. However, I had such a high regard for my friends that I did pray earnestly about the invitation, expecting that I would eventually decline. Just the opposite. Much to my surprise, it turned out to be one of those rare occasions when God spoke directly to me. He clearly said (not in an audible voice), "My son, I want you to pay strict attention to the church in the workplace." My inexperience was trumped by my desire to obey God, so I knew I had no option but to accept the invitation.

As a part of my normal routine of attempting to keep up with unfolding developments in the Christian world, I had become cognizant of what was commonly known as the Faith at Work Movement. Its roots could be traced back to the 1930s, when the evangelical Christian Business Men's Committee was first launched, and the 1950s, when its charismatic counterpart, Full Gospel Business Men's Fellowship International, was founded. As the years went by, other similar organizations emerged, but a significant escalation of attempts to give a voice and a greater influence to believers who were associated with the business world occurred during the late 1990s. I was aware of these developments but was only mildly interested. I had no inclination to become a part of this movement until I received that word from the Lord in 2001.

Once I did, I began to move. Being a scholar by nature, I first wanted to research what God's people had been saying about faith in the workplace, so I purchased and read (with different degrees of thoroughness) between 100 and 110 books on the subject. I built an annotated bibliography. I began to discern certain historical trends and how the seasons had changed with time. I took notes and proceeded to organize my thoughts. I became acquainted with some of the recognized leaders of the movement and learned much from them. I began receiving invitations to do some teaching on what I was finding out.

Silvoso's Tipping Point

It was just then that my close friend Ed Silvoso released his book *Anointed for Business.* Reading that book turned out to be the tipping point for my paradigm shift. Ten years later I still recommend Silvoso's book as the best port of entry for anyone who wants to be introduced to the concept of ministry in the workplace. Silvoso is aware of the decades of development of Faith at Work, which I have just mentioned, but his book is far from a rehash of the old. It convincingly takes us into entirely new arenas of understanding what contributions toward the future God's people in business, government and education can and should be making.

Not only has Ed been a close friend for a long time, but also, at one point in the past, he was my student in Fuller Seminary. He took my course on spiritual gifts and heard me teach that the gifts were only supposed to be used for ministry in the church, not in the workplace. I don't know if he agreed with me or not back then, but he passed his exams and got a good grade.

However, when it later came time for writing *Anointed for Business,* Silvoso made a point to include a section called "Gifts in the Marketplace." In it, he argues that Jesus' promise to fill believers with the Holy Spirit and give them spiritual gifts applies "*primarily* to ministry in the marketplace."[4] The italics are his, indicating that he had moved 180-degrees from what he had heard in my class. Now that I have shifted my paradigm and agree with him, I love what he goes on to say. He quotes Jesus' command to go into all the world and preach the gospel to all creation (see Mark 16:15), and then he adds, "The process described by Jesus is *definitely* centrifugal and expansive. The entire world, the totality of creation, must be the focus of the mission entrusted to us, not just a church building or a gathering of believers."[5]

Not only am I thankful for all that Ed Silvoso writes in *Anointed for Business,* but I hasten to add that, when he wrote it, he graciously chose to honor me by dedicating the book to me. Only modesty prevents me from quoting his very flowery dedication in full. However, I can encourage you to read it on your own!

The Church in the Workplace

When I used to say that all ministry through spiritual gifts needed to be done in the church, one of my problems was that I had too narrow a concept of the church. I was thinking of the church as a place where believers gather together on a regular basis. It usually had a church building of one sort or another. It was led by a pastor. It had a congregation with a defined membership. That is the traditional concept of the church.

When Jesus said, "I will build My church" (Matt. 16:18), He used the Greek word *ecclesia.* Back in those days in the Roman Empire, the *ecclesia* was a group of citizens in a city who convened for legislative purposes. I deal with that function a bit more in the next chapter. Right here, however, I want to stress that the most fundamental New Testament meaning of *ecclesia* is simply "the people of God." Wherever they happen to be, the people of God constitute the church. Sometimes, usually on Sunday, the people of God are gathered together in an assembly, just like I described above. That is the true church, since it is made up of the people of God.

However, Monday through Saturday the same people of God are not gathered together; they are scattered throughout the workplace. Do they stop being the church six days a week? Of course not. By definition they are the true church seven days a week whether they are gathered or whether they are scattered. Actually, if you get a concordance and check the use of "church" or *ecclesia* through the New Testament, you will find that about half the time it is used in the traditional way of believers gathered, but the other half it is used for believers scattered. For example, in the book of Ephesians, Paul makes nine references to the *ecclesia* and not one of them signifies a church building, a geographic location or a certain congregation. They all refer to the people of God scattered out among society.

While I was searching for some new terminology to describe these two forms of the church, my friend Leo Lawson suggested that we take a look at the well-known sociological distinction between the nuclear family and the extended family as a starting point. That terminology is widely recognized and commonly accepted in our society. Why not refer to the gathered church as the nuclear church and the scattered church as the extended church? I liked the idea, and I have been using "nuclear church" and "extended church" for years with very satisfactory acceptance.

One of the obvious implications of this is that there actually *is* a church (people of God) in the workplace, namely, the extended church. Unfortunately, in most workplace situations, this church has never had much influence. This is because the church in the workplace has never had the organization and the biblical government that it needs in order to be effective. I will expand on this later.

Ministry in the Workplace

Meanwhile, once we understand that the church is both the nuclear church and the extended church, my classic view that all ministry must be done in the church would be acceptable. My problem, however, was that I really meant that ministry was supposed to be done only in the *nuclear* church. Now that I have cleared up my view of the church, I see that Christian ministry is supposed to be done *both* in the nuclear church *and* in the extended church, or the workplace. This is a hugely important paradigm shift, and you can imagine how liberating it would be to believers who are neither ordained ministers nor regular church volunteers. What they do in the workplace counts!

For example, Ephesians 4:12 speaks of "equipping of the saints for the work of ministry." I would think that this refers to *all* of the saints, not just the 20 percent or so who have nuclear-church jobs, whether paid or unpaid. It also means that the 80 percent whose activities Monday through Saturday in the extended church consume most of their time are also doing bona fide ministry. Believers who are bus drivers, nurses, lawyers, schoolteachers, auto mechanics, CEOs, retail clerks or stay-at-home moms are all engaged in ministry just as legitimate as singing in the choir, leading a small group or even pastoring a church.

A good way to understand what I have just written is to look at the Greek word for "ministry," which I just quoted from Ephesians 4. It is *diakonia,* which you can probably see is the root word for "deacon." It appears dozens of times in the New Testament, and about half the time it is translated "ministry" and half the time "service." What does this mean? It means that whenever you are serving anyone, you are ministering to them. If you are waiting on customers in a restaurant, you are ministering to them. If you are filling someone's teeth, you are ministering to them. If you are selling someone insurance, that is a ministry. When you look at it this way, just about any job you can think of can be seen as a ministry.

A Job and a Ministry

When does a job become a ministry? I believe that a job becomes a ministry when God leads you into the arena, and you take the voice of God, the anointing of God and biblical principles with you as you work, minister and serve others in whichever ways your gifts, your experience and your learned skill sets allow you to function. Here is what businessman John Beckett writes after discovering this principle:

> In stark contrast to my prior thinking, the Bible enabled me to view my work as having great worth to God, provided I would bring it into harmony with him in every way possible. As a believer and a business person, I was no longer a second-class citizen. Nor did I need to leave my Christian convictions and biblical values outside the office entrance when I headed into work on Monday mornings.[6]

John Beckett found real freedom once he understood the church in the workplace.

Let me take this one step further. If, for a moment, we can assume a Hebrew mindset (remember chapter 10), we can see that, biblically, work is actually *sacred*. When God created Adam and Eve, even before they sinned, the Bible says that He put them in the Garden to work (see Gen. 2:15). Work was part of God's original design for humans, not some inferior nuisance in a lower realm that we had to learn to endure, as Plato's Greek mindset would imagine. In fact, for the Hebrews, work actually constituted *worship*! Mark Greene has studied this a great deal, and here is his conclusion:

> Work is ordained by God. And it should be dedicated to God. . . . The Hebrew word for work is *avodah,* the same as the word for worship. "Service" captures the flavor best. Work is a seven-letter word—service—to God and people. And though I would lose my job if I built a theology on the basis of that observation alone, we can see elsewhere in scripture that work is a part of "everything" we do "to the glory of God." For God, work is part of our worship. It is part of our service to Him.[7]

Two Cultures, Two Rule Books

One reason that the extended church does not have the influence it might have in most sectors of the workplace is that the nuclear church and the extended church have not been as supportive of each other as they could be. What is going on? The fact of the matter is that the majority of pastors in the nuclear church have not yet gone through the paradigm shift that I am describing in this chapter.

How do I know that we are dealing with the majority of nuclear-church pastors? It is because of a social scientific study done by Laura Nash of Harvard University and Scotty McLennan of Stanford University, published in the book *Church on Sunday, Work on Monday.* Although they don't use the same terminology as I do, "church on Sunday" would mean the nuclear church and "work on Monday" would mean the extended church. This study uncovers many cultural differences between the two forms of the church. They found that "businesspeople and clergy live in two worlds. Between the two groups lie minefields seeded with attitudes about money, poverty, and the spirit of business."[8]

As I have analyzed this information and applied it to the church in the workplace, I have come up with a list of four facts that have huge implications for moving ahead and activating the extended church:

1. *Each of the two forms of the church, the nuclear church and the extended church, has a distinct culture.* Peter Tsukahira writes, "Culture contains values and expectations that lie beneath our conscious thoughts. There is a church culture and there is a business culture. Although the two coexist in the believing community, it is as if they have different values and goals, speak different languages, and have entirely different customs."[9]

2. *The cultural gap is enormous.* I always knew there was a cultural gap between the nuclear church and the extended church, but Nash and McLennan's study showed me how deep it really is. I was amazed! Building bridges between the two will require a good bit of determination and hard work on both sides.

3. *Each culture has its own rule book.* Sometimes the rules are quite different. I attempted to describe the differences relating to eight of those rules in my book *The Church in the Workplace.*

4. This is the most sensitive point: *Most extended-church, or workplace, leaders understand both rule books, while most nuclear-church leaders understand only one rule book—namely, theirs.* To complicate matters, many nuclear-church leaders think that their rule book is the only one that is right. They disdain certain workplace rules as wrong, and some go on to pass spiritual judgments against their church members who know that they will not influence their sector of the workplace if they do not have the liberty to flow with those elements of their workplace culture that are not ungodly.

With all this, it may appear that the differences between the nuclear church and the extended church are irreconcilable. This cannot be the case, however, because mobilizing and activating the church in the workplace is one of the things that the Holy Spirit is saying to the churches in this season. In fact, for the past 10 years or more there has been a discernable trend among nuclear-church leaders to begin to accept their workplace parishioners at face value and to recognize and applaud their vocations as legitimate Christian ministries. Some pastors are even becoming bi-vocational by moving into the workplace themselves. Paradigm shifts for individuals may come quickly, but for whole institutions, such as the church, more time is usually needed.

Governing the Extended Church

Back in chapter 9, I described my paradigm shift from denominational government to apostolic government. When the apostle Paul wrote, "He Himself gave some to be apostles, some prophets, some evangelists, and some pastors and teachers" (Eph. 4:11), this was not intended to be a history lesson, but a statement of the ongoing nature of the church. All of these offices are active today, including apostles and prophets. Paul also wrote, "God has appointed these in the church: first apostles, second prophets, third teachers" (1 Cor. 12:28). In chapter 9, I applied this to the church in general.

However, now that we are distinguishing the nuclear church from the extended church, we must recognize that the extended church, the church in the workplace, is also "built on the foundation of apostles and prophets" (Eph. 2:20). Even those of us who identify with the Apostolic-Prophetic Movement must admit that most of the teaching, preaching and writing we have done on apostles and prophets has been directed to the nuclear church. Just a glance at my library on the New Apostolic Reformation will show that virtually all books written about apostolic government up to now assume that apostles will minister in the context of the nuclear church.

Some are resisting the notion that there can be apostles in the workplace. To make it personal, a while ago I was being hosted for lunch in the home of one of America's most recognized nuclear-church apostles. He had invited four of his top leadership team to be with us. To open the conversation he said, "Peter, what are some of the things that God has been revealing to you these days?" I mentioned one or two other things, but when I came to apostles in the workplace, the room went silent. My friend gave me a wry look, got up from the table, came around to my side, knelt on the floor in front of me and said, "Peter, I beg of you on bended knees not to move forward with this idea of apostles in the workplace!" I made some kind of a humorous comment in an attempt to reduce the tension, and then I quickly changed the subject. From then on, I understood what a serious threat the activation of extended-church apostles can be to certain nuclear-church apostles.

Salt and Light

God's people in the workplace know that they are salt and light (see Matt. 5:13-16). They have been taught that since day one in the nuclear church. However, many of them have done their best to be salt and light in their workplace for 10 or 20 years and nothing has changed. Why? The answer undoubtedly lies in the fact that the spiritual government of the extended church has not yet come into place.

The people of God in the workplace ordinarily are affiliated with any number of different denominations or apostolic networks. Their nuclear churches typically will have certain characteristics or emphases that prove to be disagreeable to other nuclear-church leaders. This makes it extremely unlikely that a nuclear-church pastor or apostle could come into a certain sector of the workplace and provide effective government for all of God's people there. Furthermore, the cultural gap between the nuclear church and the extended church is too wide.

Leaving room for possible exceptions, the rule would be that workplace apostles will need to emerge from within a specifically defined area of the workplace. I believe that they are already there. God has given certain workplace people the spiritual gift of apostle. Our problem is that the majority of these gifted apostles have not been identified, recognized, affirmed, encouraged and activated by God's people around them. A few have, and we are grateful for their example. However, activating large numbers of apostles in the workplace should become a top agenda item for the body of Christ over the next 10 years.

If and when this happens, believers will become the army of God that the Bible tells us about. Apostles in the workplace will be the principal leaders of that army for advancing God's kingdom and for eventually seeing the tangible answer to the prayer that Jesus taught us: "Your kingdom come, Your will be done on earth as it is in heaven" (Matt. 6:10). I want to pick this theme up and deal with it in further detail in the next chapter.

Notes

1. C. Peter Wagner, *Your Spiritual Gifts Can Help Your Church Grow* (Ventura, CA: Regal Books, 2005), p. 33.
2. Jack W. MacGorman, *The Gift of the Spirit* (Nashville, TN: Broadman Press, 1974), p. 31. Emphasis in the original.
3. Wagner, *Your Spiritual Gifts Can Help Your Church Grow*, p. 35.
4. Ed Silvoso, *Anointed for Business* (Ventura, CA: Regal Books, 2002), p. 34.
5. Ibid., emphasis in the original.
6. John D. Beckett, *Loving Monday* (Downers Grove, IL: InterVarsity Press, 1998), p. 74.
7. Mark Greene, *Thank GOD It's Monday: Ministry in the Workplace* (Bletchley, England: Scripture Union, 2001), p. 104.
8. Laura Nash and Scotty McLennan, *Church on Sunday, Work on Monday* (San Francisco: Jossey-Bass, 2001), p. 128.
9. Peter Tsukahira, *My Father's Business* (published by Peter Tsukahira, P.O. Box 7231, Haifa, Israel, 2000), p. 19.

14

From **Extending** the **Church** to **Reforming Society**

Of all the paradigm shifts I unfold in this book, this one is the most radical. Let me explain why. Since the day I was saved back in 1950, I had committed my life to do everything within the power that God chose to give me to help fulfill the Great Commission. My first career was a field missionary in Bolivia for 16 years. My second career was teaching missiology at Fuller Seminary for 30 years. Regretfully, I now realize that during those first two careers I had only a partial understanding of the meaning of Jesus' words, "Go therefore and make disciples of all the nations" (Matt. 28:19).

Here is what I thought the Great Commission meant: Go to as many of the nations of the world as possible, faithfully make the gospel known to all, win as many souls to Christ as you can, nurture them to maturity in their Christian walk, and multiply churches throughout the nation under the direction of national leaders. That constitutes making disciples. Undoubtedly, there are many reading these words who would still think that what I have just written does, indeed, describe the essence of the Great Commission. I certainly know where you are coming from.

Evangelism and Church Planting

The part of the Great Commission that I was teaching and trying to obey was correct and helpful. What was the problem? The problem was that I didn't really understand the stated goal of the Great Commission. During my tenure at Fuller Seminary, my specialty within the general field of missiology was church growth. Extending the church was my passion. I wrote several textbooks that were used in a number of seminaries and Bible schools. In all of them I stressed that evangelism and church planting were our goals.

For example, I emphasized to my students and my readers alike that in order to serve the Lord fully they needed to "recognize how vitally important it is to understand the Great Commission: for without a thorough understanding of it, no one could be sure he or she was obeying it properly."[1] I thought that it was essential to distinguish the *end* from the *means* in the Great Commission. The means would be witnessing and preaching. Mark tells us that Jesus said, "Go into all the world and *preach* the gospel to every creature" (Mark 16:15, emphasis added). Luke records this statement from Jesus: "Repentance and remission of sins should be *preached* in His name to all nations, beginning at Jerusalem" (Luke 24:47, emphasis added). Then in Acts, "You shall be *witnesses* to Me in Jerusalem, and in all Judea and Samaria, and to the end of the earth" (Acts 1:8, emphasis added).

If witnessing and preaching the gospel are means, what, then, would be the end? Matthew 28:19 tells us that we are to "make disciples." The evidence that we have fulfilled the Great Commission is that we leave behind true disciples of Jesus Christ. One problem is that some missionaries and evangelists feel that they have fulfilled the Great Commission if they have preached to large numbers of people and have seen some raise their hands or come forward at the invitation. I don't think this, by itself, is fulfilling the Great Commission. They have used proper means, but they typically do not go back and check as to how many of those who came forward ended up being true *disciples*. Only then could they know whether their preaching was successful or not.

You can imagine that some became upset when they first heard these ideas, especially so when whole denominations agreed with me and changed the way they began to measure the effectiveness of their evangelists and their evangelism programs. To go one step further, I began to address how you tell the difference between professed converts and true disciples. I insisted that the only valid, measurable sign for a true disciple was responsible church membership. After all, I was professor of church growth, so I might be expected to argue that the end of missions and evangelism would be the growth and multiplication of churches. One of the statements of mine that has been quoted the most through the years is, "The single most effective evangelistic methodology under heaven is planting new churches."[2] Actually, I still believe this is true for evangelism, but I no longer believe that evangelism and church planting are the legitimate *ends*—or final goals—of the Great Commission.

I taught these things fervently, but I have since gone through a paradigm shift.

What Are We Aiming For?

If winning souls and multiplying churches is not the authentic end of Jesus' Great Commission, what, then, is it? I am now convinced that it amounts to taking Jesus' words, "Make disciples of all the nations," literally. Notice that the unit to be discipled here is not individuals who happen to live in a nation, but the nation itself.

To get a clear view of what "all the nations" means, it helps to go to the original Greek, *panta ta ethne*. *Panta* is the word for "all," and *ta* is "the." Now, take a look at the word *ethne*. You can probably see that we get our English word "ethnic" from it. *Ethne* doesn't necessarily mean "nations" in the way we usually use the word, as in "United Nations." It means groups of people who live with each other because of a certain set of commonalities that bind them together. A very accurate translation of *ethne* would be "people groups." The idea behind this is that whole people groups can and should become disciples of Jesus Christ.

A Slow Change

I'll get into the way that my paradigm shift came about in due time, but first I feel that I should make a professional public confession. My church growth mentor was Donald McGavran, a missionary statesman and educator who had spent 60 years in India. I eventually became his successor and the first incumbent of the Donald A. McGavran Chair of Church Growth at Fuller.

When I studied under him, I learned that he interpreted the Great Commission literally and understood *panta ta ethne* to mean that we should aim to disciple whole people groups. However, when I tried to apply this to America, after I had returned from Bolivia, I found myself so immersed in my paradigm of saving souls and multiplying churches that I intentionally downplayed McGavran's position and took the individualistic approach that I told you about in the beginning. It was only after McGavran had gone to his eternal reward that I finally struggled through my paradigm shift and learned to take Jesus' words literally. I now believe that Donald McGavran was right and that we must aim for discipling whole nations.

Some of my paradigm shifts came rather quickly, but this one was quite drawn out. The best I can recall, the first nudge came from John Dawson's influential book *Taking Our Cities for God,* which became a bestseller in 1990. Dawson, whom I greatly admire, was the first in the circles with which I was moving to set as a goal changing a whole social unit, such as a city. At that time, I must admit, I used his book more for its sound principles of spiritual warfare than for its missiological implications.

He was followed by George Otis, Jr., who began making persuasive *Transformation* videos, documenting social changes around the world that resulted from prayer and spiritual warfare. Then came Ed Silvoso with his epic *Transformation,* still my choice for the most solid, foundational textbook in the field. By the time Silvoso's book came along, I was already on board with this new paradigm, but the time span I just described was around 15 years.

The Dominion Mandate

My theology of the fall of Adam and Eve, particularly touching the role of Satan in the Garden, is now far different from what I learned when I went to seminary. In seminary, the issue was how sin entered the human race and was subsequently passed down from generation to generation. Satan entered the Garden as a deceiver in order to make Adam and Eve sin, and he succeeded. Adam and Eve ate the forbidden fruit, God banished them from the Garden, and Satan had accomplished his purpose. From then on, most of the ills of the human race could be blamed on what some theologians have called the total depravity of humanity.

Now that I have shifted my paradigm, I still begin in the Garden of Eden, but I begin with God's stated purpose for creating Adam and Eve. God spent the first five days creating everything else; then on the sixth day He created Adam and Eve. The first thing He said was, "Be fruitful and multiply; fill the earth and subdue it; have dominion over the fish of the sea, over the birds of the air, and over every living thing that moves on the earth" (Gen. 1:28). Apparently, God made His whole creation for Adam and Eve, and He wanted to put them in charge of it. That is what "have dominion" signifies. God gave to Adam what I like to call the dominion mandate.

God made Adam and Eve in His image. This means, among other things, that they could communicate with God and that they could love Him. However, true love cannot be forced; it must be a choice. The first humans had to choose whether or not they would love and obey God. This means that God created them as free moral agents. An extension of this principle would have to do with God's offer that they take dominion over the creation. Adam would have authority to take dominion, but he would also have authority to give dominion away.

Satan's Role

In light of this, let's reexamine Satan's role. Satan did not go into the Garden of Eden just to make Adam sin, although that was part of it. Rather, Satan went there primarily to usurp the dominion over creation that God had given to Adam. Why was this important to Satan? Let's refresh our memories concerning our enemy.

Satan was originally created as one of the finest of angels, "the anointed cherub who covers" (Ezek. 28:14). He was so brilliant that one of his names was Lucifer. God had made Lucifer a powerful angel and had given him great authority in heaven. However, Lucifer was not satisfied with the authority that God had given him—he wanted more—so he gathered some other angels, went into rebellion and tried to overthrow the government of God. He, of course, failed and was thrown out of heaven with about one-third of the angels.

At that point, Satan found himself without authority. He still had his power, which was the way he had been created, but he no longer had the authority to use that power. One of his greatest desires was to regain his authority, and that is the main reason he went into the Garden of Eden disguised as a serpent. Satan knew something. He knew that Adam was a free moral agent. He knew that God had given Adam authority to take dominion of the creation, but that Adam also had the ability to give this authority away.

The Worst Possible Decision

Satan tempted Adam and Eve to eat the forbidden fruit (see Gen. 3). Think of the magnitude of Adam's choice. The word "Adam" in Hebrew is not just a proper name; it also means the whole human race. Consequently, Adam was making a decision not just for himself but for you and me as well. As we know, he made the worst possible decision. He decided to obey Satan rather than God. One result was that he sinned, passing original sin down to the whole human race. Most of us have always known that, but we have not always been aware of an even greater implication: At that moment, Satan took over the dominion of God's creation, the dominion originally intended for the human race made in the image of God.

I realize that some people will question this theology. Some like to think that Satan has no intrinsic power or authority, especially after Jesus died on the cross. This is a nice thought, but it is only a dream. It does not line up with either biblical revelation or the history of the human race. The Bible, even after Jesus' death and resurrection, labels Satan "the prince of the power of the air" (Eph. 2:2) and "the god of this age" (2 Cor. 4:4). Jesus Himself referred to Satan as "the ruler of this world" (John 14:30). It is difficult to trivialize this strong biblical language.

The case gets even stronger if we recall Jesus' third temptation. This is where Satan took Jesus up on a high mountain and showed Him "all the kingdoms of the world and their glory" (Matt. 4:8). The fact that Satan had the power to show Jesus *all* the kingdoms is remarkable enough, but then Satan went on to display his authority. He offered to give those kingdoms, over which he ruled, to Jesus if only Jesus would worship him (v. 9). The notable thing here is that Jesus never questioned whether Satan had the right to make that offer. As a matter of fact, if by chance Satan did not have such authority, the whole temptation would have been nothing but a charade!

This, of course, plays out in human history. Early on, Satan's dominion became so evil that God had thoughts of discontinuing the whole human race and only Noah's obedience saved a tiny fraction of it (see Gen. 6). Human existence through the centuries is a story of misery. Wars and genocide are a common thread. Human sacrifice has been rampant through history. Slavery has been an accepted way of life. Disease and natural disasters produce their own trail of human affliction. Oppression, injustice, poverty and abuse have characterized human existence. Add to this natural disasters that victimize whole innocent populations.

I could go on, but what some theologians call the problem of evil, or theodicy, is difficult to explain solely on the basis of human sinfulness. The apostle Paul describes some of this as "[conducting] ourselves in the lusts of our flesh, fulfilling the desires of the flesh and of the mind, and [being] by nature children of wrath" (Eph. 2:3), and he attributes this sad state of human affairs to "the prince of the power of the air, the spirit who now works in the sons of disobedi-ence" (v. 3). It is necessary to bring Satan, the prince of the power of the air, into the picture to properly deal with the deeply imbedded problem of evil.

Arguably, the most stimulating and convincing exponent of the problem of evil in our day is my friend Gregory Boyd. His amazing twin books on the subject, *God at War* and *Satan and the Problem of Evil,* more than 400 pages each, have no match in contemporary literature. Greg helped greatly to reinforce my paradigm shift. He persuasively re-futes the traditional theology that God controls everything that ever happens and that even the tragic things that occur through human beings or natural disasters are somehow within the sovereign will of God, even though we might not understand them. He, instead, advo-cates a warfare worldview through which to understand Scripture.

Boyd argues that "there is a dominant motif running throughout Scripture that depicts God as warring against human and angelic op-ponents who are able in some measure to thwart his will."[3] He goes on to point out that God continually strives against rebellious creatures. "According to Scripture," Boyd argues, "the head of this rebellion is a powerful fallen angel named Satan. Under him are a myriad of other spiritual beings and humans who refuse to submit to God's rule."[4] Think about this: Without recognizing that our enemy has superhu-man power, it is difficult to make sense of a great deal of the Bible.

The Second Adam Changes Things

Because of Adam's wrong choice, the original plan that God had for the human race to rule His creation did not materialize. Neverthe-less, His purpose never changed. For that reason God intervened by sending His Son, Jesus Christ, who is also known as the Second or Last Adam (see 1 Cor. 15:45), a designation indicating a new start. Since the beginning, the course of human history has made two 180-degree turns. The first turn-around happened with the First Adam, and the second with the Second Adam. Since Jesus, human history has been heading back in the right direction, even though it is still far from being complete.

Why did Jesus come? Yes, He came to save us from our sins, but there is an even larger picture. What is it? "For this purpose the Son of God was manifested, that He might destroy the works of the devil" (1 John 3:8). Jesus came to turn around the misery and evil throughout the human race that Satan has been getting away with since the Garden of Eden. Cindy Jacobs says it well: "Jesus wasn't looking for converts to a new religion; He was inviting people into a new kingdom, with a new government and a new King. He was inviting people to live heaven on earth."[5]

About Himself Jesus said, "For the Son of Man has come to seek and to save that which was lost" (Luke 19:10). Most sermons we hear on this Scripture assume that it really means that Jesus came to seek and save *those* who were lost, stressing individual salvation. I see that as a *pastoral* application of Jesus' statement. However an *apostolic* view takes the verse literally—saving *that* which was lost. What is it that was lost? Obviously, the dominion that God intended for humans to have over creation. I like the way that Joe Mattera of New York City puts it: "The main purpose of Jesus dying on the cross was not so that you can go to heaven. The main purpose of His death was so that His kingdom can be established in you so that, as a result, you can exercise kingdom authority on earth (Luke 17:21) and reconcile the world back unto Him (2 Cor. 5:19)."[6]

Reconciliation Is Our Task

In the previous statement, Joe Mattera brings up the matter of reconciliation. This actually ends up putting the implementation of the dominion mandate squarely in our laps. Here is the perspective of God the Father: "For it pleased the Father that in Him all the fullness should dwell, and by Him to *reconcile* all things to Himself, by Him, whether things on earth or things in heaven, having made peace through the blood of His cross" (Col. 1:19-20, emphasis added). Jesus shed His blood not only to reconcile all *people* to the Father but, beyond that, to reconcile all *things*. Jesus paid the price not just for individual reconciliation but also for social reconciliation. He paid the price to replace the kingdom of Satan with the kingdom of God.

God's desire for reconciliation is clear, but how is it to be implemented? Apparently, He is not planning to take some sovereign, divine action to force it to happen. No, He expects us, His Kingdom-minded servants, to implement His desire. "Now all things are of God, who has reconciled us to Himself through Jesus Christ, and has given us the ministry of reconciliation" (2 Cor. 5:18). When we put these Scriptures together, here is what I think they mean:

- Jesus paid the *price* (His blood) for the reconciliation of all things.
- God gave us the *task* of making it happen here on earth.

This is an awesome responsibility and obviously one that we cannot attempt in our own power. I believe that is why Jesus, just before He left the earth, said these famous words: "But you shall receive power when the Holy Spirit has come upon you; and you shall be witnesses to Me in Jerusalem, and in all Judea and Samaria, and to the end of the earth" (Acts 1:8). With the power of the Holy Spirit, nothing is impossible.

Jesus' witnesses are those who are willing to act and speak on His behalf. Jesus' agenda was to destroy the works of the devil, to seek and save that which was lost, and to reconcile all things to God. This allows us to take literally the Great Commission that tells us to disciple whole nations.

It is important to extend the church of Jesus Christ around the world, but that is only one step toward fulfilling the final objective of the prayer that Jesus taught us: "Your kingdom come, Your will be done on earth as it is in heaven" (Matt. 6:10). It is an enormous assignment, but it clearly is the mandate we have from God!

Notes

1. C. Peter Wagner, *Frontiers in Missionary Strategy* (Chicago, IL: Moody Press, 1972), p. 21.
2. C. Peter Wagner, *Church Planting for a Greater Harvest* (Ventura, CA: Regal Books, 1990), p. 11.
3. Gregory A. Boyd, *Satan and the Problem of Evil* (Downers Grove, IL: InterVarsity Press, 2001), p. 15.
4. Ibid.
5. Cindy Jacobs, *The Reformation Manifesto* (Minneapolis, MN: Bethany House Publishers, 2008), p. 63.
6. Joseph Mattera, *Ruling in the Gates* (Lake Mary, FL: Creation House Press, 2003), p. 5.

15

From **Society** as **One Mass** to the **Seven Mountains**

Once I began to understand that if we were to take the Great Commission literally and believe that God wants to disciple whole nations, not just individuals within those nations, I began to look toward the next step, which would be practical implementation. Where do we start?

In the previous chapter I pointed out that the literal translation of "nations" (*ethne*) was "people groups." "Nations" gives you the idea of territorial boundaries, while "people groups" implies ethnic or cultural boundaries. Both are valid. Whichever you choose, or even if you blend them together, you end up with a mass of people as the target. Social transformation means that the whole society, including all its networks and infrastructures, needs to be transformed so that it becomes characterized by the values and the blessings of the kingdom of God.

Practical Action

How do you break a whole society down for practical action? Suppose you have a huge nation such as the United States, with more than 300 million people? For most people, targeting the entire country is an overwhelming, not to say discouraging, thought. Most of us who began taking literally discipling the whole nations realized this, so as we began casting the vision for social reformation, we would ordinarily mention praying for nations, regions, states, cities, neighborhoods, people groups, and the like. It made the whole project a bit more manageable. For several reasons, some of us ended up using cities as our goal more than anything else. We would undoubtedly still be using cities as our major point of reference if it weren't for the appearance of a man named Lance Wallnau around the early 2000s. Lance, who has since become a close friend, turns out to be a paradigm shifter par excellence.

This paradigm was a bit different from the others I have been describing. Possibly we shouldn't think of it so much as a paradigm *shift* as a paradigm *upgrade*. It wasn't like being set in a former belief, for example, that churches should be governed democratically and then later realize that they should actually be governed apostolically. Nor was it like changing from a theological conviction that God foreknew everything that would ever happen to understanding that there are certain things that He chooses not to know ahead of time. No, we were correct in advocating that we target social units such as cities for fulfilling our dominion mandate, but we needed help in getting our minds around the way that these social units were shaped, or molded. Like a jigsaw puzzle, we could see the picture on the cover of the box, but we didn't have the pieces that needed to be put together to arrive at the whole.

A Ringside Seat

I was fortunate enough to have a ringside seat as this new paradigm began to emerge. For around 20 years, Global Harvest Ministries, the organization that I led, sponsored a number of public conferences every year. My purpose was to help equip the body of Christ for serving God by highlighting some of the newer things that the Holy Spirit was saying to the churches at the time.

I would set a conference theme and then recruit a speaking team of the most visible and articulate individuals who were attempting to address various aspects of that theme. You might recall that in chapter 13 I told of how the Lord spoke to me about concentrating on the church in the workplace in 2001. As an outcome, I organized several conferences relating to the church in the workplace. On the strong recommendation of some friends, I invited Lance Wallnau to speak at one of these events. As I listened to him, it was the first time I had been exposed to his teaching on the Seven Mountains.

I wish I could say that I was instantly converted. I should have been! However, the truth of the matter is that my mind was not sharp enough to grasp the profound implications of what Lance was saying the first time I heard it. Still, I was fascinated by his quickness of thought, his acute skill in the use of English meta-phors, his sustained originality that blindsided most listeners, and his thorough grasp of the subject matter without referring to notes—all filtered through what was obviously a committed King-dom mindset—so I cultivated Lance's friendship and persuaded him to join the speaking team for a number of conferences to come.

By about the third time I heard Lance speak, I became convinced that he was articulating something unusually important that the Spirit was saying to the churches. The idea that religion, family, ed-ucation, government, media, arts and entertainment, and business—the Seven Mountains, or mind-molders—were the principal units that actually determined the culture of a whole society provided the template we had been searching for. Rather than attempting to vi-sualize a whole society change at once, we could better visualize the transformation of each of the Seven Mountains, along with numer-ous sub-divisions of each one, together bringing cities, nations or re-gions into the flow of the kingdom of God. Lance writes, "If the world is to be won, these are the mountains that mold the culture and the minds of men. Whoever controls these mountains controls the direction of the world and the harvest therein."[1]

Lance Wallnau never claimed to be the originator of what we now call the 7-M Template. He invariably told the story of what has turned out to be a historic luncheon involving Bill Bright, founder of Campus Crusade, and Loren Cunningham, founder of Youth With A Mission (YWAM). In preparation for the luncheon, which was the first time the two had met personally, they had each drawn up a list of the seven spheres that they thought shaped society more than anything else. Astoundingly, their lists were virtually identi-cal! With a bit of fine-tuning needed to standardize the terminol-ogy, the paradigm of the Seven Mountains has now become common currency among those committed to a literal fulfillment of the Great Commission.

Government Counts

You may recall that in chapter 13, when I was writing about the church in the workplace, I mentioned that God's people in the workplace, by and large, recognize that they are supposed to be salt and light in order to change their particular environment for good. However, for most of them, years have gone by and the changes have not come. Why?

I suggested that a major reason was that the government of the church in the workplace (unlike the government of the nuclear church) has not yet come into place. In addition, if I may be permitted another flashback, to chapter 9 this time, it is the apostles, properly aligned with prophets, who are the ones chosen by God to give leadership to this church government in the workplace. However, all apostles, whether in the nuclear church or in the workplace, are assigned specific spheres in which their authority is to be exercised. Understanding the Seven Mountains, particularly the Six Mountains of the workplace, provides an excellent starting place for defining what those apostolic spheres for workplace apostles might be.

To be a little bit more specific, this would mean that there are true, biblical apostles in the Media Mountain, the Government Mountain, the Education Mountain, and all the rest; and there are apostles, more specifically, within the many subdivisions of each. Take the Business Mountain as an example. Some apostles there would be specifically assigned to the health care industry, which would be an apostolic sphere different from the financial sector, automobile manufacturing or agriculture. Within health care, we would expect to find apostles to pharmaceuticals, cancer research, dentistry, anesthesiology, family practice, orthopedics, nutrition, health insurance, and on and on. With biblical government fully operational in each one of these spheres, society in general can be transformed to reflect the blessings and the prosperity of the kingdom of God.

As we move forward in this way of thinking, we will need to wrestle with some aspects of language. To date, most of our attempts toward understanding the biblical government of the church have related to the Religion Mountain. In the Religion Mountain, the biblical term "apostle" is understood, at least by those moving in the stream of the New Apostolic Reformation. However, for Kingdom-minded believers embedded in the cultures of the other six mountains, "apostle" might not be the best choice of language. If not, what term would be better? At this writing, I do not have a good answer to that question. In due time, however, I'm sure it will come.

A Few Can Do It

Some may suspect that transforming society might not be possible because we have too few Kingdom-minded believers in any given mountain. This, however, is not a correct assumption, as proven, unfortunately, by the homosexual community in America. Years ago, the ungodly equivalent of the apostolic leadership of the homosexual community decided to begin to work on making a fundamental change in the American Family Mountain. Specifically, they set out to attack our deeply cherished Judeo-Christian concept of marriage's being exclusively heterosexual, between a man and a woman. Their agenda was to change American culture enough so that same-sex marriage would be considered acceptable to the general public, both morally and legally.

They systematically mobilized their advocates in the Media Mountain, the Education Mountain, the Government Mountain, the Arts and Entertainment Mountain and even the Religion Mountain to coordinate their immoral campaign focused on manipulating our Family Mountain. Despite vociferous protests, intense prayer and fasting, public demonstrations, apostolic/prophetic decrees, impassioned sermons, fervent warnings on radio and television, and enormous investments of finances by organizations such as Focus on the Family and the American Family Association—all emerging from America's majority Christian community—the gay agenda, to all intents and purposes, has attained its desired cultural changes in our nation within only one generation.

What point am I making? Depending on which surveys you use, something less than 2 percent of the American population are practicing homosexuals. A full 85 percent of Americans believe that marriage should be exclusively heterosexual. America is a democratic country. However, in this case, the majority did not rule. We battled courageously, but arguably we all but lost the war. A tiny minority succeeded in molding culture by proactively gaining influence in the different mountains. In retrospect, the gay community outfoxed the Christian community because (1) it had a government, (2) it had a strategy of using the mountains that molded culture, and (3) it had access to enormous sources of funding. One lesson we can learn from this is that with only a few Kingdom-minded people in the right places, huge changes can occur if their efforts are skillfully coordinated. Let's take this as a challenge for bringing about a better future, perhaps even reversing the gay agenda.

Cultural Rulebooks

When I wrote about the church in the workplace, I brought up the cultural gap between the nuclear church and the extended church, or the church in the workplace. Now that we know that what I am calling the workplace is composed of six of the seven mountains, we must go one step further and recognize that each of the six mountains has a distinct culture of its own with a corresponding cultural rulebook.

The culture of the Education Mountain, for example, is quite different from the culture of the Media Mountain, and so on. This becomes very important when we analyze the process necessary to bring a certain mountain into the stream of the kingdom of God. Influence in each mountain comes from the top down, not from the bottom up. Therefore, our strategy must be to encourage Kingdom-minded leaders to move up as far as they can possibly go in their respective mountain. Obviously, the only way that one could move upward in their mountain would be to conform, in every way possible, to the cultural rulebook of that mountain.

By this I am not suggesting that apostles in any of the mountains leave behind their biblical principles of ethics, morality and righteousness. Every culture, unfortunately, is tainted with certain ungodly principles and practices that must be dealt with. Obviously, some lines must be drawn. However, this raises the question of who would be the best qualified to know where to draw the lines. Most, I believe, would agree that the Kingdom-minded apostolic leaders in any given mountain would be the ones to wrestle with the sensitive issues that might be as simple as black and white but that are, more often than not, complex shades of gray.

These Kingdom-minded leaders are those who best understand the nuances of their cultural rulebooks. Especially those of us in the Religion Mountain need to display the necessary humility to recognize that our peers in the other mountains may be just as spiritual as we are and may come to conclusions about drawing certain lines that we, from the perspective of our Religion Mountain rulebook, might question. When this happens, open dialogue and prayer are called for, and we need to trust God to bring us to a win-win situation.

A common mistake of the past has been to assume that people from the Religion Mountain should be called upon for guidance in delicate matters of biblical morality in all of the mountains. However, superimposing the rulebook of the Religion Mountain on the other six mountains carries the subtle danger of actually retarding the flow of Kingdom principles in whichever mountain.

Speaking of cultural differences, influence is attained one way in the Religion Mountain and another way in the other six. In the Religion Mountain, *spirituality* is a chief factor contributing to influence. However, spirituality is not considered to be a prerequisite for influence in any of the other six. In the other six mountains, *success* is the determining factor. Successful people are the ones to whom colleagues and co-workers ordinarily look for guidance and mentoring.

Ironically, this brings to mind numerous sermons in which I have heard success denigrated as sin by various pastors who unintentionally discourage workplace believers in their congregations, who are following another rulebook. Furthermore, in the workplace, successful people are more than likely rich. This offends some Religion Mountain leaders because they tend to succumb to a knee-jerk association of the accumulation of wealth with greed and conclude that sin must inevitably be involved. I detail the implications of the actions of what I consider this pernicious spirit of poverty in the final chapter.

Thoughts from the Religion Mountain

I am firmly rooted in the Religion Mountain. For more than 50 years I have earned my living from the Religion Mountain. This, I believe, gives me a measure of expertise in examining some of the attitudes and actions of the Religion Mountain, particularly before we began to understand the church in the workplace and the 7-M Template. I will list four of them.

First, we have hyper-spiritualized the Religion Mountain. Because spirituality is such an important attribute for Religion Mountain leaders, we have tended to assume that the most spiritual believers end up in the Religion Mountain. Our traditional distinction between clergy and laity reflects this attitude. We have sent out the message that fully committed Christians in another mountain who sincerely want to serve God should consider going into full-time ministry. What would this imply? It would suggest that the most dedicated believers, if they are really sincere, should make a spiritual sacrifice, give up their jobs in the "world," come into the Religion Mountain and serve as pastors or missionaries.

This persistent attempt to pull leaders out of the six Non-Religion Mountains into the Religion Mountain has, of course, weakened the other six and reduced their potential for being transformed. It would be a good thing for Religion Mountain leaders to encourage the development of apostles, prophets, evangelists, pastors and teachers in the other Six Mountains and to recognize that, although they might not display their spirituality in the same manner as those in the Religion Mountain, deep down they might well turn out to be just as spiritual as their Religion Mountain counterparts.

Second, we have overestimated the influence of the Religion Mountain. We in the Religion Mountain have, somewhat arrogantly, imagined that we routinely influence the other six mountains and thereby affect our society. This is because, if our congregation is a decent size, we ordinarily have representatives of all the mountains in church every Sunday, sitting under the teaching of their pastors. They are supposed to take what they learn on Sunday and apply it to their lives and activities Monday through Saturday. Good-hearted workplace leaders agree with the premise, but most of the time they end up being able to implement it only partially.

Why is this? It is because, with some notable exceptions, church pastors across denominational lines teach principles derived from the Religion Mountain rulebook. After all, this is what their professional training in seminary and Bible school has provided for them. Few have had significant life experience in any of the other Six Mountains. Typical sermons offer helpful guidance in developing personal character, in maturing a spiritual relationship with God, in applying supernatural power to the challenges of daily life, in deeper understanding of the Word of God, and in building a strong and functional family life. However, with all of this, there is little content that helps parishioners become successful in their mountain of choice.

I indicated that there are some notable exceptions. These would be the small percentage of pastors who, indeed, have accumulated life experience in one or more of the Non-Religion Mountains. They would also include life-centered and positive-thinking pastors such as Robert Schuller of a generation ago and Joel Osteen of this generation, who, interestingly enough, have been severely criticized as shallow, self-help preachers by many of their Religion Mountain counterparts.

Third, we have failed to activate the other Six Mountains. This is a corollary of what I have just written, taken from the personal level to the corporate level. As the call for social reformation and the dominion mandate is being embraced by more and more Religion Mountain leaders, sincere attempts are being made toward changing society through religious means.

The recent history of American evangelical Christianity has made this undertaking more difficult than it might otherwise be. Actually, 100 years ago, American society was significantly influenced by the Religion Mountain. Believers, or at least those who espoused Judeo-Christian principles, were at or near the top of most mountains. Today, that picture has drastically changed for the worst. Why?

It was my friend Mark Pfeifer who first pointed out to me that two significant religious movements during the twentieth century contributed to a tragic migration of influential Christian leaders from the Six Mountains to the Religion Mountain. The first was Fundamentalism, which taught that the devil is getting stronger, the world is getting worse, the church will be raptured in order to escape the despotic rule of the Antichrist, and, meanwhile, there is nothing we can do about it, so why try? I deal with this in some detail in the next chapter. The second was the Holiness Movement, which taught that committed believers should turn their backs on the sinful "world" (meaning the workplace) and separate themselves from it. The safe place, of course, would be the Religion Mountain. Many churchgoing workplace believers who did not feel they should disobey their pastors made the unfortunate switch.

When church leaders began hearing the Holy Spirit speak about social reformation, some of them took inventory and realized that their influence in the other six mountains in America was very weak. Action was needed, so Religion Mountain leaders decided that if they did more of what they are good at, it would affect all of the other six mountains. They agreed to instruct the body of Christ to pray harder, worship longer, fast more frequently, intensify spiritual warfare and live more holy lives. However, with all of this, American society was moving further and further away from Kingdom principles, not closer.

The lesson to be learned from this is that all six of the mountains of the workplace will be changed only from within, not from the actions of other mountains, especially the Religion Mountain. What the churches should do is to equip their workplace saints to function more effectively and to rise to positions of influence in their mountains. The problem is that, at least according to my informal estimate, 95 percent of pastors have not been trained to do this either in seminary or through real-life experience. Somehow, we in the Religion Mountain need to find creative ways to activate our workplace apostles, prophets, evangelists, pastors and teachers.

Fourth, we have developed a shortsighted battle plan. As I tried to explain in chapter 7, our efforts to see God's will done here on earth as it is in heaven inevitably bring us into warfare, because Satan is attempting to maintain his dominion over society. While we in the Religion Mountain have learned a great deal about spiritual warfare, especially through the decade of the '90s, workplace leaders, by and large, have not. Consequently, when situations obviously demanding spiritual warfare have arisen in any of the six mountains, leaders have called upon those in the Religion Mountain to help them with the warfare, which they did in most cases. However, when the battles have ended, the Religion leaders have gone back to their mountain. This has been a short-term, stopgap strategy.

What must happen long term is for those of us in the Religion Mountain to find ways and means to train workplace leaders in the strategic use of the weapons of spiritual warfare *within* each of the six mountains. When this is done and when the generals of spiritual warfare in each mountain are in communication with each other, the possibilities of Kingdom-minded individuals to become the head and not the tail in their mountain will dramatically increase. We then will begin to see sustained social transformation in our cities or in our nation.

Conclusion

I am painfully aware that in this chapter I have not offered many practical action steps for taking dominion of the six Non-Religion

Mountains. In a relatively new arena like this, however, it is good to establish the foundation of a sound theory upon which appropriate action can be taken, and that is what I have attempted to do.

Meanwhile, three individuals, Johnny Enlow of Daystar Church in Atlanta, Robert Henderson of Wellsprings Church in Colorado Springs, and Tommi Femrite of GateKeepers International also in Colorado Springs, have provided us with excellent books designed to give us a good start for practical action.

Enlow's first book, *The Seven Mountain Prophecy*, which is a manual of spiritual mapping for each of the mountains, identifies the spiritual principality that Satan uses to keep each mountain in the kingdom of darkness, preventing it from moving into the kingdom of light: The Religion Mountain is dominated by the spirit of religion, the Family Mountain by Baal, the Government Mountain by Lucifer, the Media Mountain by Apollyon, the Education Mountain by Beelzebub, the Arts and Entertainment Mountain (which Enlow calls Celebration) by Jezebel, and the Business Mountain (which he calls Economy) by Mammon.

In his second book, *The Seven Mountain Mantle,* Johnny Enlow visits each of the mountains and provides valuable insights as to what kinds of steps need to be taken in order to bring Kingdom reformation. Enlow's vision is that Christian revolutionaries "will not be content to live in a Christian subculture that has little influence on society. They will zealously endeavor to bring entire nations into the kingdom of God."[2]

In *A Voice of Reformation,* Robert Henderson assumes the unenviable task of describing how each mountain would actually look if it were transformed. His argument is that, in order to begin to pray and act intelligently, we need to know precisely what we are aiming for. As a part of the process, Henderson has characterized the Religion Mountain as the Impetus Mountain, the Family Mountain as the Values Mountain, the Education Mountain as the Equipping Mountain, the Government Mountain as the Empowering Mountain, the Business Mountain as the Finance Mountain, the Arts and Entertainment Mountain as the Prophetic Mountain, and the Media Mountain as the Watchman Mountain. His challenge is that "we must be proactive in the developing of reformers and the commissioning of them into the mountain of their calling."[3]

Tommi Femrite, one of America's most respected intercessors, has gone one step further and has established a for-profit company to provide professional-level intercession for Kingdom-minded leaders in all seven mountains. Called AIN (Apostolic Intercessory Network), she has set a goal to enable all 50 intercessors currently on the AIN team to earn a full-time living by praying. Tommi explains the whole philosophy behind this unusual ministry in her book *Invading the Seven Mountains with Intercession*.

I applaud forerunners like Johnny Enlow, Robert Henderson and Tommi Femrite. Beyond them I see in the very near future a whole library packed with new thoughts, new revelation from the Holy Spirit, new steps for implementation, and story after story of how mountains of society or segments of those mountains have been transformed, confirmed by professional sociological measurements, to reflect the blessings and the prosperity of the kingdom of God!

Notes

1. Lance Wallnau, "A Prophetic, Biblical, and Personal Call to the Workplace" (privately circulated paper, n.d.), n.p.
2. Johnny Enlow, *The Seven Mountain Mantle* (Lake Mary, FL: Creation House, 2009), p. 142.
3. Robert Henderson, *A Voice of Reformation: An Apostolic and Prophetic View of Each of the Seven Mountains in a Reformed State* (Colorado Springs, CO: Robert Henderson Ministries, 2010), p. 165.

16

From **Escapist Eschatology** to **Victorious Eschatology**

When I grew up and left home back in the 1940s, I had received no Christian or religious orientation from my family or friends. I was raised in one of the only 13 percent of American households that did not even own a copy of the Bible. Nevertheless, the hand of God must have been on me because, before I left to go to college in another state, I inexplicably felt that I needed to buy two books to take with me, namely, a dictionary and a Bible, which I did. I forget where I bought the Bible, but I know that I would have had no preference at all as to what kind of a Bible it might be. It so happened that my Bible turned out to be a Scofield Reference Edition.

Scofield and Larkin

Right after I was saved, I became a voracious Bible reader. I somehow knew that the Scofield notes were not part of the real Bible, but, as far as I was concerned, they were to be taken at face value. I had nothing else to compare them to, and they helped me understand Bible passages that otherwise would have made little sense. As time went by, I learned a huge amount from the Bible, but I was a bit frustrated because I had no understanding of how all the parts of the Bible fit together as a whole. I was at a loss to figure out how Genesis, 1 and 2 Chronicles, Daniel, Ezekiel, Luke, Romans and Revelation were all part of a bigger picture.

Then, through a certain set of circumstances, I made contact with a Plymouth Brethren family who began to mentor me and who provided me a copy of a fascinating book, *Dispensational Truth* by Clarence Larkin. The book contained page after page of hand-drawn charts and accompanying explanations, showing in intricate detail exactly how the whole Bible fit together and even how all of history from "eternity past" to "eternity future" fit into what the Bible taught. I devoured Larkin's book just as I had previously devoured the Bible and Scofield's notes, and everything finally came together!

Little did I suspect that this process had programmed me with one particular framework of biblical interpretation that not everyone else in the body of Christ agreed with. The church I finally joined, New Brunswick Bible Church, did follow Scofield and Larkin. I enrolled in Fuller Seminary, and my English Bible professor, Wilbur M. Smith, agreed as well. The mission board under which I first went to Bolivia, South America Indian Mission, fit the same mold. I found myself a thoroughgoing dispensationalist! To all intents and purposes, the tenets of dispensationalism reflected to me the true Word of God.

Dispensationalism

Dispensationalism teaches that God's design for creating the earth and the human race, from beginning to end, revolved around seven dispensations: the Age of Innocence (Gen. 1-3), the Age of Conscience (Gen. 3-8), the Age of Civil Government (Gen. 9-11), the Patriarchal Age (Gen. 12-Exod. 19), the Age of Law (Exod. 20 to Pentecost), the Age of the Church (Pentecost to the rapture), and the Millennial Kingdom (Rev. 20 onward). In each one of the dispensations, God entered into certain covenantal relationships with human beings that usually were broken, precipitating the next dispensation. My purpose here is not to detail the intricacies of dispensationalism but to explain the paradigm of eschatology, or the doctrine of the end times, with which I became programmed early in my Christian life.

We dispensationalists were known as pre-tribulationists and pre-millennialists, or pre-trib and pre-mil for short. What does this mean? The theological term for this is the futurist view of eschatology. It was introduced in the late 1800s by John Darby of England and then picked up by C. I. Scofield and many others, permeating much of American evangelicalism in the 1900s.

Dispensationalists believe that the world will continue to get worse and worse. We can expect nation to rise up against nation, earthquakes and famines, wars and rumors of wars, persecution of believers, exponential increase in wickedness, through which the true church survives, barely hanging on as a faithful remnant of God. Finally, when God decides that enough is enough, He will rapture the church, taking every true believer from earth to heaven without passing through death. Then comes a seven-year Great Tribulation, when Antichrist and the False Prophet will take over and produce the most miserable epoch of depravity that the human race has known. At the end of the seven years, the notorious battle of Armageddon will erupt, and Jesus will emerge victorious. He will then rule the world for a millennium (1,000 years) of peace, and we will rule with Him. Satan will then rise up again, but he and his demons will be cast into the lake of fire and consumed once and for all. Then the people of God will end up in the New Jerusalem forever.

When you read this, you can see that it makes an appealingly neat package, and you can be assured that numerous selected Bible verses would back up each step. We were called pre-tribulationists because we believed that the church would be raptured before the Great Tribulation. We were called pre-millennialists because we believed that Jesus would come back to earth before the millennium. We prayed, "Your kingdom come, Your will be done on earth as it is in heaven" (Matt. 6:10), but we believed that the prayer we prayed would only be fulfilled when the millennium arrived sometime in the future, not before.

The Role of Believers

To get more to the point, what is the role of believers in the world under this futurist view of eschatology? First and foremost, it is to preach the gospel to as many people as possible, to save as many souls as possible and to do this quickly, because no one knows when Jesus might come and rapture the church. It could be today, and woe to those who are left behind! As far as society is concerned, we wait. We have faith. We have hope. Someday Jesus will come and bring righteousness to earth, all in God's sovereign timing.

Remember, for most of my career as a Christian leader, I held the futurist view. It carries some very positive aspects, not the least of which is the urgent call for evangelism and world missions. The unprecedented surge of the missionary movement during the twentieth century and the explosive growth of world Christianity was significantly fueled by futurists. For example, the Pentecostal Movement turned out to be the strongest driving force for world missions during the last century, and virtually all Pentecostals would be what theologians would call eschatological futurists. Eschatological futurists view all the end-time prophecies in the future tense, and I was one of them.

With all this, then, why change a paradigm? Well, the Bible says that "we know in part" (1 Cor. 13:9). In other words, nobody knows everything, and I believe that this applies especially to the field of eschatology. Good people have good biblical and practical reasons for holding each one of the three main views: futurist, preterist and partial preterist. I will soon explain why I switched from being futurist to partial preterist. I personally think the partial preterist view is the best way to understand what the Bible teaches about the future, but I also respect those who have come to other conclusions. As a matter of fact, I strongly suspect that God never intended for any of us to have a completely detailed and accurate road map of where He is taking the human race. Lee Grady puts it well when he warns us against becoming infected with "last days fever."[1]

I have already explained the futurist position in some detail. The word "preterist' means past. The *full preterist* view believes that all the end-time prophecies of the Bible have already been fulfilled, including the marriage feast of the Lamb, Jesus' appearance on a white horse, the resurrection of the dead, the separation of the sheep and goat nations, the new heaven and new earth, and several other things that seem to others like they still belong in the future. *Partial preterists* agree that much end-time prophecy has, indeed, been fulfilled, but that some things, including those that I just mentioned, are still in the future. I do not believe that I need to give details as to why I disagree with full preterism, but I will mention that my good friend John Eckhardt espouses this position and explains it quite thoroughly in his book *Come Quickly, Lord Jesus*.

Shifting the Paradigm

Shifting out of the futurist understanding of eschatology was a long, though rather painless, process for me. While in Bolivia, I taught systematic theology in seminary, and I presented the standard futurist view of eschatology. As time went on, however, I felt myself harboring a few doubts as to whether dispensationalism might really be as air-tight an explanation of God's plan for the human race as C. I. Scofield and Clarence Larkin supposed it was. I never attempted to specialize in eschatology, so the subject always was a rather low priority for me. Furthermore, pre-millennialism happened to be embedded in my mission's statement of faith, and I was in no mood for a quarrel of any kind over a matter that I considered fairly insignificant. In fact, I never recall waking up in the morning sincerely believing that Jesus might return that very day!

When I began my second career, teaching at Fuller Seminary, my subjects were missiology and church growth. Over the years I saw no need of bringing eschatology into the picture, so I put the matter on the back burner and gave it little thought.

Things first began to change, however, when I became involved in spiritual warfare back in the early 1990s, as I related in chapter 7, "From Tolerating Satan to a Declaration of War." Instead of just sitting back and allowing Satan to have free rein in promoting his schemes of wickedness and injustice, I learned that God had provided powerful weapons of spiritual warfare that He expected us to use against the principalities of darkness to help neutralize the enemy's evil advances. As we moved out, we discovered that if we used these weapons broadly enough and effectively enough, whole previously unreached people groups could break Satan's stranglehold and receive messengers of the gospel or the good news. This planted some doubts in my mind as to whether the world was supposed to get worse and worse in preparation for the rapture.

These doubts escalated significantly around the turn of the century, give or take a couple of years on both sides. That is when I began adopting many of the new paradigms that I have been discussing, such as the kingdom of God, the church in the workplace and reforming society. One after the other had as its driving force a vision for the world to get better and better, not worse and worse. By that time, whenever I thought about eschatology, I realized that I could no longer remain a dispensationalist. However, I avoided discussing the matter with anyone because I had a real problem: I knew what I was *not*, but I did not yet know what I *was*! This was embarrassing, especially for someone who had the reputation of being a scholar! However, as I wrote before, eschatology had never been my forte.

Victorious Eschatology

The tipping point came when, in 2006, my friend Harold Eberle gave me a copy of a book that he, along with Martin Trench, had just published, *Victorious Eschatology*. Reading that book produced one of those unforgettable experiences when, page after page, new lights began to go on in my mind. By the time I had finished the book, I finally knew what I *was*—a partial preterist, like Harold Eberle! Here is his vision: "The eschatological view presented in this book reveals that the kingdom of God will grow and advance until it fills the earth. The church will rise in unity, maturity, and glory before the return of Jesus. We will present to you a victorious eschatology."[2]

I agree because this statement accurately reflects the dominion mandate, or the literal interpretation of the Great Commission that tells us to make disciples of whole nations. A futurist eschatology that expects to escape from the world through a rapture of the church does not fit this viewpoint. I like the way that Mark Pfeifer puts it: "The church is not sitting around *waiting* for the return of Jesus. It is *working* for the return of Jesus. It is the job of the redeemed sons and daughters of God to make disciples of every nation and prepare the earth for His return."[3]

The two most detailed biblical passages concerning the end times are Matthew 24–25, commonly called the Olivet Discourse, and the book of Revelation. Let me explain how they reflect victorious eschatology, with thanks to Harold Eberle, who provided me with many of these thoughts.

The Olivet Discourse

Starting with the Olivet Discourse, here is where Jesus mentions a series of cataclysmic events, such as the sun's being darkened, thunder and lightning, earthquakes, the appearance of false messiahs and false prophets, wars and rumors of wars, the Great Tribulation, and things like that. Previously I relegated all of that to the future. Still, I was always puzzled by this statement from Jesus: "Assuredly,

I say to you, this generation will by no means pass away till all these things take place" (Matt. 24:34). By itself, this seems like a clear declaration that the people listening to Him would actually experience these things in their lifetime.

At the beginning of Matthew 24, we get a closer look: "Then Jesus went out and departed from the temple, and His disciples came up to show Him the buildings of the temple" (v. 1). It is good to understand that this was the real temple in Jerusalem that they were looking at. What did Jesus say? "Do you not see all these things? Assuredly, I say to you, not one stone shall be left here upon another, that shall not be thrown down" (v. 2). Nothing could be clearer. The sacred temple itself was to be completely destroyed.

Next, Jesus went to the Mount of Olives, where we get the term "Olivet Discourse." They could see the temple from there. The disciples were puzzled, so here is what they asked Jesus: "Tell us, when will these things be? And what will be the sign of Your coming, and of the end of the age?" (v. 3). This is where Harold Eberle helped me a great deal. He points out that the disciples asked Jesus three questions: (1) When will these things happen, including the destruction of the temple He had just told them about? (2) What will be the sign of Jesus' coming? (3) When would the end of the world come? In the Olivet Discourse, Jesus answers all three questions.

1. *The things that Jesus said would happen in that generation did (see Matt. 24:4-28).* The persecution began when Rome was burned in AD 64. Nero initiated seven years of tribulation, climaxed by the destruction of Jerusalem in AD 70. This wasn't something for the distant future—many of the people who actually saw Jesus were wiped out by the Roman attack.

2. *The signs of this destruction are presented in Matthew 24:29-34.* Eberle and Trench describe how every one of the signs was literally fulfilled during the Roman massacre. I won't detail them all here, but I will try to help us understand the diabolical anti-Semitism by a series of quotes from the book. First, "20,000 Roman soldiers, under the command of General Titus, surrounded the

city and cut off all supplies of food for four months so the people would starve. Then the soldiers came into the city and mercilessly killed more than one million Jews. The soldiers set the Temple on fire and led away 97,000 Jews as captives."[4] Next, "The Roman commander ordered the Temple in Jerusalem to be demolished so completely that each and every stone was carried away and the land upon which the Temple had stood was plowed over completely."[5] Finally, "[Josephus] narrates a vile account of a [Jewish] woman murdering her small son, cooking him, and eating half of him, then arguing with thieves, who broke into her house looking for food, as to who would eat the other half."[6] These are just samples of this abomination of desolation!

3. *The "end of the age" did not take place then (as full preterists would argue).* It is future, and it is covered in Matthew 24:35–25:46, the rest of the Olivet Discourse. Please notice that Jesus changes the subject in Matthew 24:35: "Heaven and earth will pass away, but My words will by no means pass away." This refers to when Jesus Himself returns to earth. Unlike the destruction of Jerusalem, there are no signs for this one: "Of that day and hour no one knows, not even the angels of heaven, but My Father only" (Matt. 24:36). While there are no specific signs, certain things still must happen before Jesus will come again, as we will soon see.

The Book of Revelation

The most important question for interpreting the book of Revelation has always been when it was written. At this time, I do not intend to deal with the details of the content of Revelation, but I do want to give my opinion about the date. I don't profess any scholarly expertise on Revelation, but I have checked the writings of a good number of heavyweight scholars. It turns out that some of them conclude from the evidence that John wrote Revelation during the reign of Emperor Nero when Rome burned in AD 64. Nero used

Christians as the scapegoats and launched a great anti-Christian persecution. Other scholars, emphasizing different evidence, argue that Revelation was not written until the reign of Emperor Domitian, around AD 95. As far as fixing the date is concerned, there is no clear winner. However, as you can see, the dates are 30 years apart. The significant thing for biblical interpretation is that one date occurs before the destruction of Jerusalem in AD 70 and the other after its destruction.

I personally side with those scholars who arrive at the earlier date. All things considered, it is the only date that fits what I just explained from the Olivet Discourse in Matthew 24–25. Once we are comfortable with this, we can then understand that much of the content of the book of Revelation was actually fulfilled during the destruction of Jerusalem in AD 70, although, as we partial preterists believe, much is yet to be fulfilled in the future. If you are interested in reading more about the content of Revelation, I strongly recommend Eberle and Trench's *Victorious Eschatology*, which I have been referencing.

Our Finest Hour Is Coming

The major change in my personal paradigm shift was to look toward the future and believe that the power of God is active, the kingdom of God is advancing, and the people of God are being prepared for their finest hour. Satan has had too much dominion over this earth for too long a time. Let's look at what the Scriptures say.

First Corinthians 15:24 begins, "Then comes the end." This is what we mean by "eschatology." "When He [Jesus] delivers the kingdom to God the Father." If Jesus delivers the Kingdom, the implication is that God's kingdom has by then indeed come, and His will is actually being done here on earth as it is in heaven. "When He puts an end to all rule and all authority and all power." Jesus first came to earth and died on the cross to destroy the works of the devil, and this passage concerning the end times affirms that before it is all over, Jesus will have finished whatever it takes to destroy the works of the devil. This has not happened as yet. It is still sometime in the future.

Revelation 11:15 records the words of the seventh angel: "The kingdoms of this world have become the kingdoms of our Lord." Remember Jesus' third temptation, when Satan offered to give Him all the kingdoms of the world (see Matt. 4:8-9)? It was a legitimate offer because at that time Satan still had dominion over all the kingdoms. However, Jesus then died on the cross, rose again and gave the power of the Holy Spirit to His disciples in order to complete His Great Commission of making disciples of all the nations. Revelation 11:15 shows that by the end times, this will literally have happened. Satan will no longer rule; instead, "He [Jesus] shall reign forever and ever!"

In Acts 3:21, Peter is speaking to a crowd after he and John had healed the lame man at the temple gate. Not too long before that, Jesus had been raised from the dead, had spent 40 days with His disciples, and had been taken to heaven in a cloud. Peter now speaks of Jesus, "whom heaven must receive until . . ." Until when? Heaven had just received Jesus, but for how long? Jesus came to the earth once, but when would He come back? This is one of the most important eschatological questions of all, and Peter gives us the answer: "until the times of restoration of all things."

This is worth looking into for a moment. Jesus came to reconcile the world, which Satan had usurped from Adam, back to the Father. He gave the ministry, or the implementation, of that reconciliation to us, His disciples. Since Jesus died on the cross, huge progress has been made. The world and the quality of life of the human race is much better now than it was 2,000 years ago. One day the restoration of all things will be completed, but that day has not yet come. Jesus is still in heaven. Do you think He could come today? Not if we take this Scripture at face value, because all things have not yet been restored. This is one of the compelling reasons why I have found my old paradigm of futurist eschatology deficient.

This is my opinion:

- We do not need a *defeatist* eschatology; we need a *victorious* eschatology.
- We do not need a *negative* eschatology; we need a *positive* eschatology.
- We do not need an *escapist* eschatology; we need a *dominion* eschatology.
- We do not need a *passive* eschatology; we need an *active* eschatology.

There Is Work to Do!

I find it very interesting that Peter, in his second epistle, brings up the "day of the Lord," which "will come as a thief in the night, in which the heavens will pass away with a great noise, and the elements will melt with fervent heat" (2 Pet. 3:10). All this, of course, is painting the picture of the end times. As he writes this, Peter admonishes his readers not only to look for the coming day of God but also to hasten it (see v. 12). I take that to mean that we have work to do. If we do certain things, God's kingdom will advance more rapidly and Jesus will return sooner. Peter stresses our need for "holy conduct and godliness" (v. 11), which are essential starting points on which I elaborated in chapter 8, "From Reformed Sanctification to Wesleyan Holiness." However, our responsibility goes beyond that to active participation in fulfilling the dominion mandate.

We cannot afford to be passive and expect that things will somehow work out with or without us. God has given us the ministry of reconciliation, and we are to hasten the day when the reconciliation will be complete. The final victory will be ours, and our victorious eschatology will help point the way.

Notes

1. Lee Grady, "Fire in My Bones" (newsletter, August 25, 2009), p. 1.
2. Harold R. Eberle and Martin Trench, *Victorious Eschatology: A Partial Preterist View* (Yakima, WA: Worldcast Publishing, 2007), p. 1.
3. Mark W. Pfeifer, *Dominion Eschatology* (Chillicothe, OH: SOMA, 2008), p. 15. Emphasis in the original.
4. Eberle and Trench, *Victorious Eschatology*, p. 14.
5. Ibid., p. 15.
6. Ibid., p. 44.

17

From a **Spirit** of **Poverty** to a **Spirit** of **Prosperity**

I don't know if you've ever heard the vernacular expression from my generation, "So-in-so is as poor as a church mouse!" The meaning was that the person referenced would be about as poor as you could get. Why didn't they use "a house mouse," "a barn mouse," "a field mouse" or any mouse in general? It seems obvious that the person who coined the phrase wanted to choose the poorest environment, with the least resources, for the unfortunate mouse, so the church was the best candidate. It was a good choice because typically the church has indeed been considered an institution characterized by poverty.

The Spirit of Poverty

How did the church end up embracing poverty? I personally believe that embracing poverty is one of what the Bible calls "the wiles of the devil" (Eph. 6:11). Satan recognizes that it is to his advantage if the church is poor, and he assigned one of his most powerful principalities of darkness to oversee this delusion. As good a name as any for this demon might be the spirit of poverty. The main strategy that the spirit of poverty has used for centuries—and quite successfully, I might add!—is to plant the thought among believers that there is a positive correlation between piety and poverty. The idea is that full-time Christian ministers gain their status by their spirituality and that poverty is a commendable personal attribute for clergy.

Poverty as a virtue became institutionalized only after the Greek mindset, which I dealt with in chapter 10, began to permeate the thinking of the church back at the time of Emperor Constantine. Greek dualism separated the material world from the spiritual world and associated issues of wealth with the supposedly inferior material world. Truly spiritual people were to avoid a desire to accumulate wealth as much as possible. From this emerged the monastic movement, in which monks were required to authenticate their superior spirituality with vows of poverty.[1] Since then, unfortunately, poverty has persisted in the church as one of the characteristics of piety. The spirit of poverty has been having its way!

To get a bit theological, I will contend that poverty is *not* the will of God, for clergy or for anyone else. Take, for example, Deuteronomy 28. This is one of the earliest and longest chapters in the Bible. The first part (vv. 1-14) talks about prosperity, while the second part (vv. 15-68) talks about poverty. Prosperity is held up as a blessing: "The LORD will grant you abundant prosperity—in the fruit of your womb, the young of your livestock and the crops of your ground" (v. 11, *NIV*). Prosperity is the will of God. On the other hand, poverty is a curse: "Therefore you shall serve your enemies . . . in hunger, in thirst, in nakedness, and in need of everything" (v. 48). Poverty is the will of the devil. Additionally, in the New Testament, we read, "Beloved, I pray that you may prosper in all things" (3 John 2).

Our challenge is to use our weapons of spiritual warfare to bind the strongman, called the spirit of poverty, off our personal lives, our ministries and our environment and to invite the divine spirit of prosperity, as I like to call it, to take its place.

The Necessities of Life

I can speak directly to this because, for the first 40 years of my ministry, I was severely oppressed by the spirit of poverty. I was born one year after the Great Depression started, and our family got along on only the bare necessities of life, never a surplus. No sooner did the Depression end when World War II began, and America as a whole went on an austerity program, with the rationing of food, shoes, gasoline, and the like.

Then I became a student in college and seminary, most of the time not knowing how I was going to pay last week's bills. What did all of this prepare me for? Nothing less than 16 years as a field missionary in Bolivia, where living on a subsistence income was a sign of true obedience to God. We missionaries had to raise our own salaries, and I turned out to be a very mediocre fundraiser. Soon the spirit of poverty had become my friend and had convinced me that it would be wrong to live any kind of a life that might be tinged with prosperity.

In the early 1970s I left Bolivia and joined the faculty at Fuller Theological Seminary. I was in my 40s and, with a family of five, had no savings, no real estate, no investments and no retirement fund. I was able to sell some things as my family and I left Bolivia, enough for a down payment on a car. I was only able to purchase a house because some friends loaned me money for a down payment, interest-free. The salary I began receiving appeared astronomical to me—I think I would have worked for half of it!—but even once I found myself enjoying a decent cash flow, the spirit of poverty still gripped me, and I had little desire to spend what I earned.

Even though we lived in the heat of Southern California, I would not allow the family to have an automobile with air conditioning. I could afford department stores, but for years I insisted on buying my clothing used, from the Salvation Army thrift store. We were not poor, but somehow I could not shake off the ingrained idea that poverty would keep me closer to God.

Why a Change Was Needed

I did not consider the lifestyle I chose as any kind of personal hardship. It never bordered on suffering. Our family enjoyed life. I eventually allowed cars with air conditioning. If I were honest, I would be forced to suspect that all of this might well have elicited a bit of spiritual pride! Nevertheless, the pernicious spirit of poverty continued to dominate me until around the turn of the century.

What changed things? The change began to come after I was first introduced to several of the paradigms I have already written about, such as kingdom theology, ministry in the workplace and reforming society. It gradually became clear that transforming society costs money. Throughout human history, three things have transformed society more than anything else: violence, knowledge and wealth—and the greatest of these is wealth! Even the Bible says, "Money answers everything" (Eccles. 10:19). It was a tedious process, but I began admiring wealth for what it could do for God's kingdom, not scorning it as if it were a spiritual disease.

After some time, I began seeing how several pieces of the social transformation puzzle were fitting together, and I designed the following graphic:

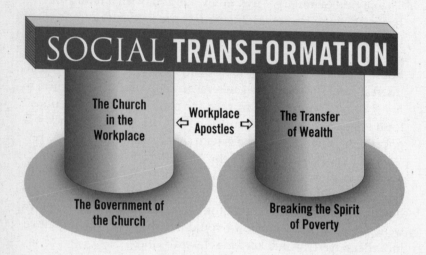

As you will see, this diagram relates to much more that I have been talking about in this book other than wealth, so let me explain. The centerpiece is the bar that reads "Social Transformation," which is the goal, covered in chapter 14. The bar stands on two pillars, and the more I work with this, the more I am convinced that these are the two main pillars: "The Church in the Workplace," which you will find in chapter 13; and "The Transfer of Wealth," which I will mention in this chapter. Each pillar has its foundation, without which the pillar could not stand. "The Church in the Workplace" stands on the foundation of "The Biblical Government of the Church," covered in chapter 9. "The Transfer of Wealth" stands on the foundation of "Breaking the Spirit of Poverty," which I am dealing with right now. The only component with arrows, indicating practical action, is "Workplace Apostles." I would go so far as to declare that we are not going to see sustained social transformation unless and until workplace apostles are properly activated, encouraged and aligned, and I say as much in chapter 13.

Issues concerning polluting "The Land" affect everything from the bottom up, and "The Cosmic Powers" try to nullify efforts toward Kingdom transformation from the top down. These are both spiritual enemies against which we are assigned to do battle, as I explain in chapter 7.

When I looked at this graphic, it became obvious to me that without breaking the grip that the spirit of poverty had maintained so strongly in my life, God could never use me effectively in championing the reformation of society or the advance of the Kingdom. Without that pillar, the whole structure would collapse. I knew I had to shift my paradigm, but I did not know what direction to take. Basically, I needed deliverance, which, praise God, eventually came.

Breaking the Curse!

The best I can recall, the curse of the spirit of poverty was broken off me in three steps.

The first step came through my friend Yonggi Cho of Korea, known as the pastor of the world's largest church. Several years previously we had first connected with each other. He had invited me to become a member of his Church Growth International board, so I visited Korea once a year for board meetings and his annual conference. Through a series of events, it turned out that in 1984 God used me to pray for a lady from his church who had flown over from Korea for that purpose with Cho's encouragement, and she was quite miraculously healed. Before she returned to Korea, she brought me the medical evidence of her rather dramatic healing and left me an envelope containing a generous sum of money. Not suspecting that the spirit of poverty was working behind the scenes, I took the money to church the next Sunday, told the people of the healing and piously put the cash in the offering box for the poor.

Remember that I just admitted that subjecting myself to the spirit of poverty tended to encourage spiritual pride? Well, this is a good example. I thought that I had acted so nobly by giving that money to the poor that I could hardly wait to get back to Korea and tell Cho. When I flew over and we spoke, I asked him how his church member was, and he told me that she was doing wonderfully. Then, in an attempt to score some points with the pastor of the largest church in the world, I tried to put on a humble tone of voice and told him how I decided to give her gift to me to the poor. Cho's response? I was shocked! He got a stern look on his face and said, "Peter, I am ashamed of you! If our sister wanted to give her money to the poor, she would have done it. She didn't want that money to go to the poor: she wanted to bless you personally! You violated the desire of her heart!" When he said that, I immediately knew that he was right. I knew he had pricked my pride balloon; I admitted I shouldn't have done it, and I decided not to do it again!

Even though I never forgot learning this lesson, it fell short of liberating me completely from the spirit of poverty. From then on I have kept personal gifts (although I do tithe from them), but I still imagined that there was something less than spiritual connected with a desire for prosperity. The change came 12 years later, in 1996, through my friend Bill Hamon. He was attending a high-level conference of Christian leaders that I was convening at Fuller Seminary.

I had known of Hamon's reputation as one of America's most respected prophets, but this was the first time we had met personally. Much to my surprise, on the second day Hamon told me that he wanted to meet with me in a side room during the break. When we did, he brought with him four or five colleagues from his apostolic network, Christian International. He said, "God has told me that I am to break off of you the spirit of poverty that you have had since your missionary days. Do you agree?" Rather stunned, I told him that I agreed. Bill immediately raised his voice to a high level and fervently began to pray a rather long prayer of deliverance from that demon of poverty, with all his friends verbally agreeing. In my spirit I felt that a change was taking place and that I was willing to let poverty go and to allow it to be replaced with a spirit of prosperity.

When Hamon finished, he took out a wad of cash from his pocket and held it over my head, encouraging his friends to do the same thing. He collected all their money, held it high and shouted, "Peter, this money is for you, and you alone! You are not to tithe it; you are not to give it away; you are to spend it only on you and your wife. This is a prophetic symbol that the spirit of poverty is now gone from you and will never return!" It worked! Since then I have welcomed prosperity and joyfully received it. The cash was $170; I took Doris out to a restaurant we could never otherwise have afforded; we wined and dined extravagantly; and I had been set free!

This could have been all, but God was good enough to give me one more confirmation. This came nine years later, in 2005, during an annual meeting of the International Coalition of Apostles, an organization that I was leading. The protagonist was once again Bill Hamon. At the conclusion of this meeting attended by several hundred apostles, Hamon took charge and had Doris and me sit on chairs at the front of the room. He reminded the crowd that I had been leading them for several years and had been taking no remuneration, but that this was the time to show their appreciation. He invited them to come forward and lay money at our feet, which they enthusiastically did. I went home with a pocketful of money.

When we landed in Colorado Springs, I said to Doris, "We're not going straight home. Instead, we're first going to the Toyota dealer." Her Toyota Camry was 10 years old and had over 100,000 miles on it. It was time for a new car. We went to the Toyota dealer and made a substantial down payment on a brand-new Camry from the gift we had received from the International Coalition of Apostles. The net result of that prophetic act persuaded me once and for all that the curse of the spirit of poverty was finally gone for good!

Inviting the Spirit of Prosperity

As radical as it may sound, I believe that God wants His people to be rich. Poverty is a characteristic of the kingdom of darkness. Prosperity is a characteristic of the kingdom of light. Heaven is, quite evidently, a prosperous place. Jesus once told us to ask the Father to have His will be done here on earth as it is in heaven (see Matt. 6:10). I think this implies that we should ask God to give us a divine spirit of prosperity.

Those of us who have come to an agreement that the essence of the Great Commission is to make disciples of whole nations, meaning reforming our society (see chapter 14), have also come to agreement on what our final, measureable goal should be. Reformation will take place only when we eradicate systemic poverty! When systemic poverty prevails, every baby born will be predestined by the surrounding social systems to be poor throughout life. This is not the will of God. This is not what heaven is like. The first change needs to be a move from poverty to sufficiency, but mere sufficiency is not the goal either. With sufficiency alone, a person cannot help others less fortunate, to say nothing about influencing positive changes in society as a whole.

Here is what the Bible says about prosperity: "You shall remember the LORD your God, for it is He who gives you power to get wealth, that He may establish His covenant" (Deut. 8:18). Obviously, according to this Scripture, God wants us to be wealthy, providing (1) we recognize that the ultimate source of our prosperity is God Himself and (2) the overriding purpose of the forthcoming wealth is to establish His covenant, which is Old Testament language for extending the kingdom of God. A prerequisite for receiving this spirit of prosperity is to be a Kingdom-minded and a Kingdom-motivated believer.

In the New Testament, Paul speaks of the grace of Christ, who "though He was rich, yet for your sakes He became poor, that you through His poverty might become rich" (2 Cor. 8:9). Let me say two things about this Scripture. First, Jesus' becoming poor is a reference to His incarnation. Poverty is relative. Most poor people in Sudan, for example, wish they could be as "rich" as poor people in the United States. An African friend of mine once said, "I love America—it is the only place I know of where poor people are fat!" For Jesus, life on earth was poor only compared to life in heaven.

Having said that, however, let's not persist in the common mistake of imagining that Jesus lived in earthly poverty while He was here. His father, Joseph, presumably was a skilled carpenter who had a small business and who made a respectable living for his family in Nazareth. True, Jesus was born in a stable, but not because His family was poor. When they arrived in Bethlehem, they first attempted to register in the equivalent of a Hilton, so they must have had the money necessary to pay the bill.

Soon after that, the three wise men showed up and brought gifts extravagant enough to honor an Eastern monarch. Some scholars have estimated the value as several million of today's U.S. dollars. However much it was, it at least allowed Joseph to take his family on a two-year vacation to Egypt. During Jesus' ministry, He had no financial lack. He was accompanied by several women of means, one of whom was the wife of Herod's equivalent of Secretary of the Treasury. These women "provided for Him from their substance" (Luke 8:3). Jesus and His disciples did not make a connection between poverty and piety!

Second, one of the purposes of Jesus' incarnation was to enable His followers to "become rich" (2 Cor. 8:9). The Greek word for "rich" is *plouteo,* which means, according to Strong, "increased with goods."[2] In this context it does not mean spiritually, psychologically or socially enriched, as some preaching on this verse (influenced, I believe, by the spirit of poverty) might indicate. The lexicon places *plouteo* in the area of material wealth, money or abundance. This is why I was bold enough to begin this section by suggesting that God wants us to be rich.

Prosperity Must Not Be Abused

Good things can be abused. Eating can be abused, drinking can be abused, sex can be abused, and also wealth can be abused. One of the most ubiquitous promoters of the abuse of wealth is a demonic principality named Mammon. We easily recall Jesus' words: "No one can serve two masters; for either he will hate the one and love the other, or else he will be loyal to the one and despise the other. You cannot serve God and mammon" (Matt. 6:24).

The *New Living Translation* and the *English Standard Version* both use "money" instead of "mammon." This is an unfortunate mistake by the translators, some of whom were probably influenced by the spirit of poverty. Mammon is not a synonym of money. In fact "mammon" in my *New King James Version* really should have been translated with a capital *M,* because it is the proper name of an evil spirit like Apollyon, Beelzebub or Baal.

I think that Mammon works in conjunction with a number of other wealth-abusing demons, such as the spirit of greed (an excessive desire for material possessions), the spirit of covetousness (a lust for forbidden things), the spirit of parsimony (stinginess and hoarding), and the spirit of self-reliance (personal pride in acquisitions). One of the tactics of Mammon is also to empower the spirit of poverty. If we are Kingdom-minded, we will not allow any of these pernicious forces of darkness to gain a foothold in our lives.

The Prosperity Gospel

A generation ago a significant step forward towards opening the doors for the spirit of prosperity was the Word of Faith Movement, led by such as Kenneth Hagin, Kenneth Copeland, Fred Price, and others. Unfortunately, some of the pioneers succumbed to the tactics of Mammon that I just described, fell into a distasteful public display of opulence, boasted of their superior faith as measured by their visible accumulation of wealth, and incurred the displeasure of large numbers of recognized Christian leaders.

That was the bad news. The good news is that they did help change attitudes toward wealth, and now the second-generation Word of Faith leaders have learned from their predecessors and, by and large, have avoided their excesses. Even some first-generation leaders are now receiving long-due recognition. I would argue, for example, that for 20 years Fred Price of Crenshaw Christian Center in Los Angeles brought more African-Americans out of poverty than the city and county governments combined! I was disappointed by a recent prestigious public statement that condemned the prosperity gospel as a "false gospel." The statement misrepresented its proponents, whose "practices and lifestyle are often unethical and un-Christlike" and who "replace the call to repentance with the call to give money to the preacher's organization."[3] This unkindly caricature of biblical prosperity is highly offensive to our current generation of Word of Faith leaders, and I believe it plays into the hands of the spirit of poverty.

Philip Jenkins, professor of history at Penn State University, has made a tremendous contribution by researching and reporting the explosion of Christianity in what he calls the Global South in his books *The New Christendom* and *The New Faces of Christianity*. On the subject of poverty and prosperity, Jenkins reports, "Around the world, many highly successful churches teach some variant of the gospel of prosperity, the controversial belief that Christians have the right and duty to seek prosperity in this world, to obtain health and wealth here and now."[4]

He goes on to mention my friend David Oyedepo of Nigeria, who regularly fills his 50,000-seat sanctuary to overflowing with believers and their families who have broken the curse of the spirit of poverty and have been set free from bonds of systemic poverty.

Oyedepo "claims a divine mandate to 'make My people rich.'"[5] In analyzing why such a thing might be so controversial, Jenkins writes, "However sincere their complaints, leaders of old established churches have a vested interest in painting their prosperity-oriented rivals in the bleakest and most mercenary terms, precisely because they are such successful competitors for the souls of the faithful"[6]

I am encouraged. God's people are moving into a new season when, instead of being "as poor as a church mouse," they are believing that God will give them the power to get wealth for the purpose of extending the kingdom of God, reforming their society and seeing the Lord's prayer, "Your kingdom come, Your will be done on earth as it is in heaven" (Matt. 6:10), answered.

Conclusion

To conclude this chapter, as well as the book, please allow me to recommend taking seriously the three steps commonly attributed to John Wesley:

1. *"Earn all you can."* Don't be lazy. Develop a solid work ethic. Serve your employer so well that you land at the top of the list for promotions. Make profitable investments. Set as a goal owning your own company. Strive for five independent streams of income for you and your family. Expect a high salary, and always believe it can be increased.

2. *"Save all you can."* David Oyedepo of Nigeria expects all of his church members to save 10 percent of their income, and most of them do. In order to help facilitate this, his church, Winners Chapel, has founded its own corruption-free bank, protecting parishioners from the greed-infested and corruption-riddled national banking system. John Wesley would have loved it! I dare say that you could save more than you are currently saving if you set your mind to it.

3. *"Give all you can."* John Wesley applied this. It is said that his only personal possessions when he died were a

silver spoon plus some coins found in his pocket and in his dresser drawer. Please establish an airtight giving lifestyle, characterized by tithe (the first 10 percent of your income), offerings (gifts over and above the tithe), alms (giving directly to the poor), and firstfruits (extra giving over and above the other three, as God bestows His blessings on you). The Bible says, "Give, and it will be given to you" (Luke 6:38). If you give extravagantly and cheerfully, you can expect to dismiss the spirit of poverty and welcome the spirit of prosperity into your life and into your community!

Notes

1. It is interesting to note that, while the personal spirituality of monks was supposedly enhanced by the vow of poverty, the monastic orders themselves had no aversion to accumulating vast amounts of wealth. For example, sociologist Rodney Stark reports, "Throughout the medieval era, the church was by far the largest landowner in Europe, and its liquid assets and annual income far surpassed not only those of the wealthiest king, but probably those of all of Europe's nobility added together." *The Victory of Reason: How Christianity Led to Freedom, Capitalism, and Western Success* (New York: Random House Trade Paperbacks, 2005), p. 58.
2. James Strong, *Strong's Exhaustive Concordance*, s.v. *plouteo*, Greek #4147.
3. "The Cape Town Commitment: A Confession of Faith and a Call to Action," *International Bulletin of Missionary Research* (April 2011), p. 77.
4. Philip Jenkins, *The New Faces of Christianity: Believing the Bible in the Global South* (New York: Oxford University Press, 2006), p. 90.
5. Ibid., p. 91.
6. Ibid., p. 94.

Scripture Index

Genesis 1-3; 196
Genesis 1:28; 143, 177
Genesis 2:15; 167
Genesis 3; 178
Genesis 3-8; 196
Genesis 6; 178
Genesis 6:5, 144
Genesis 6:6, 144
Genesis 9-11; 196
Genesis 12-Exodus 19; 196
Exodus 20; 196
Deuteronomy 8:18; 214
Deuteronomy 28; 208
Deuteronomy 28:1-14; 208
Deuteronomy 28:11; 208
Deuteronomy 28:15-68; 208
2 Kings 20:1; 144
2 Kings 20:5-6; 144
Psalm 24:1; 154
Psalm 90:10; 9
Psalm 103:12; 111
Proverbs 6:16-19; 144
Ecclesiastes 10:19; 209
Isaiah 9:6; 96
Jeremiah 18:7-10; 135, 145
Ezekiel 28:14; 177
Daniel 10:13; 157
Daniel 10:20; 91
Nahum 1:3; 144
Matthew 2:2; 27, 152
Matthew 3:2; 152
Matthew 4:8; 178
Matthew 4:8-9; 204
Matthew 4:9; 178
Matthew 4:17; 152

Matthew 4:23; 83
Matthew 5:13-16; 170
Matthew 6:9-13; 111
Matthew 6:10; 135, 152, 171, 181, 197, 213, 217
Matthew 6:13; 111
Matthew 6:24; 215
Matthew 6:33; 153
Matthew 10:1; 156
Matthew 10:7; 152
Matthew 10:34; 96, 155
Matthew 11:12; 96, 155, 158
Matthew 13; 152
Matthew 13:54-58; 26
Matthew 16; 155
Matthew 16:18; 149, 153, 164
Matthew 16:19; 153, 155
Matthew 24-25; 200, 203
Matthew 24:1; 201
Matthew 24:2; 201
Matthew 24:3; 201
Matthew 24:4-28; 201
Matthew 24:29-34; 201
Matthew 24:34; 201
Matthew 24:35; 202
Matthew 24:35-25:46; 202
Matthew 24:36; 202
Matthew 26:39; 147
Matthew 27:46; 27
Matthew 28:19; 57, 97, 173, 174
Matthew 28:20; 55
Mark 1:24; 156
Mark 1:27; 156
Mark 4:3-20; 58
Mark 5:6; 27

Mark 13; 20
Mark 13:32; 22, 27
Mark 16:15; 77, 97, 163, 174
Luke 1:44; 8
Luke 2:11; 151
Luke 2:49; 26
Luke 6:38; 218
Luke 7:28; 154
Luke 8:3; 215
Luke 9:1-2; 83
Luke 10:2; 59
Luke 10:9; 83, 152
Luke 10:17; 154
Luke 10:19; 98
Luke 10:24; 154
Luke 11:11,13; 110
Luke 11:20; 26
Luke 15:4; 61
Luke 17:2; 74
Luke 17:21; 153, 180
Luke 19:10; 97, 180
Luke 23:46; 27
Luke 24:47; 174
Luke 24:49; 61
John 1:1,14; 21
John 1:29; 151
John 2:23; 83
John 3:3; 103
John 4:39-42; 71
John 5:19; 26
John 5:22; 26
John 5:30; 26
John 9:38; 27
John 10:18; 27
John 12:50; 27
John 14:12; 28
John 14:30; 178
John 16:8; 110
John 21:11; 61

Acts 1:3; 152
Acts 1:6; 27
Acts 1:7; 28
Acts 1:8; 174, 181
Acts 3:21; 204
Acts 8:6; 83
Acts 8:7; 83
Acts 8:12; 83, 152
Acts 10; 71
Acts 10:38; 25
Acts 11; 71
Acts 11:19; 71
Acts 13:46; 72
Acts 15; 15, 17
Acts 15:13; 17
Acts 15:19; 17, 72
Acts 19; 159
Acts 19:8; 152, 158
Acts 19:10; 158
Acts 19:11-12
Acts 21:8; 83
Acts 28:31; 152
Romans 6:23; 103
Romans 7:15; 102
Romans 8; 102
Romans 12; 33, 37
Romans 12:2; 14, 17, 35, 127
Romans 12:6; 35
Romans 15:18-19; 84
1 Corinthians 4:4; 123
1 Corinthians 4:16; 123
1 Corinthians 7:7; 38
1 Corinthians 9:2; 124
1 Corinthians 12; 33, 37
1 Corinthians 12:1; 30
1 Corinthians 12:7; 35
1 Corinthians 12:18; 35, 122
1 Corinthians 12:28; 123, 169
1 Corinthains 12:29-30; 122

1 Corinthians 13:3; 38
1 Corinthians 13:9; 198
1 Corinthians 15:45; 180
1 Corinthians 15:45,47; 24
2 Corinthians 4:3-4; 97
2 Corinthians 4:4; 178
2 Corinthians 5:18; 181
2 Corinthians 5:19; 180
2 Corinthians 8:9; 214, 215
2 Corinthians 9:7; 144
2 Corinthians 10:3; 98
2 Corinthians 10:4; 98
2 Corinthians 10:8; 124
Galatians 2:7-8; 72
Galatians 2:11-13; 16
Galatians 2:14; 72
Galatians 3:1; 16
Galatians 5:2; 72
Ephesians 1:22-23; 34
Ephesians 2:2; 178
Ephesians 2:3; 179
Ephesians 2:20; 169
Ephesians 3:6-9; 38
Ephesians 3:10; 99
Ephesians 4; 33, 37, 166
Ephesians 4:11; 169
Ephesians 4:12; 46, 165
Ephesians 6:11; 105, 154, 169, 207
Ephesians 6:12; 91, 98, 157

Philippians 2; 23
Philippians 2:5-8; 23
Philippians 2:8; 27
Philippians 2:13; 39
Colossians 1:19-20; 181
Colossians 1:24; 34
Colossians 2:21-22; 109
Colossians 3; 109
1 Timothy 3:1-7; 48
1 Timothy 3:2; 123
Titus 1:5-9; 48
Hebrews 5:8; 26
Hebrews 11:6; 144
James 2:17-18; 107
James 3:1; 123
James 4:7-8; 106
1 Peter 1:15; 106, 107, 110
1 Peter 4:9; 38
1 Peter 4:10; 35
2 Peter 2:11; 205
2 Peter 2:12; 205
2 Peter 3:10; 205
1 John 1:9; 111
1 John 3:8; 180
3 John 2; 208
Revelation 2:7; 66
Revelation 11:15; 203, 204
Revelation 12:12; 158
Revelation 20; 196

Subject Index

120 Fellowship Sunday School, 107

7-M Template, 185, 189

abortion, 7-8

Abraham (biblical), 131, 136, 154

Adam (biblical), 24-25, 89, 102, 103, 107, 142, 143, 144, 166, 176, 177, 178, 179-180, 204

Africa(n), 12, 86, 116, 120, 121, 214, 216

African Independent Churches, 116, 120

Ahn, Apostle Ché, 49, 50

Alexander the Great, 128

American Family Association, 187

American Independent Charismatic Movement, 120

American Jewish community, 133

Anaheim Vineyard, 82

Andes, 81

Andrew (disciple), 20

Annacondia, Carlos, 85

Anointed for Business, 163, 164

anthropology, 9, 42, 68, 131

anthropomorphisms, 145

Antichrist, 191, 197

antiwar movement, 93-94, 95, 96, 97

apartheid, 15

Apostolic Council for Educational Accountability (ACEA), 49, 50

Apostolic Intercessory Network (AIN), 194

apostolic sphere, 124, 186

Apostolic-Prophetic Movement, 169

Aquinas, Thomas, 130

Arabic, 74

Aramaic, 26

Aristotle, 128, 129

Armageddon, 197

Arminianism, 142

Arts and Entertainment Mountain, 187, 193

ascension, 152

Ashamed of the Gospel, 62

Assemblies of God, 120, 121

atonement, 103, 138, 140

Augustine, 130

authoritarianism, 122

Authority to Tread, 158

avodah, 167

Baal, 193, 215

Babylonian Empire, 128

Bakke, Ray, 151

Barna, George, 44, 62, 108

Barnabas (biblical), 15, 16, 17, 71

Barrett, David, 86

Beckett, John, 166

Bible Institute of Los Angeles (Biola), 30, 41

biblical holiness, 108, 110

Billy Graham Crusades, 80

Billy Graham Evangelistic Association, 57, 77

Body Life, 32
Boyd, Greg, 142, 146, 147, 179
Breaking the Bonds of Evil, 157
Bridges of God, The, 53, 55
Bright, Bill, 77, 78, 185
Brown, Colin, 24, 25
Brown, Rick, 73, 74
Business Mountain, 186, 193
Cabrera, Omar, 85, 90
Calvin, John, 32, 102, 137, 143
Calvinism/Calvinist(ic), 102,
    138, 139, 140, 141, 142
Campus Crusade for Christ, 77
Carey, William, 114
Carnell, Edward John, 23, 24
Catholic(s), 66, 78, 107, 113, 117
cessationist/cessationism, 80,
    81, 82, 89, 134
charis, 35
charisma, 35
charismatic(s), 36, 37, 58, 86,
    87, 117, 118, 120, 162
China/Chinese, 13, 26, 70, 84,
    85, 86, 116, 121
Chinese house church, 120
Cho, David Yonggi, 84, 91, 211,
    212
Christian and Missionary Al-
    liance, 120
Christian Business Men's Com-
    mittee, 162
Christian International, 212
Christian perfection, doctrine
    of, 105
Christianity in Culture, 10, 127
Christianity Today, 74, 142, 146
Christianizing the Roman Empire,
    159

Christology, 24, 25
Church Growth International,
    211
Church in the Workplace, The, 168
Church of God, 105
Church of the Nazarene, 105
*Church on Sunday, Work on Mon-
    day*, 167
circumcise(d)/circumcision, 15,
    16, 17, 71, 72, 124
Clinton, Bobby, 35, 36
Cochabamba, Bolivia, 43, 78
Come Quickly, Lord Jesus, 198
Congregationalists, 116, 120
Congress on World Evangeliza-
    tion, 90
Constantine, 207
contextualization, 70-71, 72,
    116
convergence, 35, 36, 37
Cook, Bruce, 153
Copeland, Kenneth, 216
Cornelius (biblical), 25, 71
corporate spirit of religion, 93,
    94
Corumbá, Brazil, 11
Costa, Paul, 78
Council of Jerusalem, 16, 72, 74
Crenshaw Christian Center,
    216
cross-culture/cultural, 9, 42,
    65-75
Crusaders Ministry, 94
Cullmann, Oscar, 91
cultural, 11, 66, 117, 129, 133,
    167, 187
    anthropology, 9, 42, 68
    boundaries, 183

counter-, 108
gap, 15, 168, 170
mandate, 150-151
paradigms, 9-11
rulebooks, 188-189
Cultural Revolution, 84, 116
Cunningham, Loren, 185
Damascus Road, 15
Daniel (biblical), 157
Darby, John, 196
Dawson, John, 91, 156, 176
Daystar Church (Atlanta), 193
Decker, Ken, 31
Decker, Ruth, 31
Deliver Us from Evil, 157
democracy, 34, 114, 115, 119, 120
diakonia, 166
dialectical method, 129
Diana (goddess), 159, 160
Dictionary of Pentecostal and Charismatic Movements, 117
dispensation(s), 196
Dispensational Truth, 195
dispensationalist/dispensation-alism, 196-197, 199
divine nature, 19, 20, 21, 22, 23, 25
Does God Have a Future? 146
dominion eschatology, 204
dominion mandate, 176-177, 180, 184, 191, 200, 205
Domitian, 203
dualism, 129-130, 132, 207
Eastern Bible Institute (*Instituto Bíblico del Oriente*), 42
Eastern Orthodox, 32
Eastern religions, 92, 157

Eberle, Harold, 143, 200, 201, 203
ecclesia, 164, 165
ecclesiastical sphere, 124
ecclesiology, 151
Eckhardt, John, 94, 95, 198
Education Mountain, 186, 187, 188, 193
Edwards, Jonathan, 32
Egyptian Empire, 128
election, 138, 140
Elizabeth (biblical), 8
Emmaus Bible Institute, 43, 44
Engaging the Enemy, 91
Enlightenment, the, 93
Enlow, Johnny, 193, 194
Episcopalians, 29
eradicated/eradication, 103-104, 105, 213
Eternity (magazine), 31
ethnic sphere, 124
ethnocentric, 16
evangelical, 21, 29, 30, 31, 32, 33, 37, 41, 42, 45, 58, 78, 79, 80, 102, 117, 150, 162, 191
Evangelical Theological Society (ETS), 146
evangelicalism, 196
evangelistic mandate, 150, 151
Eve (biblical), 89, 107, 143, 166, 176, 177, 178
extended church, 165, 167, 168, 169-170, 188
Faith at Work Movement, 162, 163
False Prophet, the, 197
Family Mountain, 187, 193
Femrite, Tommi, 193, 194

First Apostolic Age, 125

Focus on the Family, 187

Foster, Richard, 147

Fourth Dimension, The, 84

Freemasonry, 92, 157

Full Gospel Business Men's Fellowship International, 162

Fuller Evangelistic Association, 82

Fuller School of Theology, 46

Fuller School of World Mission, 80, 115, 130, 150

Fuller Theological Seminary, 22, 30, 41, 46, 54, 77, 209

functional sphere, 124

futurist, 196, 197, 198, 199, 200, 204

Gabriel (biblical), 157

Garden of Eden, 89, 142, 143, 167, 176, 177, 180

GateKeepers International, Colorado Springs, 193

Generals International, 105

Gentile(s), 15, 71, 72, 132

George Allan Theological Seminary, 44

Gilbert, P. J., 90

Glasser, Arthur F., 150

Global Dictionary of Theology, 90

Global Harvest Ministries, 184

Global South, 86, 87, 125, 155, 159, 216

Global Spheres, Inc., 94

Glory of Zion International, 37

God at War, 142, 179

God of the Possible, 142

Government Mountain, 186, 187, 193

Grady, Lee, 198

Graham, Billy, 57, 77, 78

Great Commission, 55, 57, 61, 77, 91, 92, 97, 173, 174, 175, 181, 183, 185, 200, 204, 213

Great Depression, 208

Great Tribulation, 197, 200

Greek(s)

    Empire, 128

    language, 43, 102, 108, 131, 164, 166, 175, 215

    mindset, 127-136, 167, 207

    mythology, 19, 73

    people, 129, 132, 135, 158

    philosophy, 128, 129

Green, Michael, 91

Greene, Mark, 167

Greenwood, Rebecca, 157, 158

Hagin, Kenneth, 216

hagios, 108-109

Hall, Christopher, 142, 146

Hammond, Frank, 156

Hamon, Bill, 50, 212, 213

Harvard University, 167

Hay, Alexander Rattray, 31, 32, 33

Hayford, Jack, 33, 91, 147, 156

Hebrew(s)

    culture, 12, 71, 131, 133

    language, 43, 108, 131, 167, 178

    mindset, 127-136, 166

    people, 129, 132, 134, 135, 167

Hellenists, 71

Henderson, Robert, 193, 194

Henry VIII, 113

hermeneutics, 43

Herod (biblical), 215

Hezekiah (bibilical), 144, 145

Hiebert, Paul, 130, 131
Holiness Movement, 104, 105, 109, 110, 191
Hollywood Presbyterian Church, 77
homogeneous unit principle, 68, 69
How to Cast Out Demons, 157
How to Have a Healing Ministry in Any Church, 83
Human Jesus Theory, 21
human nature, 19, 20, 21, 22, 23, 24, 25, 27, 28, 104
humanism, 129, 132
Hyde, Praying, 101
immutability, 138
impassibility, 138
incarnation, 19, 23, 24, 214, 215
Incarnation-theology theory, 22-24, 28
India(n), 60, 68, 130, 131, 175
Inter-Varsity Christian Fellowship, 29
International Coalition of Apostles, 44, 94, 122, 213
International Society of Deliverance Ministers, 157
Invading the Seven Mountains with Intercession, 194
Isaac (biblical), 136
Jacob (biblical), 136
Jacobs, Cindy, 50, 105, 156, 157, 158, 180
James (disciple), 20,
James of Jerusalem, 15, 16, 17, 71, 72, 152
Jehovah's Witnesses, 21

Jenkins, Philip, 86, 87, 125, 216, 217
Jerusalem Council, 15
Jews/Jewish, 15, 16, 17, 26, 71, 72, 124, 132, 133, 135, 151, 154, 158, 202
John (disciple), 20, 159, 160, 202, 204
John the Baptist, 8, 96, 152, 154, 155
Joseph (and Mary, biblical), 16, 24, 26, 214
Josephus, 202
Judaism, 16, 17, 72, 135,
Judaizers, 16, 17, 71-72,
kadosh, 108-109
Kelly, John, 94, 95
Key '73, 80
kingdom of God, 61, 75, 83, 86, 94, 95. 97, 103, 149, 150, 151, 152, 153, 154, 155, 156, 158, 160, 181, 183, 185, 186, 188, 193, 194, 199, 200, 203, 217
Korea(n), 68, 84, 86, 211
Kraft, Charles H. ("Chuck"), 10, 12, 66, 127
Larkin, Clarence, 195-196, 199
Latin America Mission, 78
Latin American Grassroots Churches, 117
Latter Rain, 120
Lausanne Committee for World Evangelization (LCWE), 90
Lausanne II (Congress on World Evangelization), 90-91
Lawrence, Carl, 85
Lawson, Apostle Leo, 49, 165

Lazarus (biblical), 21

legalism, 109-110,

Look Out! The Pentecostals Are Coming, 33, 82

Lord's Prayer, 111, 217

Luther, Martin, 32, 93, 102, 107, 137

Lutheran(s), 113, 116, 120, 137

Lutheran China Study Center, 85

MacArthur, John, 62

MacGorman, Jack, 161

MacMullen, Ramsay, 159, 160

Mammon, 193, 215, 216

Manila, Philippines, 90-91

Mao, 116

Mary (mother of Jesus), 8, 16, 19, 24, 26, 73

Mattera, Joe, 180

McGavran, Donald, 45, 46, 53, 54, 56, 68, 70, 79, 81, 175, 176

McLennan, Scotty, 167, 168

Media Mountain, 186, 187, 188, 193

Medo-Persian Empire, 128

Methodist(s), 106, 120

missiology/missiological, 17, 31, 42, 53, 54, 68, 70, 72, 73, 79, 116, 117, 120, 131, 151, 173, 176, 199

mission strategy, 31, 56-57

Modern Missionary Movement, 114

moral relativism, 129

Mormons, 21

Mosaic Law, 72

Mount of Olives, 20, 201

Mueller, George, 101

Muslim(s), 69, 70, 72, 73, 74, 86

Nash, Laura, 167, 168

Neocharismatics, 86

Nero, 201, 202

New Age, 92, 157

New Apostolic Reformation, 46, 48, 120, 121, 169, 186

New Brunswick Bible Church, 196

New Christendom, The, 86, 87, 216

New Faces of Christianity, The, 86, 87, 216

New Testament Missionary Union (NTMU), 31

New Testament Order for Church and Missionary, The, 31

Noah (biblical), 178

Nobel Prize, 133

Northern Baptist Seminary, 151

nuclear church, 165, 167, 168, 169, 170, 186, 188

occult, 92, 97, 98, 151, 156, 157, 159

Olivet Discourse, 200-202, 203

omnipotent/omnipotence, 138, 139

omnipresence, 138

omniscient/omniscience, 20, 22, 23, 138

original sin, 24, 103, 104, 178

Orthodox Church, 113

Osteen, Joel, 191

Otis, George Jr., 176

Our Kind of People: The Ethical Dimensions of Church Growth in America, 151

Oyedepo, David, 216, 217
Packer, J. I., 58
panta ta ethne, 175
Paul (biblical), 15, 16, 17, 30, 35, 71, 72, 83, 90, 98, 102, 109, 123, 124, 152, 157, 158-160, 164, 169, 179, 214
Peninsula Bible Church, 32
Penn State University, 86, 216
Pentecostal(s)/Pentecostalism, 29, 31, 33, 36, 80-81, 82, 86, 117, 198
Pentecostal Holiness, 105
Peter (disciple), 16, 17, 20, 25, 72, 124, 152, 153, 204, 205
Pfeifer, Mark, 191, 200
Philip (disciple), 83, 152
Pierce, Chuck, 50, 94, 95
Pinnock, Clark, 142, 146
Plato, 128, 129, 130, 131, 132, 167
plouteo, 215
Plymouth Brethren, 195
Possessing the Gates of the Enemy, 158
Power Evangelism, 82
pre-millennialism/pre-millennialists, 196, 197, 199
pre-tribulationists, 196, 197
pre-Vatican II, 78
Presbyterian, 45, 77, 137
preterist(s), 198, 200, 202, 203
Price, Fred, 216
Princeton Seminary, 81
principalities (and powers), 90, 91, 92, 96, 98, 99, 105, 157, 160, 199, 207
Protestant(ism), 29, 41, 66, 78, 79

Protestant Movement in Bolivia, The, 80
Protestant Reformation, 102, 113, 120, 137
rapture(d), 135, 191, 196, 197, 199, 200
rationalists, 93
Reformed doctrine of sanctification, 102-103, 104, 105, 106
Religion Mountain, 186, 187, 188, 189, 190, 191, 192, 193
Restoration Movement, 120
resurrection, 27, 132, 152, 178, 198
Roman
    (Catholic) Church, 32, 78, 113, 117
    Empire, 71, 87, 98, 131, 158, 159, 164
    massacre, 201
    people, 201, 202
Saddleback Church, 121
Salvation Army, 105, 209
Sanders, John, 142, 144, 146, 147
Santa Cruz, Bolivia, 11
Santería, 157
Santiago de Chiquitos, Bolivia, 30
Satan and the Problem of Evil, 179
satanism, 92, 157
Saul (biblical) (*see* Paul)
School of World Mission, 45, 54, 67, 70, 77, 80, 81, 83, 115, 130, 150
Schuller, Robert, 191
Schwartz, Christian, 44

Scofield, C. I., 195-196, 199

Scofield Reference Bible, 195

Second Apostolic Age, 47, 51, 93, 94, 99, 124-125

second blessing, 104

Seven Mountain Mantle, The, 193

Seven Mountain Prophecy, The, 193

shamanism, 157

Shaw, Daniel, 46

Shaw, Gwen, 156

Shepherding Movement, 120

Signs and Wonders Today, 83

Silbiger, Steven, 135

Silvoso, Ed, 91, 156, 163-164, 176

Smith, Wilbur M., 196

So Free, 157

social reformation, 135, 191

social transformation, 183, 192, 210

Socrates, 128, 129

South America Indian Mission (SAIM), 30, 196

Southern Baptist, 119, 121

Spirit Christology, 24, 25

spiritual gift(s), 29-39, 48, 80, 122, 134, 149, 161-162, 163, 164, 170

spiritual warfare, 89, 91-93, 94, 95, 96, 97, 98, 99, 105, 111, 134, 140, 142, 155, 156, 157, 158, 159, 176, 191, 192, 199, 208

Spiritual Warfare Network (SWN), 91-93, 156,

Spiritual Warfare Strategy, 158

Stanford University, 167

statistical analysis, 61

Stedman, Ray, 32, 33, 34

Strachan, Kenneth, 78

Strachan Theorem, The, 78

Sudduth, Bill, 157

Taking Our Cities for God, 176

Tan, Dr., 70

Tao Fung Shan, Hong Kong, 85

Taylor, Hudson, 101

territorial
   boundaries, 153, 183
   sphere, 124
   spirit(s), 90, 91, 92, 157, 159,

Territorial Spirits, 91

That You May Believe, 24

theism, 132, 135, 140, 142, 143, 145, 146, 147, 148

Theological Education by Extension (TEE), 45-46

Transformation, 176

Trench, Martin, 200, 201, 203

Trinity, the, 19, 20, 24, 70, 72

Tsukahira, Peter, 168

Turned-on Church in an Uptight World, A, 32

Two-Channel Theory, 21-22, 23, 24, 28

Urbana Missionary Conference, 30

University of California at Los Angeles (UCLA), 77

United Nations, 153, 175

United States Congress, 95

Unmoved Mover, 129

Urban House Church Movement, 116

Vasa, King Gustavus, 113

vere deus et vere homo, 19

Victorious Eschatology, 200, 203
Vietnam War, 95
Vineyard Movement, 82
Voice of Reformation, A, 193
voodoo, 92, 157
Wagner, C. Peter, 61, 62,
Wagner, Doris, 157
Wagner Leadership Institute (WLI), 49, 50, 51
Wallnau, Lance, 183, 184, 185
Warfare Prayer, 158
Warfield, Benjamin, 80, 81
Warren, Rick, 121
Wellsprings Church, Colorado Springs, 193
Wesley, John, 32, 105, 108, 110
Wesleyan holiness, 101-112, 205, 217
Western Christian(s), 74
Western Christian missions, 131
Westminster Shorter Catechism, 138

wicca, 157
Wimber, John, 82-83, 89, 90
wineskin(s), 48, 49, 51, 93, 125
Wink, Walter, 147
Winners Chapel, 217
Winter, Ralph, 45, 67
witchcraft, 92, 157
Wizard of Oz, 90
Wood, George, 121
Word of Faith Movement, 216
workplace apostles, 170, 186, 192, 210,
World Vision, 79
World War II, 95, 120, 121, 155, 156, 208
Wycliffe Bible Translators, 73
Yale University, 159
Yoido Full Gospel Church, 84
Young, Brad, 134
Your Spiritual Gifts Can Help Your Church Grow, 29, 161
Youth With A Mission (YWAM), 185

Lessons from a Lifetime in the Church

Wrestling with Alligators, Prophets and Theologians
ISBN 978-0-8307-5531-8
ISBN 0-8307-5531-4

For the past half-century, Dr. C. Peter Wagner has been at the leading edge of key spiritual paradigm shifts guided by the Holy Spirit. He has led the Church from one great move of God to the next, riding the wave of the Spirit through different changes he never imagined were possible when he first answered God's call to ministry. In his memoir, *Wrestling with Alligators, Prophets and Theologians*, Dr. Wagner invites you to experience these spiritual paradigm shifts as they happened—just as he did—and he shares how these surprising moves of the Spirit impacted his own ongoing transformation. You'll witness the seismic changes in the Church's recent history through the eyes of one leader who has seen it all unfold!

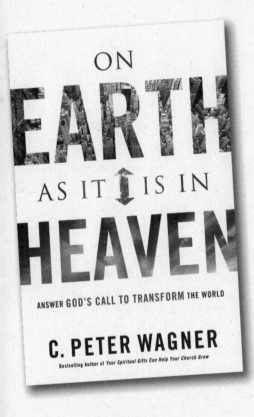

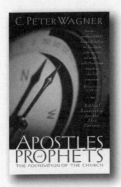
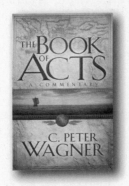

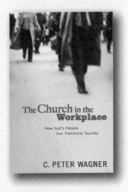
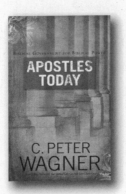
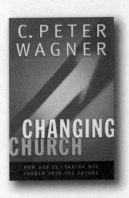